THE FRANCIS BOOK

THE FRANCIS BOOK

THE FRANCIS BOOK

800 Years with the Saint from Assisi

Compiled and Edited by Roy M. Gasnick, O.F.M.

Collier Books

MACMILLAN PUBLISHING COMPANY

NEW YORK

Collier Macmillan Publishers

LONDON

Collier Books
Macmillan Publishing Company
866 Third Avenue, New York, NY 10022
Collier Macmillan Canada, Inc.

Library of Congress Cataloging-in-Publication Data
Main entry under title:
The Francis book.
    Bibliography: p. 208
    1. Francesco d'Assisi, Saint, 1182–1226—Addresses,
essays, lectures.   I. Gasnick, Roy M.
BX4700.F6F72   1980   282′092′4   80-20211
ISBN 0-02-542760-1
ISBN 0-02-003200-5 (pbk.)

First Collier Books Edition 1980

Macmillan books are available at special discounts for bulk
purchases for sales promotions, premiums, fund-raising, or
educational use. For details, contact:

    Special Sales Director
    Macmillan Publishing Company
    866 Third Avenue
    New York, NY 10022

10 9 8 7 6 5

Printed in the United States of America

Designed by Jack Meserole

Dedicated to my families: GASNICK
LUCAS
LUKACH
IGLODY
PUSKAS
LENT
JASKOT
CAPKO
PUSZTAY
FILIPPELLI
LANE
KOPEC
HARTSUIKER
VASTA
PAOLONI
MULZET
SEES
WATTERSON
TREMMEL
WIND

and especially to my families Franciscan: THE FRIARS MINOR
THE CONVENTUALS
THE CAPUCHINS
THE THIRD ORDER REGULAR
THE POOR CLARES
THE SECULAR FRANCISCANS
THE ANGLICAN FRANCISCANS
THE LUTHERAN FRANCISCANS

Contents

His Universal Appeal, 169

Epilogue, 206

Foreword

A portrait of Saint Francis hangs in a private collection in London, rare not just because it is by Rembrandt, nor because it can be viewed only by the privileged few. It is rare because it is one of the two or three nonbiblical saints Rembrandt ever painted.

Rembrandt was a Protestant who in much of his art reflected his religious outlook on life. Hence, he was alienated by the Catholic devotional attitudes toward saints. Yet he painted a Saint Francis. Why?

The painting shows Francis kneeling. Before him is a large Bible. Clasped in his hands is a crucifix. In Rembrandt's day, as up to the Second Vatican Council, the Bible had been the rallying sign of Protestants, just as the crucifix had been for Catholics. Reinhold Schneider, in his excellent little work on Saint Francis in art, makes this interpretation: "Bible and crucifix, tokens of a divided Christianity, unite in Francis."

Rembrandt's *Saint Francis* provides a clue to understanding the perennial popularity of the "universal saint" whose birth eight hundred years ago will be commemorated by his admirers of every faith and of no faith throughout the world in 1982.

Francis seems to touch everyone.

Historians recognize him as one of the most influential figures to rise out of the Middle Ages because of his personal concern for the poor and oppressed, his disarmingly simple approach in dealing with the Church and with civil authorities, and the thousands of followers who flocked to him and then carried his vision to the ends of the earth.

Artists from Cimabue and Giotto through Rembrandt, Bellini, and El Greco to modern Americans such as John La Farge and Beniamino Bufano have celebrated his communion with nature and his mystical embrace of the cross.

Dante placed him on the highest steps of *Paradiso*. Gerard Manley Hopkins, absorbing Francis's understanding of the individuality of every created thing, gave the modern world a new kind of poetry.

G. K. Chesterton called him "the world's one sincere democrat," and the "first hero of humanism."

Presidents Eisenhower and Ford have quoted the famous prayer attributed to him, "Lord, make me an instrument of your peace." The city named after him, San Francisco, is proud of its statue, *St. Francis of the Guns*, cast from melted-down handguns voluntarily turned in to the city's mayor after the assassination in 1968 of Senator Robert Kennedy.

Francis is truly a multimedia person. Franco Zeffirelli made a film in 1972, *Brother Sun, Sister Moon*, about his early life. In 1976 NBC News produced an hour-long documentary, "Francis of Assisi: the Man and His Meaning," on the occasion of the seven hundred fiftieth anniversary of his death. *Marvel Comics* this year published their first religious "comic" or illustrated book, *Francis, Brother of the Universe.*

His presence is felt in America, not only in history, art, and artifact, but also through the spiritual and social service of some one hundred thousand of his American followers, clerical and lay, male and female, Catholic, Anglican, and Protestant.

New York's *Cue* magazine referred to Francis as "the man about whom more has been written than about any other saint." A glance at the table of contents of *The Francis Book* will confirm this at once. And what a galaxy of names!

Many authors have written *about* St. Francis. But the authors selected for *The Francis Book* are concerned with what Saint Francis *was about*. Each author selected here brings out a different (and usually personal) perspective about St. Francis. Each, then, is intended to help readers not only to learn something about Saint Francis, but also to learn something about themselves.

Those who read this book are not expected to agree with all the opinions and interpretations about Saint Francis contained herein. The editor himself does not. But our times call for honesty, openness, and objectivity, and hence the need to present as broad a picture of Francis as possible.

Do with this book what you will: flip through it, read it, study it, delight in it, be inspired by it, but most of all, be forewarned that you may have to do something about it. Francis-fever is contagious. And Francis himself always kept saying, "Let us begin again, for up to now we have done nothing."

ROY M. GASNICK, O.F.M.

New York City, 1980

Acknowledgments

MICHAEL MEILACH, O.F.M., who makes typewriters sing—and sometimes melt because of his speed—who made a manuscript out of the dozens of copies of sections of books and articles from magazines as well as other sources.

CYRIL SEAMAN, O.F.M., and the staff of the Dawson Memorial Library at Siena College in New York, who opened all resources to me, helped with some of the research, and reproduced some of the materials I needed. Apart from clippings I had been collecting over the years, all the sections of *The Francis Book* were researched at the Dawson Library. Would that all college libraries were so endowed.

JAMES C. G. CONNIFF, a literary agent who took the idea of *The Francis Book* and ran with it so fast that, though leaving me breathless in trying to match pace, the book was sold before it was finished, and finished when it should have been just beginning. As a total communications man, he makes things happen.

MY BROTHER AND SISTER FRANCISCANS across the country who gave me leads to many of the selections in the book as well as sending me some of the photos and illustrations that accompany the text of *The Francis Book*.

CASSIAN A. MILES, O.F.M., who kept the information flowing from the New York Franciscan Communications Office on those days when I was wrangling with the manuscript. His fraternal and literary support keeps me Franciscan and keeps me literate.

Prologue

What Is This Francis?

NIKOS KAZANTZAKIS

I swear I shall tell the truth. Lord, aid my memory, enlighten my mind, do not permit me to utter a single word I might later regret. Arise and bear witness, mountains and plains of Umbria; arise, stones sprinkled with his martyr's blood, dusty, bemired roads of Italy, black caves, snow-covered peaks; arise, ship that took him to the savage East; arise, lepers and wolves and bandits; and you, birds who heard his preaching, arise—Brother Leo needs you. Come, stand on my right, on my left; help me to tell the truth, the whole truth. Upon this hangs the salvation of my soul.

"Put yourself out, Brother Francis," I used to cry. "Put yourself out before you burn up the world."

I tremble, because many times I find I cannot distinguish what is true from what is false. Francis runs in my mind like water. He changes faces; I am unable to pin him down. Was he short? Was he immensely tall? I cannot put my hand over my heart and say with certainty. He often seemed squat to me, all skin and bones, with a face that bore witness to his penury—scant, chestnut-colored beard, thick protruding lips, huge, hairy ears erect like a rabbit's and listening intently to both the visible and invisible worlds. His hands, though, were delicate, his fingers slender—indications of descent from a noble line. . . . But whenever he spoke, prayed, or thought he was alone, his squat body shot forth flames that reached the heavens: he became an archangel with red wings that he beat in the air. And if this happened at night when the flames were visible, you recoiled in terror to keep from being burned.

"Put yourself out, Brother Francis," I used to cry. "Put yourself out before you burn up the world."

Then, lifting my eyes, I would watch him as he headed directly for me, calm and smiling, his face once again characterized by human joy, bitterness, and penury. . . .

I remember once asking him, "Brother Francis, how does God reveal himself to you when you are all alone in the darkness?"

And he answered me: "Like a glass of cool water, Brother Leo; like a glass of water from the fountain of everlasting youth. I'm thirsty, I drink it, and my thirst is quenched for all eternity."

"God like a glass of cool water?" I cried, astonished.

"And what did you think, Brother Leo? Why be alarmed? There is nothing simpler than God, nothing more refreshing, more suited to the lips of man."

But a few years later when Francis was a doubled-over lump of hair and bones, devoid of flesh, nearly breathing his last, he bent forward so that the friars would not hear him, and said to me, trembling, "God is a conflagration, Brother Leo. He burns, and we burn with him."

So far as I can gauge his height in my mind, I can say only this with certitude: from the ground trodden by his feet, from there to his head, his stature was short; but from the head upward it was immense.

There are two parts of his body, however, which I do remember with perfect clarity: his feet and his eyes. I was a beggar, had spent my entire life among beggars, had seen thousands of feet that passed every day of their existence walking unshod over rocks, in dust, mud, upon the snow. But never in my life had I seen feet so distressed, so melancholy, so feeble, gnawed away by journeys, so full of open wounds—as his. Sometimes when Father Francis lay sleeping I used to bend down stealthily and kiss them, and I felt as though I were kissing the total suffering of mankind.

And how could anyone forget his eyes after having once seen them? They were large, almond-shaped, black as pitch. They made you exclaim that you had never viewed eyes so tame, so velvety; but scarcely had you completed your thought when the eyes suddenly became two open trapdoors enabling you to look down at his vitals, heart, kidneys, lungs; whereupon you discovered that they were ablaze. He would often stare at you without seeing you. What did he see? Not your skin and flesh, not your head—but your skull. One day he caressed my face

slowly with the palm of his hand. His eyes had become filled with compassion and sweetness, and he said, "I like you, Brother Leo. I like you because you leave the worms free to stroll over your lips and ears; you do not chase them away."

"What worms, Father Francis? I don't see any worms."

"Surely you do see them when you are praying, or asleep and dreaming about paradise. You see them but do not chase them away because you know full well, Brother Leo, that they are emissaries of God, of the Great King. God is holding a wedding in heaven, and he sends them with invitations for us: 'Greetings from the Great King, who awaits you. Come!' "

When Francis was among others, he would laugh and frolic—would spring suddenly into the air and begin to dance, or would seize two sticks and play the "viol" while singing sacred songs he himself had composed. Doubtless he did so to encourage his companions, realizing perfectly well that the soul suffers, the body hungers, that man's endurance is nil. When he was alone, however, his tears began to flow. He would beat his chest, roll in the thorns and nettles, lift his hands to heaven and cry, "All day long I search for thee desperately, Lord; all night long while I am asleep thou searchest for me. O Lord, when, when, as night gives way to day, shall we meet?"

Another time I heard him cry, his eyes pinned on heaven: "I don't want to live any more. Undress me, Lord. Save me from my body. Take me!"

Each dawn, when the birds begin to sing again, or at midday when he plunged into the cooling shade of the forest, or at night, sitting in the moonlight or beneath the stars, he would shudder from inexpressible joy and gaze at me, his eyes filled with tears. "What miracles these are, Brother Leo!" he would say. "And he who created such beauty— what then must he be? What can we call him?"

"God, Brother Francis," I answered.

"No, not God, not God," he cried. "That name is heavy, it crushes bones. . . . Not God—Father!"

One night Francis was roaming the lanes of Assisi. The moon had come up fully round and was suspended in the center of the heavens; the entire earth was floating buoyantly in the air. He looked, but could see no one standing in the doorways to enjoy the great miracle. Dashing to the church, he ascended the bell tower and began to toll the bell as though some calamity had taken place. The terrified people awoke with a start thinking there must be a fire, and ran half-naked to the courtyard of San Ruffino's, where they saw Francis ringing the bell furiously.

"Why are you ringing the bell?" they yelled at him. "What's happened?"

"Lift up your eyes, my friends," Francis answered them from the top of the bell tower. "Lift up your eyes; look at the moon!"

That was the kind of man blessed Francis was; at least that was the way he appeared to me. I say this, but I am really not sure. How can I ever know what he was like, who he was? Is it possible that he himself did not know? I remember one wintery day when he was at the Portiuncula, sitting on the threshold sunning himself. A young man arrived, out of breath, and stood before him.

"Where is Francis, Bernardone's son?" he asked, his tongue hanging out of his mouth. "Where can I find the new saint so that I may fall at his feet? For months now I have been roaming the streets looking for him. For the love of Christ, my brother, tell me where he is."

"Where is Francis, Bernardone's son?" replied Francis, shaking his head. "Where is Francis, Bernardone's son? What is this Francis? Who is he? I am looking for him also, my brother. I have been looking for him now for years. Give me your hand and let us go find him!"

His City

Assisi Is . . .

BY ABOUT FIFTY WRITERS,
RECORDED BY
RAPHAEL BROWN

A city on a hill that cannot be hidden—a holy city—the unique town—the unchanged town—one of the holy cities of our Western world—one of the most sacred cities on earth—the mystical city par excellence—an enchanted city—one of the sacred refuges where art and prayer unite—the town at whose feet everything base dies—a temple—a house of prayer—a house of God—a holy reliquary—a shrine—a citadel of the spirit—a beacon—a lighthouse.

A city of light—a city of silence and eternity—a place of and at peace—a town of peace and love—a nest of peace—a haven of peace suspended between heaven and earth—a Sabbath-day town—an asylum of silence—an oasis.

A vast convent—a heavenly cloister—a holy hive—a kind of monastery—a blessed place—a lost paradise—a particle of paradise—the gate to heaven—the way that leads to heaven—the entrance hall of eternity.

A gardenland—a garden of peace and bliss—the most beautiful garden in all the world—the chosen home of dreams, silence, and serenity.

A fountain of grace—a cascade of blessings—a fountain of life and compassion—a center for inner renewal and healing—a heavenly pharmacy—a little city of the soul—one of the most glorious cities of the world of the spirit—a place on earth where the kingdom of God has resided—one of the capitals of the spiritual life—the last asylum of peace and joy—the finest capital in the world, the capital of love.

Assisi is a heart—an affair of the heart—You speak to the heart.

In Assisi one feels close to the heart of Christ.

The soul of this dear town is summed up in these two words: charity and love.

Umbria and Assisi

FODOR'S ITALY, 1978

In Umbria, known as the Green Heart of Italy, the works of God take precedence over human accomplishment. Umbrian scenery wants nothing for variety. Though small, the region includes mountains, hills, valleys and plains, lakes and rivers. Although it is simple enough to catalogue these geographical features and even to grow lyrical over their combined effects, the true characteristics that make Umbria remarkable escape easy description. The subtlety of the country's influence on the visitor is the reason it is difficult to try to recreate its visual impression in words.

It is a pity to see Assisi before doing any other town. Assisi has such charm that other spots have a tendency to seem drab by comparison.

Even among the hills, the country is undramatic, but the strange, bluish haze that diffuses the landscape and has caused so many writers to characterize Umbria with the adjectives *mystic* and *ethereal,* lends the area a special charm. The colors, mostly soft tones of grays and greens, further add to the sense of peace.

Hills covered with olive groves, or in the less-cultivated parts, with pines, rise with deceptive gentleness from the flatness of the broad plain. It is only from directly below, or from one of the many towns built on them, that you realize how steep the hills really are. On the terraced lower slopes and on the plain are the famous Umbrian grapevines, carefully trained to grow over dwarf elms. Slim poplars divide the fields and shade the dusty white roads. Everything seems as motionless as if the scenery were painted. . . .

It is a pity to see Assisi before doing any other town. Even though it is so near Perugia, Assisi has such charm that other spots have a tendency to seem drab by comparison. This is high praise when you consider that even the enormous number of tourists and pilgrims who visit the tiny city and its important shrines have not detracted from its atmosphere.

Although Assisi lived through a history very similar to that of its neighbor and bitter enemy, Perugia (in 1492 a Perugian army, led by one of the Baglioni, sacked Assisi), it is today completely associated with the cult of Saint Francis. This saint and founder of the monastic order that bears his name was born in c. 1182, the son of a well-to-do cloth merchant. His young manhood gave no indication of the future development of his character, for he led the carefree life of a twelfth-century rake. The great change followed a serious illness he had contracted on his return from a spell in a Perugian jail, where he was held after capture in one of the frequent clashes between the two cities.

Francis became convinced that the root of all evil in mankind lay in the desire for possessions, and promptly changed his life, remodeling it on that basis. Tradition has it that not only did he himself give up all worldly things, but also that he tried to have his most unwilling father share his sacrifice by selling his stock of cloth and giving the proceeds to the church of San Damiano.

In 1210, Francis, by then a well-known religious figure, organized the Franciscan Order of Mendicant Friars, whose basic tenets are those he had adopted for himself: poverty and asceticism. Preaching his simple faith in an era sadly needing reform, Saint Francis won many converts.

Women flocked to join the order begun by his follower, Saint Clare, whose first convent, incidentally, was the church of San Damiano. These movements were to spread all over Europe and survive today as Franciscans, Capuchins, and Conventuals for men, and as the so-called Poor Clares for women.

Almost everything of importance to be seen in Assisi is in some way associated with the memory of the saint. The huge basilica was started to honor him in the two years between his death in 1226 and his canonization. Originally, the land on which the church stands had served as the execution ground for condemned criminals and bore the suggestive title of Infernal Hill. Saint Francis, in his humility, had asked to be buried there. His wish was granted, and by order of the Pope the name of the spot was changed to Hill of Paradise. Funds flowed in. The saint's great popularity brought many to work on his memorial without pay, and the lower church was completed in the record time of twenty-two months. About ten years later, the upper church and the huge, double-arched cloisters were added.

To prevent the saint's remains from being stolen,

5

Francis's indefatigable follower, Brother Elias, who also seems to have been largely responsible for the building of the lower church, had the body removed to a secret vault cut in the living rock under the church. This tomb defied all attempts to locate it until 1818. Two flights below the floor of the lower church the visitor can see the coffin containing the body of the saint. The crypt is se-

verely handsome, and its four corners hold the bodies of Francis's four closest followers.

Artistically, both the upper and lower churches, which together make up the big, two-level basilica, are treasure-houses. The lower level, dim and crypt-like on the brightest of days, is marvelously frescoed by master artists of several periods. The oldest of these paintings are classified as primitives and are attributed to a mid-thirteenth-century artist, known only as the Master of St. Francis. Afterward, at different times, Cimabue, Giottino (pupil of Giotto), Simone Martini, and Pietro Lorenzetti were commissioned to add to the glory of the building. Lorenzetti's fresco of the Virgin, Child Jesus, and Saint Francis, to the left of the altar, is particularly sensitive and is considered to be one of the finest pieces produced by the Sienese School of that period (1330). To get the most pleasure from this visit, a flashlight is invaluable.

Also to the left of the altar, in the sacristy, are preserved a number of relics of the saint. Among them are his patched, gray cassock, the cruel cord, made of camel's hair and needles, which belted his waist, and the crude sandals, which he wore when he received the stigmata in 1224. The stigmata, according to Roman Catholic belief, are the five wounds that Christ suffered at his Crucifixion, supernaturally inflicted on an individual.

The top portion of the walls of the upper church are decorated with a number of frescos by unidentified artists, probably of the Roman school. More important are the twenty-eight scenes from the life of Saint Francis with which Giotto enriched the lower half of the walls of the nave. Beside the basilica is a lovely and little-visited cloister, enclosing a small cemetery.

Assisi is well worth the stiff walk up Via San Francesco to the central Piazza del Commune, flanked by thirteenth-century palaces and the Roman Temple of Minerva, still used as a church. In the baptismal font of the Romanesque twelfth-century Cathedral of Saint Rufino, Saint Francis, Saint Clare, and the Emperor Frederick II were baptized.

The thirteenth-century Basilica of Saint Clare is most impressive in its simplicity. The saint's body, quite blackened by time, lies open to view in the crypt, while the closed cloisters of her followers adjoin the church.

In a side chapel can be seen one of the most famous and best-loved crucifixes in the world. Before this cross Saint Francis prayed and first recognized his mission, and later was to have his visions of Christ and the Virgin.

In contrast, a trip out of town to the tiny church of San Damiano is pure sunshine. Originally, the cross discussed above hung in the chapel here. A jolly young friar in his brown habit acts as guide. He will show you the little court where Saint Francis wrote, the table where Saint Clare performed a miracle, and the choir with its legends. It is an exquisite spot with a glorious view.

A road climbs Mount Subasio, offering magnificent panoramas above Saint Francis's favorite retreat, the *Eremo delle Carceri*, located in a dense forest three miles behind the town. The formidable papal stronghold built by Cardinal Albornoz in the fourteenth century also is worth a visit.

Below the town is the ostentatious, frescoed Santa Maria degli Angeli, built over the cell with its adjoining chapel, the Portiuncula, where Saint Francis died. Nearby is the garden where, ever since the saint rolled among the roses while wrestling with temptation, the bushes have been thornless.

Assisi

ALFRED NOYES

I know a city on a hill, a mountain's castled
  crown,
Where, like the stairs the angels tread, the streets
  go up and down,
A city very small and kind and full of strange
  renown.

It stands upon an eastern height and looks toward
  the west.
Far off, it sees Perugia, its ancient foe, at rest;
And all the birds of Italy are gathered to its
  breast.

So small, so kind, but smaller far in the dim
  gulf below,
The world of men and all the tides that toss them
  to and fro,
While on its crag that city stands, crowned with
  the sunset glow.

Still, like a lean dark cypress there, against the
  clouds on high,
Brother of sun and moon and star, he towers into
  the sky,
As long ago, with arms upstretched, while all
  things else went by.

Assisi, 1926

W. STEPHEN BUSH

Assisi, in Umbria, is filled with pious and devoted pilgrims, who have come to his birthplace to celebrate with prayer and meditation the virtues of Saint Francis. For this year marks the seven-hundredth anniversary of the death of that famous man who founded the Franciscan Order. This is the "Franciscan Year," as decreed by the heads of the order and approved by the Pope. Pilgrimages and celebrations have been in progress several weeks and will continue until October 14, when the majestic honors of the Catholic Church will be bestowed upon the *poverello* or "little poor one," who is also called Giullare di Dio—the minstrel of God.

Umbria, which holds so much of Italy's natural beauty and so many of Italy's treasures of art, this country of Raphaello Sanzio with its air of crystalline clearness and the soft green and brown tints of its landscape—this Umbria gently inviting to contemplation and peace—is quite the finest vestibule there could be for the ancient cloistral city on the hill. To this day Umbria echoes everywhere, with memories of the singing saint, who addressed Brother Sun and Brother Water and Brother Wind, who preached to the birds at Bevagna, and who at Cannara wanted the whole world to join his happy brotherhood.

Much has been restored and renovated in the ancient city of *Ascesi*,* but the spirit of her people and of her people's neighbors has little need of revival. Walk for an hour or two after the heat of the day in the squares and streets and byways of the ancient city, and you will find that the centuries have changed it little inwardly or outwardly since the day the son of Pietro Bernardone made his pact with Lady Poverty. Umbria is that lady's kingdom.

The religious ceremonies that attest the veneration in which the church holds this saint are free from pomp or gorgeousness, for such things were an abomination to the spirit of the man whose memory is honored. All the functions and festivities on the long program are characterized by simplicity and have much in them that seems touching. Indeed it is this unique aspect that will make

* Old form of Assisi.

the events of the Franciscan Year memorable to the pilgrims. The ceremony with which the series was begun here was exceedingly simple—nothing more than a tribute paid in passing the house of a dear friend.

From every part of Umbria, from Perugia, Foligno, Spoleto, and Trevi had come the artless folk of the countryside, which the Italian with a sweep describes as *contadini,* and the flowers they had gathered in the fields or their own gardens they tenderly deposited at the shrine of the man whom they probably understand better than anybody else in the world. That was the keynote of the first celebration—if the simple act can be thus described. The strewing of flowers, the ringing of the bells in friendly harmony, the singing of the old Franciscan hymns—such are the features of the Franciscan Year in which pilgrims and contadini join in happy accord.

Through some misunderstanding or blunder in tact, a brass band had come up from Rome. The natives regarded it in silent wonder. The bandsmen felt ill at ease, but the leader plucked up courage at last and in some street not far from the city hall the instruments blared forth. It seemed like setting off firecrackers in the peaceful shades of a cathedral. The shock thereof was great. Strange to say, no protest was needed; the sounding brass was chidden into silence by the very atmosphere of the place.

By writers of every nation, representing every shade of religious belief, the husband of Lady Poverty has been proclaimed as an apostle of humanity, and one of the possessions common to all mankind.

Medieval costumes were worn late in the afternoon. There will be many other ceremonies on the civil side, tributes of the city, when men and women will appear again in the garb of the Middle Ages. But this bit of color will detract nothing from the outspokenly informal and neighborly character of the proceedings. And not all who have come to Assisi are in the strict sense of the word religious pilgrims.

No saint in the roster of Rome has as many admirers outside the circles of orthodoxy as the saint who went his way singing not in the official tongue of the Church but in the language of the plain people. By writers of every nation, representing every shade of religious belief, the husband of the Lady Poverty has been proclaimed as an apostle of humanity, and one of the possessions common to all mankind. . . .

John Paul II at Assisi

Here I am in Assisi on this day that I have wished to dedicate specially to the patron saints of this country, Italy; a country to which God has called me in order that I may serve as St. Peter's successor. Since I was not born in this land, I feel more than ever the need of a spiritual "birth" in it. And therefore, on this Sunday, I come as a pilgrim to Assisi, at the feet of Saint Francis, the Poverello, who wrote Christ's gospel in incisive characters in the hearts of the people of his time. We cannot be surprised that his fellow citizens have

wished to see in him the patron saint of Italy. The Pope, who, owing to his mission, must have before his eyes the whole universal Church, the bride of Christ, in the various parts of the globe, particularly needs the help of the patron saint of Italy in his See in Rome; he needs the intercession of Saint Francis of Assisi.

And so he arrives here today.

He comes to visit this city, which is always a witness to the marvelous divine adventure that took place between the end of the twelfth and the beginning of the thirteenth century. It is a witness to that surprising holiness that passed here like a great breath of the Spirit. A breath in which Saint Francis of Assisi participated, as well as his spiritual sister Saint Clare and so many other saints born from their evangelical spirituality. The Franciscan message spread far beyond the frontiers of Italy, and very soon it also reached Polish soil, from where I come. And it still operates there with abundant fruits, as, moreover, in other countries of the world and in other continents.

You [Francis], who brought Christ so close to your age, help us to bring Christ close to our age.

I will tell you that, as Archbishop of Cracow, I lived near a very ancient Franciscan church, and from time to time I went there to pray, to make the *Via Crucis* (Way of the Cross) and to visit the Chapel of Our Lady of Sorrows. Unforgettable moments for me! One cannot fail to mention here that it was just from this magnificent trunk of Franciscan spirituality that the blessed Maximilian Kolbe came, a special patron in our difficult times.

I cannot pass over in silence the fact that just here, in Assisi, in this basilica, in the year 1253, Pope Innocent IV proclaimed saint the Bishop of Cracow, the martyr Stanislaus, now the patron saint of Poland, whose unworthy successor I was until a short time ago.

Today, therefore, setting foot here for the first time as Pope, at the sources of this great breath of the Spirit, of this marvelous revival of the Church and of Christianity in the thirteenth century, linked with the figure of Saint Francis of Assisi, my heart opens to our patron saint and cries: "You, who brought Christ so close to your age, help us to bring Christ close to our age, to our difficult and critical times. Help us!" These times are waiting for Christ with great anxiety, although many men of our age are not aware of it. We are approaching the year A.D. 2000. Will they not be times that will prepare us for a rebirth of Christ, for a new Coming? Every day, we express in the eucharistic prayer our expectation, addressed to him alone, our Redeemer and Savior, to him who is the fulfillment of the history of man and of the world.

Help us, Saint Francis of Assisi, to bring Christ closer to the Church and to the world of today.

You, who bore in your heart the vicissitudes of your contemporaries, help us, with our heart close to the Redeemer's heart, to embrace the events of the men of our time. The difficult social, economic, and political problems, the problems of culture and contemporary civilization, all the sufferings of persons of today, their doubts, their denials, their disorders, their tensions, their complexes, their worries. . . . Help us to express all this in the simple and fruitful language of the Gospel. Help us to solve everything in an evangelical key, in order that Christ himself may be "the Way—the Truth—the Life" for modern man.

This is asked of you, holy son of the Church, son of the Italian land, by Pope John Paul II, son of the Polish land. And he hopes that you will not refuse him it, that you will help him. You have always been kind, and you have always hastened to bring help to all those who appealed to you. . . .

A greeting and special thanks to the ministers general of the four Franciscan families, to the Community of the Basilica of Saint Francis, to all Franciscans, and to all religious families—men and women religious—inspired by the rule and the lifestyle of Saint Francis of Assisi.

I tell you what I feel deep down in my heart:

The Pope is grateful to you for your faithfulness to your Franciscan vocation.

A City and a Saint

FRANCIS AND HELEN LINE

Rome's glory is many-splendored:
Caesars, Popes, Colosseum, St. Peter's, the Forum—
These and more are ingredients of its greatness.

The fame of Paris is such that one despairs at
listing its landmarks;
London so noted that it scarce adds or detracts
That Dickens once lived in its boundaries.

But Bethlehem, known over Christendom,
Is important for one fact alone—
There the Christ child was born.
There the Incarnation was nourished.

And Nazareth forever is chronicled
As focus for the boyhood of Jesus.

It is so with Assisi.
This Italian city of beauty
Is a repository of art and of treasure,
A city of charm and of churches
With hilltop castles and ruins,
Vineyards in Umbrian landscape below.

But pilgrims don't come for the castle,
Tourists don't come for the churches,
Franciscans from over the world
Do not seek Assisi
Just for art or for treasure.

They come because a man—
A breathing soul who altered the ages
In his manner of worship and action—
Once dwelt in this town of Assisi.

Not the city, but the saint,
Is the essence of its greatness.

The View from Assisi

ERNEST RAYMOND

You will see something of what I mean if we open our pilgrimage by sitting on the top of Assisi's hill, with the ruin of the old castle behind, the city shackled to the slope below, and the wide vale of Spoleto filling up the floor of the world.

Before us now is the theater in which most of the drama was staged. It all looks extraordinarily peaceful today. We sit among tall grasses and wild flowers, in an air pungent with the smell of mint, while innumerable butterflies flit about us—which seems to fit, somehow, the opening of a Franciscan tale. Lizards dart across the stones, and a lark, descendant perhaps of one of Francis's larks, sings its office in the limpid Italian sky. The gray olive trees go shimmering down the slope, all round and below the city walls. They carry our eyes to the great flat plain, which is a patchwork of maize fields and clover fields, with the vines festooned from maple to elm between them. In the farthest distance run fold after fold of mountains, each a lighter gray than the last. And the last has a mysterious light above it, like the light of another world.

Looking down on the city, we can see right into the streets along which Francis went rioting at midnight with his boon companions, his lute slung before him, and his voice lifted in troubadour songs, to the disturbance of graver citizens in their sleep. That was before the sword pierced him deep enough. We can see into the open piazzas where in his lifetime excited and gesticulating crowds must have discussed one sensation after another. "What's happened to Francis? He's quite different from what he used to be." "Have you heard of the awful row that is developing between that young idiot, Francis, and his father?" "Listen, all of you: old Bernardone is haling his son before the bishop for trial." "Have you heard the latest?—would you believe it?—Bernard of Quintavalle—Bernard of all people, that sober and substantial townsman!—has thrown up everything and is going to join young Bernardone in his mad game. And Dr. Peter Cataneo too, a lay canon of the cathedral, if you please—he's caught the disease. He and Bernard are giving all their goods away to the poor now in the Piazza San Giorgio." One shift of our eyes, and we can see the Piazza San Giorgio.

Then: "Listen, everybody: young Clare, the lovely daughter of Count Favorino of the Scifi—and she only eighteen!—eloped from her home at midnight last night and ran to young Francis's crazy establishment in the forest. What are children coming to?" Eighteen days later: "Agnes, Clare's sister, and only fifteen years old, has run off to join her! Her father and uncle are going with a strong force to get her back."

Yes, down there in houses whose remains are still to be found, there developed and detonated battles between children and parents not a whit different from those beneath the roofs of England today.

Far away to our right, down there in the plain, do you see a gray chapel against some cypresses? That is San Paolo in Bastia, where Clare clung to the altar when her family came to drag her home again. Look left. Do you see those haystacks against a farmhouse high up on the steep slope? That farmhouse holds the remains of the Benedictine nunnery of Sant'Angelo in Panzo, where Francis put Clare till he could find a home for her. Can you distinguish the path winding up to it? Up that path ran little Agnes to join her beloved sister. Up that path galloped knights and men-at-arms, determined to recover her. Do you see that file of cypresses marching down the hill to the left of the Porta Nuova? They mark the road to the little

convent of San Damiano. There Francis installed Clare with her clinging sister, Agnes. There she founded the order of the Poor Clares, and there she lived, perhaps the most complete of all the creations of Francis. To San Damiano they brought him dying, and there she looked after him, mending his habit and making sandals for his wounded feet. There in the garden one day—do you see the garden?—he burst into his "Canticle of Brother Sun and All the Creatures," though the sun of the East had blinded him, and he could hardly see the creatures any more. To San Damiano his brothers, knowing how Clare had loved him, brought his dead body that she might weep over it for a while and say *addio*.

And now leave San Damiano and see, right in the center of the picture, as it ought to be, the dome of the great basilica that enshrines the Portiuncula, the tiny chapel of the "Little Portion" by which Francis chose to live and to die, and in which he dreamed such dreams of us men as we have not yet been great enough to fulfil—but there is time. "Good morning, good people."

Sitting up here beneath the old ruined Rocca, are we not indeed gazing over a country where once upon a time (as Angela of Foligno said of herself with the unblushing truth of the saints) some men and women, like early envoys seeking an alliance, "walked with the Holy Spirit among the vines"?

His Life and Times

A Time for War, a Time for Servitude

OMER ENGLEBERT

In Saint Francis's day, the world known to the west was limited to Europe, North Africa, and the Near East, where the Crusaders had fought and traded for a century.

The political and social configuration of the European states was by no means that of today. France was only half as big; Spain was partly in the hands of the Moors; and England continued to exercise her suzerainty over Normandy, Brittany, and the Aquitaine. The Holy Roman Empire not only embraced Germany, Austria, Switzerland, and Bohemia, but also spilled over into the Walloons, Lorraine, Burgundy, and Provence. To this, Italy —except for the Pontifical States—also belonged.

In the Italian peninsula, however, frequent revolts flared, which Frederick I, "Frederick Barbarossa" (1152–1190), Henry VI (1190–1197), Otto IV (1197–1214), and Frederick II, "Frederick the Great" (1215–1250) had the utmost difficulty in quelling. To maintain his domination, the emperor relied on the nobility, whose members held their fiefs from him and exercised the functions of *podestàs* [mayors], judges, and consuls in his name.

Born of the necessity of keeping in check the anarchy following upon the barbarian invasions, the feudal regime comprised, as we know, two classes of men—the *majores* or *boni homines* (the great or the nobility) and the *minores* (the common people).

The *majores* were the nobles, the knights, the lords, who constituted in those times of general brigandage a permanent police force. Everyone was born into his hereditary rank (duke, marquis, count), with his local position and landed property, with the certainty of never being abandoned by his liege lord, and also with the obligation, should need arise, of dying for him. Thanks to these warriors, the *minores* were protected. They could work in peace and eat their fill—no longer in fear of

ST. FRANCIS, THE GLORIOUS POOR LITTLE ONE OF CHRIST

being liquidated or led away at the point of the lance as captives with their families. But they paid dearly for this protection, sometimes in quitrents and service, and sometimes even with the loss of freedom.

The *minores* were of two sorts: villeins and serfs. The latter, attached to the lord's land, belonged to their master like so much livestock and enjoyed no independence whatever. The others, farm laborers in the country, craftsmen, or merchants in the towns, were freemen, with the right to own property and move about freely. The serf, then, was really a slave; the villein was free in body, but subject to taxation and forced labor. The noble, who shared with the churches and monasteries nearly all the wealth of the period, was not taxed, owing only a vassal's homage to his lord.

The Crusades, which were in part commercial expeditions, transformed the feudal system. Up to then, craftsmen and laborers worked for the local market, with no other outlets than the castle or monastery. After the discovery and pillage of the treasures of the Byzantine Empire, hitherto unsuspected routes opened up to trade and industry. Innumerable ships dotted the Mediterranean; the Roman highways, destroyed by the barbarian invasions, were rebuilt; and from one end to the other of Europe raw materials and manufactured products were exchanged. Many artisans became rich, and some merchants reaped immense fortunes.

These newly rich remained nonetheless villeins or *minores,* crushed beneath the burden of quitrents and services, deprived of any voice in the government of the towns. Their fortunes, however, soon permitted their voices to be heard. They compelled the temporal and spiritual lords to grant them economic privileges and to admit them to their councils, thus becoming themselves *majores.*

From concession to concession, the lord, who up to then had made all appointments to public employment, was also constrained to grant to other citizens consuls of their own choosing, charged with lawmaking, administrating, and handing down justice. From then on, the commune was born, a sort of new suzerainty, bound like any vassal domain to its lord, and like it, obliged by the feudal oath, to place troops at his service.

The serfs did not benefit from the social transformation. For to become a freeman and lay claim to the title of "citizen," one must own a house and enjoy a certain revenue. Consequently, only a small number of privileged villeins could belong to the commune. The serfs on the glebe [soil] and of the crafts thus remained just as poor and enslaved as before. Indeed, their plight was often worse than before, so greedy and cruel did their new masters prove to be. Having no protection, the greater part among them began to form a wretched proletariat in the outskirts of the city, whose freemen were concerned only with sending them off to fight.

Now the Italian citizens of the time declared war, and fierce war, at will. These associated merchants constituting the commune were insatiable—forever having some quarrel to pick with their neighbors. When these neighbors blocked off the roads with taxes and tolls, they attacked them, if they felt themselves strong enough. If they were too weak, they allied themselves with other merchants, with some powerful lord, even with the emperor, so as to snatch the coveted river, bridge, forest, or strip of land from the rival commune.

And woe to the vanquished! Their city was razed, entire villages were destroyed, and crops burned. Prisoners—those who escaped from the massacre—were mutilated or tortured with a refinement of cruelty. At Forlì, for instance, men were shod like mules. And lest any should forget, annual festivals were celebrated in which pigs, rams, asses, and other grotesque animals appeared on the scene, charged with making the hereditary enemy seem despicable.

"Not only had war, with its orgies and disorders, become a necessity and habit, but it had become the preferred occupation, the ruling passion, and the whole life in this city, in which the word 'peace' no longer had any meaning."

Thus to the old seignoral rivalries were now joined undying hatreds and feuds between the communes, while within their walls they were often torn apart by partisan or family struggles, to the loss of their inner peace. "We learn," wrote Innocent III, "that you continue to lay waste cities, destroy castles, burn villages, oppress the poor, persecute churches, and reduce men to serfdom. Murder, violence, and rapine are rife, with quarreling and wars."

At the time of Saint Francis's youth, at any rate, these reproaches of the Pope were deserved as much by Assisi as by the communes of the Marches to which they were addressed. "Not only had war,

with its orgies and disorders, become a necessity and a habit, but it had become the preferred occupation, the ruling passion, and the whole life of this city, in which the word 'peace,' no longer had any meaning" (Fortini, *Nova Vita*, 125).

It is a mistake, then, to see in the end of the twelfth century and in the beginnings of the thirteenth a sort of golden age wherein peace and the practice of the Gospel flourished. It is true that in this period men built hospitals for the sick and abbeys whose walls resounded to the chanting of the divine praises, the land was adorned with a white flowering of churches, prayers and pilgrimages multiplied, Crusades were preached, knights professed to defend the widow and the orphan, and troubadours went all over Europe singing their courtly refrains. But if we stop to think that these hospitals, these cathedrals and monasteries were often the "remorse in stone" by means of which great sinners attempted to atone for their crimes and violence, and if we observe in addition that heresy and immorality corrupted Christian people, and that never before had the "little man" been the victim of so much social injustice, we may well conclude that the times of Saint Francis yielded to none in calamities and scandals.

The Eccentric Realist

COLMAN McCARTHY

A common assumption—widely mistaken—is that we die only once, the final tick of the physical heart that lets the sheet be pulled over our eyes and a call placed to the mortician. The literature of Christian saints, though, runs deep with another kind of mortality: the death of the self. Life does not expire but a *way* of life, and the corpse of worldly ways is buried with unpompous finality.

Few living deaths were more painful or dramatic than John Bernardone's, a young Italian of the early thirteenth century. Following a stretch as a prisoner of war—he was unhorsed in the first skirmish of a battle defending his hometown from German invaders—Bernardone suffered a strange ailment of the spirit that neither family nor friends could figure. His father, a businessman with an image to protect, said another stint in the army would bring the boy around. On wind of that, the son took to the hills and lived in a cave. When he came out one day, it was not for sunshine but to go to his father's clothing store to steal some scarlet cloth of high value. He would sell it and give the money to the poor, whom he had seen for the first time. Now he was truly crazy, his father believed; in the best traditions of mental health, the boy was locked in the cellar, in chains.

Saint Francis of Assisi is at once the most Christian of all saints . . . and the most accepted by the secular world. He is seen not as a preacher of truth or upholder of virtue, but as a practitioner of innocence.

These were the last days of John Bernardone and the first of Saint Francis of Assisi. He is at once the most Christian of all the saints—like Jesus, he owned everything because he could give it away—and the most accepted by the secular world. He is seen not as a preacher of truth or upholder of virtue, but as a practitioner of innocence. There will always be plenty of truth and virtue, but innocence?—its production is in decline, and who is making any more of it?

The beginning days of Saint Francis of Assisi,

confined to a cellar, saw the old self being slain from within. It is often the other way; Saint Paul's conversion was from without, as was Paul Claudel's in Notre Dame Cathedral. If his new life were not in the classic tradition of religious conversion, getting the works from his father was traditional family justice. Pietro Bernardone gave his boy the proverbial "best of everything." For awhile, the investment seemed to be paying off. The son dressed well, sang the newest songs to the prettiest Assisian women, and had the usual store of wild Italian oats to be sown. In fact, he earned the nickname "il Francesco"—the Frenchman—because of his fondness for fancy French ways. (If living today, Francis would be similar to our unsaintly Mafia citizens and their flair for nicknames—John [the Frenchman] Bernardone). All this changed suddenly—dapper clothes to rags, prayers in place of songs. History has been harsh on St. Francis's merchant father, but what parent today—a child comes home from college dressed in tatters and chanting mantras—cannot sympathize with old Pietro's shock? If only there were a guarantee the kids would become self-supporting and stay with it, until canonization, as Francis did!

After returning all his money and materials to his father—another custom the budding nature children of America usually overlook—Francis wandered the mountains clearing his head. For work, he settled on restoring churches, what Verlaine called "the humble life of tiresome and easy achievements." The townspeople—how often do local people everywhere have to suffer their young clowns who announce a new way of life every other week—were impressed by Francis because he persevered. Living in voluntary poverty was not a whim but was seen as a possible career.

Within a few months, friends came, and Francis established a small community—called the brotherhood—at Portiuncula. Perhaps because the Benedictines already had the market on the contemplative life, Francis decided his band should be travelers. The vocation of the road will not be easy, he warned the brothers on their first trip through the local Lombard region. "Go out, my beloved ones, and announce the gospel of peace and conversion. Be patient in trouble, give to all who insult you an humble answer, bless them who persecute you, thank those who do you wrong and slander you, because for all this your reward shall be great in heaven. And fear not because you are unlearned men, for you do not speak by yourselves, but the Spirit of your Heavenly Father will speak through you. You will find some men who are true, good and peaceful—they will receive you and your word with gladness. Others, and these in great number, you will on the other hand find to be revilers of God—they will oppose you and speak against you. Be therefore prepared to endure all things patiently."

As with all the saints, Francis said his only goal was to live according to the Scriptures, but as Nietzsche was to say, there has only been one true Christian and that was Christ. Emulating the whole Scripture is impossible, as Francis knew, so he took one part of the whole and made a wholeness out of that—detachment and voluntary poverty. "We said the office, those of us who were clerics, like other clerics, but the lay people said the 'Our Father,' and we liked to be in the churches. And we were simple (*idiotae*) and subject to all men. And I worked with my hands, and moreover wanted to work, and I desired that all the other brothers should be occupied with honorable work. And those who could do no work must learn it, not for the

desire of remuneration, but to give good example and not to be lazy. And if they will not give us pay for our work, we must have recourse to the table that the Lord has spread, as we go from door to door and beg for alms."

Down the centuries, Saint Francis has been a tempting figure for biographers. Everyone from Saint Bonaventure to G. K. Chesterton to Nikos Kazantzakis has taken a try. Historical distortions abound. One biographer, Thomas of Celano, like a modern cereal manufacturer, added excessive sugar to his product, making Francis sweet to the taste but of no substance. The *Saint Francis* (Simon and Schuster) of Kazantzakis, written as a fictional diary of Brother Leo—the saint's straight man and secretary—is a compelling account of Franciscan spirit. In Kazantzakis's words, Brother Leo tells Francis: "I know things about you that no other person knows. You committed many more sins than people imagine; you performed many more miracles than people believe. In order to mount to heaven, you used the floor of the inferno to give you your momentum. 'The farther down you gain your momentum,' you often used to tell me, 'the higher you shall be able to reach.'" The militant Christian's greatest worth is not virtue, but the struggle to transform into virtue the dishonor and malice within him or her.

Although he shared some of the Church's aberration for the Crusades—he went on one briefly but on meeting a Saracen began talking to him—Francis was a strict pacifist. As all pacifists eventually learn, often more is to be feared from one's own countrymen than from the "enemy." Kazantzakis describes a scene where Francis and Leo seek refuge with some of the good fathers. "Open the gate, brother doorkeeper," said Francis. "We are two humble servants of Christ who are hungry and cold and who seek refuge tonight in this holy monastery." The doorkeeper bellowed: "Go about your business. You—servants of God? And what are you doing roaming about the streets at such an hour? You're brigands, and you waylay men and kill them and set monasteries on fire. Off with you." "We are Christians," Francis replied. "Take pity on us." Instead, brother doorkeeper pounded the pair with a cudgel. "Do not resist," Francis called to Leo. "This is perfect joy." Leo had other ideas.

The most recent book on Francis is by John Holland Smith, in a work of readable scholarship published by Scribner's. We learn here that Francis may have had a saintly soul, but his head was often clouded with worldly stupidity. A novice who could read came once to the master for permission to own a Psalter. Never, said Francis. Books cause trouble; knowledge leads to pride. "There are too many Christians," Francis told the newcomer, "ready merely to read what the saints had done" and leave it at that. Although he continued to rail about books through the years, Francis eventually had to admit that, like sinners, they were here to stay.

With such a mentality leading what was becoming a growing religious order, the Franciscans soon had organization troubles. Moreover, the founder had a blunt tongue, quick to rebuke bishops for owning too much and his followers for praying too little. The legends of Francis talking with the sparrows and wolves are worthy of fireside repetition, but the saint also had to deal with beings considerably less lovable than animals: popes, bishops, and the crowds. He could be gentle and happy, notes historian Smith, "when it suited him. But he could also be ruthless in defending his own vision and pitiless in making either his own brothers or outsiders feel and look like fools, if he thought that would serve his ends."

Had Francis been only a dreamer among the birds, it is unlikely he would have founded the Order of Friars Minor, a congregation that has lasted to the twentieth century. In 1210, Francis walked to Rome for a meeting with the Pope to get a blessing on his work to establish his order officially. Papal assistants, ever cautious about tramps who denounced money—the assistants took it personally—advised against Francis. His rule was too hard, they said, especially the strange notion of living without property (Blessed are the property-holders . . .). For once, a Pope rejected his narrow advisers: Innocent III—a man who lived on lemons and called his clergy dogs—gave a conditional sanction to Francis's order. For the brothers, this meant little in winning the daily battles, but it was roughly similar to getting a famous name endorsement: the common people would be impressed. We're not just another roving gang of schismatics, Francis could say; the Pope backs us.

One of those apparently taken with Francis's new importance was Clara Scifi. Like Francis, she came from a wealthy Assisi family and left home for the convent only after loud scenes. Destined to found the Poor Clares, one of the Church's most heroic orders of sisters, Clare had a deep friendship for Francis until his death. There is little in contemporary life to help characterize Francis and Clare's bond; we are hot to understand everything about sex between men and women, but there is little

concern about friendship. Couples, we think, must end up in bed, or they end up in disaster. Yet Francis and Clare's friendship is truly modern; enjoying a shared consciousness, each liberated the other to do a life's work. It is odd how seldom the women's liberation movement ever calls on powerful women such as St. Clare as models of independence. Clare, forty years caring for the poor and comforting the orphans, knew more of life than do a dozen modern Greers and Friedans and their endless seminars on "oppression."

In 1220, the Franciscan movement growing, Francis found leadership not part of the spirituality he wanted. For one thing, he had to suffer a saint's most bothersome irk: other saints. In addition, few Franciscans shared their founder's uncompromising views on poverty. Calling themselves "reformers," the faction opposing Francis insisted that it was proper for the Order to use wealth so long as the members did not own it. A fine technicality, Francis said, but he dismissed it as a form of sanctified capitalism that encouraged not the spiritual life but the soft life. "Who are these men," he cried, "who have torn from my hands my own Order, the Order of my friars?"

Saddened by his brothers' adjustment to society, Francis retreated to his mountains and caves, to live as a hermit. His body—Brother Ass—was soon to give out, among the chills and drafts. For the reformers, this was high luck; soon Francis would be dead, safely canonized; a profitable shrine at his gravesite could be built, and all the while the new Franciscans could amass more real estate and ecclesiastical power.

Chesterton saw the irony in Francis's last days. "As it became more and more apparent that his health was failing, he seems to have been carried from place to place like a pageant of sickness or almost a pageant of mortality. . . . He who had become a vagabond for the sake of a vision, he who had denied himself all sense of a place and possession, he whose whole gospel and glory it was to be homeless, received . . . the sting of the sense of home."

Francis died painfully. He tried to keep the doctors outside, but they came in anyway, even cauterizing his head—the miracle antibiotic of the day. The legends differ on Francis's deathbed wish, whether he asked for a salad, a chocolate eclair, or a piece of candy. No matter. The symbol is clear: a final pleasure of innocence, after a lifetime of embracing God and owning all goods because he gave them away.

The Problem of Saint Francis

G.K. CHESTERTON

A sketch of Saint Francis of Assisi in modern English may be written in one of three ways. . . .

First, the writer may deal with this great and most amazing man as a figure in secular history and a model of social virtues. He may describe this divine demagogue as being, as he probably was, the world's one quite sincere democrat. He may say (which means very little) that Saint Francis was in advance of his age. He may say (which is quite true) that Saint Francis anticipated all that is most liberal and sympathetic in the modern mood: the love of nature; the love of animals; the sense of social compassion; the sense of the spiritual dangers of prosperity and even of property.

All those things that nobody understood before Wordsworth were familiar to Saint Francis. All those things that were first discovered by Tolstoy had been taken for granted by Saint Francis.

All those things that nobody understood before Wordsworth were familiar to Saint Francis. All those things that were first discovered by Tolstoy had been taken for granted by Saint Francis. He could be presented, not only as a human but also as a humanitarian hero; indeed as the first hero of humanism. He has been described as a sort of morning star of the Renaissance. And in comparison with all these things, his ascetical theology can be ignored or dismissed as a contemporary accident, which was fortunately not a fatal accident. His religion can be regarded as a superstition, but an inevitable superstition, from which not even genius could wholly free itself; in the consideration of which it would be unjust to condemn St. Francis for his self-denial or unduly chide him for his chastity.

It is quite true that even from so detached a standpoint his stature would still appear heroic. There would still be a great deal to be said about the man who tried to end the Crusades by talking to the Saracens or who interceded with the emperor for the birds. The writer might describe in a purely historical spirit the whole of that great Franciscan inspiration that was felt in the painting of Giotto, in the poetry of Dante, in the miracle plays that made possible the modern drama, and in so many other things that are already appreciated by the modern culture. He may try to do it, as others have done, almost without raising any religious question at all. In short, he may try to tell the story of a saint without God; which is like being told to write the life of Nansen and forbidden to mention the North Pole.

Second, he may go to the opposite extreme, and decide, as it were, to be defiantly devotional. He may make the theological enthusiasm as thoroughly the theme as it was the theme of the first Franciscans. He may treat religion as the real thing that it was to the real Francis of Assisi. He can find an austere joy, so to speak, in parading the paradoxes of asceticism and all the holy topsy-turvydom of humility. He can stamp the whole history with the stigmata, record fasts as if they were fights against a dragon; till in the vague modern mind Saint Francis is as dark a figure as Saint Dominic. In short he can produce what many in our world will regard as a sort of photographic negative, the reversal of all lights and shades; what the foolish will find as impenetrable as darkness, and even many of the wise will find almost as invisible as if it were written in silver upon white.

Such a study of St. Francis would be unintelligible to anyone who does not share his religion, perhaps only partly intelligible to anyone who does not share his vocation. According to degrees of judgment, it will be regarded as something too bad or too good for the world. The only difficulty about doing the thing in this way is that it cannot be done. It would really require a saint to write the life of a saint. In the present case the objections to such a course are insuperable.

Third, he may try to do what I have tried to do here; and, as I have already suggested, the course has peculiar problems of its own. The writer may put himself in the position of the ordinary modern outsider and inquirer; as indeed the present writer is still largely and was once entirely in that position. He may start from the standpoint of a man who already admires Saint Francis, but only for those things that such a man finds admirable. In other words he may assume that the reader is at least as enlightened as Renan or Matthew Arnold; but in the light of that enlightenment he may try

to illuminate what Renan and Matthew Arnold left dark. He may try to use what is understood to explain what is not understood. He may say to the modern English reader: "Here is a historical character that is admittedly attractive to many of us already, by its gaiety, its romantic imagination, its spiritual courtesy and camaraderie, but that also contains elements (evidently equally sincere and emphatic), which seem to you quite remote and repulsive. But after all, this man was a man and not half a dozen men. What seems inconsistency to you did not seem inconsistency to him. Let us see whether we can understand, with the help of the existing understanding, these other things that seem now to be doubly dark, by their intrinsic gloom and their ironic contrast."

I do not mean, of course, that I can really reach such a psychological completeness in this crude and curt outline. But I mean that this is the only controversial condition that I shall here assume: that I am dealing with the sympathetic outsider. I shall not assume any more or any less agreement than this. A materialist may not care whether the inconsistencies are reconciled or not. A Catholic may not see any inconsistencies to reconcile.

But I am here addressing the ordinary modern man, sympathetic but skeptical, and I can only rather hazily hope that by approaching the great saint's story through what is evidently picturesque and popular about it, I may at least leave the reader understanding a little more than he did before of the consistency of a complete character; that by approaching it in this way, we may at least get a glimmering of why the poet who praised his lord the sun often hid himself in a dark cavern, of why the saint who was so gentle with his Brother the Wolf was so harsh to his Brother the Ass (as he nicknamed his own body), of why the troubadour who said that love set his heart on fire separated himself from women, of why the singer who rejoiced in the strength and gaiety of the fire deliberately rolled himself in the snow, of why the very song that cries with all the passion of a pagan, "Praised be God for our Sister, Mother Earth, which brings forth varied fruits and grass and glowing flowers," ends almost with the words "Praised be God for our Sister, the death of the body."

Renan and Matthew Arnold failed utterly at this test. They were content to follow Francis with their praises until they were stopped by their prejudices: the stubborn prejudices of the skeptic. The moment Francis began to do something they did not understand or did not like, they did not try to understand it, still less to like it; they simply turned their backs on the whole business and "walked no more with him." No man will get any further along a path of historical enquiry in that fashion. These skeptics are really driven to drop the whole subject in despair, to leave the most simple and sincere of all historical characters as a mass of contradictions, to be praised on the principle of the curate's egg.* Arnold refers to the asceticism of Alvernia almost hurriedly, as if it were an unlucky but undeniable blot on the beauty of the story; or rather as if it were a pitiable breakdown and bathos at the end of the story.

Now this is simply to be stone-blind to the whole point of any story. To represent Mount Alvernia as a mere collapse of Francis is exactly like representing Mount Calvary as the mere collapse of Christ. Those mountains are mountains, whatever else they are, and it is nonsense to say (like the Red Queen) that they are comparative hollows or negative holes in the ground. They were quite manifestly meant to be culminations and landmarks. To treat the stigmata as a sort of scandal, to be touched on tenderly but with pain, is exactly like treating the original five wounds of Jesus Christ as five blots on his character. You may dislike the idea of asceticism; you may dislike equally the idea of martyrdom; for that matter you may have an honest and natural dislike of the whole conception of sacrifice symbolized by the cross. But if it is an intelligent dislike, you will still retain the capacity for seeing the point of a story; of the story of a martyr or even the story of a monk. You will not be able rationally to read the Gospel and regard the Crucifixion as an afterthought or an anticlimax or an accident in the life of Christ; it is obviously the point of the story like the point of a sword, the sword that pierced the heart of the Mother of God.

And you will not be able rationally to read the story of a man presented as a mirror of Christ without understanding his final phase as a man of sorrows, and at least artistically appreciating the appropriateness of his receiving, in a cloud of mystery and isolation, inflicted by no human hand, the unhealed everlasting wounds that heal the world.

The practical reconciliation of the gaiety and austerity I must leave the story itself to suggest. But since I have mentioned Matthew Arnold and Renan and the rationalistic admirers of Saint Francis, I will here give the hint of what it seems to me most advisable for such readers to keep in

* Something good in some parts but defective in others.

mind. These distinguished writers found things such as the stigmata a stumbling block because to them a religion was a philosophy. It was an impersonal thing; and it is only the most personal passion that provides here an approximate earthly parallel. A man will not roll in the snow for a stream or tendency by which all things fulfill the law of their being. He will not go without food in the name of something, not ourselves, that makes for righteousness. He will do things like this, or pretty nearly like this, under quite a different impulse. He will do these things when he is in love.

The first fact to realize about Saint Francis is involved in the first fact with which his story starts; that when he said from the first that he was a troubadour, and said later that he was a troubadour of a newer and nobler romance, he was not using a mere metaphor, but understood himself much better than the scholars understand him. He was, to the last agonies of asceticism, a troubadour. He was a lover. He was a lover of God, and he was really and truly a lover of men, possibly a much rarer mystical vocation. A lover of men is very nearly the opposite of a philanthropist; indeed the pedantry of the Greek word carries something like a satire on itself. A philanthropist may be said to love anthropoids. But as Saint Francis did not love humanity but men, so he did not love Christianity but Christ.

Say, if you think so, that he was a lunatic loving an imaginary person; but an imaginary person, not an imaginary idea. And for the modern reader the clue to the asceticism and all the rest can best be found in the stories of lovers when they seemed to be rather like lunatics. Tell it as the tale of one of the troubadours, and the wild things he would do for his lady, and the whole of the modern puzzle disappears. In such a romance there would be no contradiction between the poet gathering flowers in the sun and enduring a freezing vigil in the snow, between his praising all earthly and bodily beauty and then refusing to eat, between his glorifying gold and purple and perversely going in rags, between his showing pathetically a hunger for a happy life and a thirst for an heroic death. All these riddles would easily be resolved in the simplicity of any noble love; only this was so noble a love that nine men out of ten have hardly even heard of it. We shall see later that this parallel of the earthly lover has a very practical relation to the problems of his life, as to his relations with his father and with his friends and their families.

The modern reader will almost always find that

if he could only feel this kind of love as a reality, he could feel this kind of extravagance as a romance. But I note it here only as a preliminary point because, though it is very far from being the final truth in the matter, it is the best approach to a story that may well seem to him a very wild one, until he understands that to this great mystic his religion was not a thing like a theory but a thing like a love affair.

The Hippie Saint

JOSEPH RODDY

"Your way of living without owning anything," the Bishop of Assisi said to Francis, "seems to me very harsh and difficult."

"My lord," Francis answered, "if we possessed property, we should need arms to defend it."

No revelation that. There were always arms for the propertied, bishops for defense, and no end to the harshness and difficulties around the unpossessing. Yet there stands the scruffy, little Umbrian figure of Francis Bernardone out of that unfashionable thirteenth century, a bearded, barefoot, slightly prankish, and largely unfathomable man, but a man the world now in torment finds more alluring every day.

[The Franciscans] were the medieval precedents for his latter-day crowd hailing from the hippie communes, the unchurchable young discovering that owners are themselves fatally owned. The faith of these new Franciscans—like that of the first Christians—is in a counterculture. Their hopes are that the world will turn truly communal fast or the very roof of heaven will fall in.

It is an allure that can escape purpled bishops and the heavily propertied, to be sure, though they honor him with insipid statuary in birdbaths, ply children with pretty tales of his chats with beasts, and exclaim over the success of the religious society he started for mendicants, who now manage real estate worth maybe more than all the city of Assisi.

It was the successmongers in medieval Assisi who hustled the first Franciscan into official sainthood two years after he died in 1226. Even then, canonization was a deft way to isolate and have done with anyone whose imitation of Christ embarrassed practical Christians. "The Lord told me to become a new type of simpleton," Francis was saying while the first organization men were bringing practical-

ity, efficiency, and common sense to his band of gentle vagrants.

They were the medieval precedents for his latter-day crowd hailing from the hippie communes, the unchurchable young discovering that owners are themselves fatally owned. The faith of these new Franciscans—like that of the first Christians—is in a counterculture. Their hopes are that the world will turn truly communal fast or the very roof of heaven will fall in.

What a friend they have in Francis. He was the son of a rich man in dry goods, and right from the start he was a trouble to his father. When his son was born, Pietro di Bernardone was in France going about his fabrics. By the time he made it back to Assisi, it was to find that his French wife had already named their infant John. The father would not have it, and renamed the boy Francis, to get him started out right in life as the courtly, young French-type man the upwardbound Umbrian planned to have his son be. From the town priests, Francis learned little. But from Assisi's young sports, the youth learned to sing, drink, dance, and wench and, that the first few times around, a little revelry is not quite the vast repugnance the parish priests made it out to be.

When Perugia went to war against Assisi, twenty-year-old Francis was taken prisoner, and by all accounts found jail a good place to get on with his singing. His taste for the fleshpots slackened there and, once out, he found himself instead listening for a guiding voice of the force Saul heard on the road to Damascus, the voice Joan was to hear at the siege of Orléans. "All that which now seems to you sweet and lovely will become intolerable and bitter," was what it said. "But all that you used to avoid will turn itself to great sweetness and exceeding joy." On the road before him then was a leper, abhorrent to see, foul to smell, but with hands to be kissed, and Francis kissed them. Not only kissed them but pressed money into them—money that had lost its savor for him, though it was mostly not his, or almost entirely his father's.

When that voice he listened for told him that the Chapel of San Damiano near Assisi needed restoring, young Bernardone acted. He went back to his father's shop, loaded his horse with bolts of fine cloth, and rode off to the next town, where he sold the cloth and the horse and gave all he got for them to the old priest sitting in the sun outside San Damiano. Francis was back in the cave he had taken to living and meditating in when the senior Bernardone noticed the loss and hauled his son into the bishop's court. "My lord," said the accused, "I will give him not only the money cheerfully but also the clothes I have received from him." In a moment, Francis had them all off, had his father disowned, and faced a very unencumbered future. When he left the bishop's house, he was wearing the old cloak the gardener had discarded, and when he had fitted himself with a beggar's bowl, he had just about all he needed then to be a Franciscan.

All accounts make him out to be the merriest of mendicants, but a mystic whose overpowering faith compelled other men to follow him. First came two, giving away all they owned, then four more, then by the dozens, and then came the rock-solid Assisians who were offended by the odd ways of the beggars Francis called Friars Minor.* "Many men took the friars for knaves or madmen and refused to receive them into their houses for fear of being robbed," three followers then living with Francis wrote. "So in many places, after having undergone all sorts of bad usage, they could find no other refuge for the night than the porticos of churches or houses. . . .

"There were those who threw mud upon them, others who put dice into their hands and invited them to play, and others clutching them by the cowl made them drag along thus. But seeing that the friars were always full of joy in the midst of their tribulations, that they neither received nor carried money, and that by their love for one another they made themselves known as true disciples of the Lord, many of them felt themselves reproved in their hearts and came asking pardon for the offenses they had committed. They, pardoning them with all their hearts, said, 'The Lord forgive you,' and gave them pious counsels for the salvation of their souls."

They were so burgeoning a band in 1210 that Francis and twelve friars went to the Vatican to establish themselves as a religious society. The Pope, Innocent III, thought their way of life too severe, but since all they sought was the right to live as Christ had, to deny them would be to deny that following the Gospel was possible.

Francis was not a priest, nor were his first friars, but their audience with the Pope started them down the road to absorption. Paul Sabatier's biography of Francis, a work the Franciscans even now do not quite cherish, laments that agreement. As a

* Little brothers.

result of it, "the thoroughly lay creation of St. Francis," Sabatier writes, "had become, in spite of himself, an ecclesiastical institution. All unawares, the Franciscan movement had been unfaithful to its origin."

Others thought it foundered over the figure of Clara Scifi, the devout daughter of a noble family in Assisi. She was sixteen when she heard Francis preach and came at once to the view that she too would have to be one of his missionary troupe. By simply ignoring canon law, Francis decided that could be arranged; and late on Palm Sunday night in the year 1212, she was the first woman accepted into his society. The friars had just finished singing matins when Francis himself cut off most of her hair. In place of her shining dress, he decked her out in a black veil, a coarse woolen robe, and a knotted rope to bind it at her waist. That night he took her to live with Benedictine nuns a few miles away, where her outraged father found her but could not induce her to return home. Like Bernardone, Scifi was another status-quo parent sure to go unnoticed in Assisi had it not been for a rebellious child. Clara's younger sister joined her in a week, followed later by their youngest sister, then by their widowed mother.

The lady Franciscans, known now as the Poor Clares, lived then at San Damiano, a few miles away from the Portiuncula, the ten-foot-long chapel still there as the birth-house of the Franciscans. Francis seldom preached at San Damiano, but pious tradition has him under the olive trees and in the care of Sister Clare with his sight nearly gone when he wrote and sang "The Canticle of Brother Sun." It is among the few perfect hymns of praise that are also exalted acts of faith.

Before that, Francis was given to leaving Assisi for spells of solitary contemplation and to spread his beliefs. If he loved the birds and talked with them, it was also to tell them to be quiet while he preached. He was particularly forthright in telling a wolf in the town of Gubbio that he had to mend his ways, and that once his attacks stopped, the townsfolk would see to his care and proper feeding. He called his own body, but not without courtesy, Brother Ass. That was the brother he never subdued to his satisfaction, and he knew he had lost to that beast once more the night he found himself eating a chicken after preaching fasting and abstinence to Umbrians. The next day he had another friar lead him through the town on a halter. "Look here, you people," Francis called out as he passed, "this is the man who asks you to fast and repent while he himself feasts on a tender bird just because his stomach hurts him a little. That glutton, that reveler, that hypocrite!"

He turned up at fine dinners in episcopal palaces with his beggar's bowl. He threw money he was owed into dung heaps. And his first time in Rome, Francis was so poorly turned out when he bowed to Innocent III that the offended Pope said he should go and roll in a pigsty. Francis did, the biographers say, then returned even more redolent for his audience in the Vatican. He was the pure fool for his faith, the hard-line follower of Christ, and just maybe the precursor of Chaplin.

He was never more the man for his God, inseparable from pathos, than when he set out to convert the Muslims in Egypt while the Christian armies of the Crusade were drawn up outside Damietta to massacre them. Ministering to the Crusaders was disheartening even to Francis, for all about him he saw the Pope's legions steadily gluttonous, drunk, and dissolute. Harlots from Sicily were circulating through the tents, with all manner of relic hawkers following, and when the lucre was gone from the sacred coffers, blessed suits of armor were sold off to pay painted ladies or bartered for more pieces of a true Cross. Appalled by the Christians, Francis was conducted through the battle lines to bring the Word of God to the Muslims he thought heathens. Their Sultan, Melek-el-Kamil, in perfect civility, heard the sermons about a creed he found strange but not compelling. When the saint had given up on him, the Sultan saw him safely back to his fellow-believers. Francis continued on quickly to Assisi.

The trouble back in Italy was the trouble most saviors have with their disciples. There were thousands of Franciscans by then—men, women and near-children, each devoted in some fashion and all certain about the form their devotion took. When the Friars Minor were just a ragtag few, their begging and vagrancy were more quaint than disruptive. But beggar packs on the streets and crowds of men without homes seemed a threat to public order. Yet the larger problem was within the Order itself.

Francis was always to be the society's spiritual leader, but he found it beyond his talents to be its administering general too. Although he had never expected it of them, his Friars Minor had grown into an organization. Its administrators in Assisi were finding that most discontent stemmed from the vow of poverty that all new disciples found easy to make but arduous to observe.

Ownership was not the only problem. There were friars who wanted to change his rules on fasting and abstinence. Another, with ambitions for a splinter movement, petitioned the Pope to let him found a new society to care for lepers. In Bologna, the Franciscans were putting up a fine house of studies for themselves. Francis had forbidden them to carry anything, and now they were even planning to carry books. "There are so many in our days who want to seek wisdom and learning," he said, "that happy is he who out of love for the Lord our God makes himself ignorant." Learning was of little worth in Francis's view, but his growing society was growing its own theologians, then canon lawyers, as well as ambitious ecclesiastics who wanted dioceses, red hats, offices in the Roman Curia, and maybe the Throne of Peter itself. It was enough to make the poor saint want to start all over again, but it was too late.

A faint aura of authority still clustered about their spiritual leader, but through their ministers-general, the Franciscans came under the firm rule of Rome. To resist that would have taken administrative strength, and what little of that Francis ever had was long gone. "Where are they who have ravished my brethren from me?" he cried out one day. "Where are they who have stolen away my family?" And his Brother Ass was spent too. He suffered from hemorrhages and from stomach infections, and when thirteenth-century healers tried saving his eyesight by cauterizing his temples he showed fear. "Brother Fire," he said as the irons were brought to him, "be favorable to me in this hour; you know how much I have always loved you." But it was not favorable, and the treatment left him as unseeing as before but now hideously burned. Then came the wounds in his hands and feet, thought to be stigmata matching the wounds of Christ. When his own death was so plainly near in the fall of 1226, his closest followers brought him in a litter to the tiny Portiuncula. He was there, singing his "Canticle of Brother Sun" in a whisper the day before the life went out of him.

He left a will charging his friars to resist change and stay simple and poor, but in no time at all, it was burned to ash over the head of a friar who wanted to live by it. Gregory IX, the Pope who made being a Franciscan much easier than Francis ever had, caused a great basilica to rise up in Assisi to honor the saint. Visitors are quick to compare it to the tiny Portiuncula, and they know then how the truth of the saint can make the mighty despair.

An Eyewitness Description of Saint Francis's Appearance and Personality

THOMAS OF CELANO

O how beautiful, how splendid, how glorious did he appear in the innocence of his life, in the simplicity of his words, in the purity of his heart, in his love for God, in his fraternal charity, in his ardent obedience, in his peaceful submission, in his angelic countenance! He was charming in his manners, serene by nature, affable in his conversation, most opportune in his exhortations, most faithful in what was entrusted to him, cautious in counsel, effective in business, gracious in all things. He was serene of mind, sweet of disposition, sober in spirit, raised up in contemplation, zealous in prayer, and in all things fervent. He was constant in purpose, stable in virtue, persevering in grace, and unchanging in all things. He was quick to pardon, slow to become angry, ready of wit, tenacious of memory, subtle in discussion, circumspect in choosing, and in all things simple. He was unbending with himself, understanding toward others, and discreet in all things.

He was a most eloquent man, a man of cheerful countenance, of kindly aspect; he was immune to cowardice, free of insolence. He was of medium height, closer to shortness; his head was moderate in size and round, his face a bit long and prominent, his forehead smooth and low; his eyes were of moderate size, black and round; his hair was black, his eyebrows straight, his nose symmetrical, thin and straight; his ears were upright, but small; his temples smooth. His speech was peaceable, fiery, and sharp; his voice was strong, sweet, clear, and sonorous. His teeth were set close together, even, and white; his lips were small and thin; his beard black, but not bushy. His neck was slender; his shoulders straight; his arms short; his hands slender; his fingers long; his nails extended; his legs were thin; his feet small. His skin was delicate; his flesh very spare. He wore rough garments; he slept but very briefly; he gave most generously. And because he was very humble, he showed all

mildness to all men, adapting himself usefully to the behavior of all. The more holy amongst the holy, among sinners he was as one of them. Therefore, most holy father, help the sinners, you who loved sinners, and deign, we beg of you, most kindly to raise up by your most glorious intercession those whom you see lying in the mire of their sins.

An Analysis of Saint Francis's Handwriting

GIROLAMO MORETTI

SENTIMENT *Substantial signs:* Curve 8/10; A Angles 5/10; B Angles 3/10; C Angles 5/10; Pressure I mode 7/10; Spacing between letters 7/10; Maintains the base line 7/10; Ascending 3/10; Sinuous 7/10; Springy 5/10; Pondered 5/10; Elegant 5/10; *Modifying:* Straight strokes 7/10; Strokes bent forward 3/10; Calm 7/10; Austere 4/10. *Accidentals:* Fluid 7/10; Charming grace 5/10; Accurate 3/10.

INTELLIGENCE *Substantials:* Spacing of letters 8/10; Spacing between letters 7/10; Spacing between words 5/10; Methodical Inequality 7/10; Sinuous 7/10; Clear 8/10. *Modifying:* Accurate 3/10; Laconic 8/10.

INTELLIGENCE Quantitatively superior (*Spacing of Letters*); qualitatively capable of original concepts (*Methodical Inequality*), that is to say, an inventive intelligence. The subject has ability in psychology, and had he dedicated himself to it, he would have solved a good many questions that still remain unsolved (*Sinuous, Methodical Inequality, Curve*), inasmuch as his study would have centered on love, that being the trait he possessed to the highest degree (*Curve*). He would have been able, with great ease, to penetrate the souls of men, laying bare and objectively analyzing all human tendencies. He has offered marvelous solutions with his practical work and in the "Canticle of Brother Sun," but he could have made an incomparable contribution to the science of psychology if he had dedicated himself to this difficult and inexhaustible field.

I could not say, however, with complete certainty, if he would have had any noticeable success in scientific matters, inasmuch as it is impossible to see what the true spacing is between words in his handwriting.

There is no doubt that he does have a tendency and ability for art, an elevated lyricism lighted by love (*Curve*), and is not at all troubled by the tendencies seeking to dissolve it (*A Angles, B Angles*). He knows how to get things done (*C Angles*); his altruism is very marked; and although he has a tendency to command (*Pressure I mode*), he puts every-

26

thing entirely at the service of this altruism, even his firmness of character (*Maintains the Base Line*), his ardor (*Ascending*), and his will to perfect himself.

The subject conceivably could have created a very personal musical idiom (*Methodical Inequality, Springy*) that would have developed various motifs in a completely altruistic way. He could have captured the sounds, the chirping of birds, the soft cooing of little ones in the nest; he could have taken from the wind the delicate murmur of the breeze and the blasts of impetuous currents; and from water he could have transposed the sound of streams rushing down mountains and through gorges. It is regrettable that he did not put to music the sublime "Canticle of Brother Sun" that reveals him as a great poet.

He could have done well in art (*Elegant*), although with a tendency to design and the simple sketch (*Laconic*).

He has organizational abilities . . . , plans clearly . . . , and is capable of overcoming all opposition by his firmness of character . . . , by his decisiveness . . . , and by his knowing gentleness. . . .

His way of thinking and manner of expression are very natural (*Fluid*). He tends to intellectual and verbal terseness (*Laconic*). He has organizational abilities (*Methodical Inequality, Pondered*), plans clearly (*Clear*), and is capable of overcoming all opposition by his firmness of character (*Maintains the Base Line*), by his decisiveness (*Straight Strokes*), and by his knowing gentleness (*Strokes Inclined to the Right*).

CHARACTER As for character, he is one of those beings who by nature tend above all to altruism (*Curve*). Even though it be kept in mind that in human beings altruism cannot have one and the same common denominator and numerator, and even though allowance be made for conceding a little to the ego (2/10), it does appear that the saint had this quality to the highest degree. A generous altruism (*Spacing Between Letters*), irrepressible (*Maintains the Base Line, Straight Strokes*) but governed by the ambition of giving orders (*Pressure I Mode*) and the desire of making a good appearance (*Charming Grace*), it remains true that this ambition is mitigated greatly by his moderation (*Pondered*). There is therefore a tendency to do good for others but at the same time to act for oneself with little spirit of humility and respect for duly constituted authority. There is also the desire to have others follow his own will (*C Angles*).

Jekyll, Hyde, and Francis

ERNEST RAYMOND

You see, there are three latencies in us, not two only. Not Dr. Jekyll and Mr. Hyde only, but Dr. Jekyll, Mr. Hyde, and Young Francis. I dare almost assert that this has been proved in the clinics when the doctors have studied the phenomenon known as dissociated personality.

The classic case is that of Miss Beauchamp. The normal, everyday personality of Miss Beauchamp disintegrated into three component and warring parts, which Dr. Prince, who was in charge of the case, labeled respectively the woman, the devil, and the saint. One of these "persons" would fade right out of consciousness with all her train of memories, and another with quite different memories and motives would take command of Miss Beauchamp. By hypnotism Dr. Prince was able to dismiss one personality at will and open the chamber of consciousness to another, though I think I am right in saying he could never quite put the "devil" to sleep. The "devil" stayed always in the background watching and ridiculing the other two. I mention this famous case simply as an extreme pathological instance of something we all feel to be true: that within us contend three potential people, Dr. Jekyll, an ordinarily decent fellow, Mr. Hyde, an unspeakable person, and—very small, very little, very poor, a *poverello* (poor man), indeed—Young Francis.

Of course we could call the young and saintly one by another name than Francis if we could find in the calendar another saint whose life embodies so well all that we really believe to be the Perfect Reality of ourselves—that reality that, alas, remains for most of us always potential and unattained. The mystics of the Christian color have not hesitated to call this highest potentiality in themselves by the name of Christ, and actually to identify it with him.

A sentence of Rudolph Eucken may help us here. "Man," he says, "is the meeting place of two orders of Reality." That is to say, man alone of all the creatures in this world is visited by gleams from, or is possessed by a portion of, that invisible, eternal, ultimate Reality that is Perfection, and that lies behind the vivid but illusory "reality" of this imperfect, temporary sphere; and the result of this strange visitation or possession is that his present consciousness stands midway between an old, moribund, lower self, which cleaves to the imperfections of the lower world from which it has sprung, and a young, emergent higher self, which is happy only when it is approximating toward the perfections of Eternity.

His present consciousness stands there like a captain able to direct its will toward one or the other of these two. Most mystical writers have called this directing consciousness the Soul, the higher self the Spirit, and the lower self the Body; and if we had only grasped that this was what they meant by Body, we should have been saved a deal of misunderstanding. Soul, then, our present consciousness; Spirit, that which we long to be; and Body, that which we desire to escape: these terms have never been wholly satisfactory, but there are none better, and we shall use them on this our exciting pilgrimage, when we are getting a bit mystical.

A born artist, a natural, unconscious dramatist, a wit, he showed forth this greatest of all dramas, the clash of the Eternal on the things of Time, in a life story so stirring in its ascent to an awful climax that the world has been able to match it only with that played out by his Master twelve hundred years before.

That it is bound to be exciting I reaffirm. First, because of this personal reference that will be implicit in our talk all the way. No talk quite so interesting as that which we can relate to ourselves! And secondly, because the life story that it will compel us to retell is just about the most human and the most moving in the libraries of Christendom. There never was a more dramatic tale in the hand of a novelist. Francis would have used none of these large words written above: Ultimate Reality, Temporal Sphere, Directing Consciousness, and what not; he would not have understood them, for there was never a saint less well read in the lives of the saints, never a teacher more happily ignorant of most of the teachings of the Church that he loved, never a preacher more likely to be tripped up over a passage in the Bible; he just did with simplicity and ignorantly what you and I won't do; he dared, in the end, to let the Real come through. He dared to let the eternal truth in him conquer all; which is simply to say that he dared to let the surging love in him determine his every movement and thought. And if a man does this, he must stir up drama like dust at every step.

It is what every saint does, of course; but Francis did it more impressively, more graciously, and more amusingly than any other. A born artist, a natural, unconscious dramatist, a wit, he showed forth this greatest of all dramas, the clash of the Eternal on the things of Time, in a life story so stirring in its ascent to an awful climax that the world has been able to match it only with that played out by his Master twelve hundred years before. Strange young man, too full of love! There has been one Francis, and one only.

Pietro Bernardone: An Unorthodox Character

ANTHONY MOCKLER

In 1181 Henry the Open-Hearted died, leaving Marie his widow as Regent of Champagne till the boy-count Henry II should come of age. At about this time a merchant of Assisi, Pietro Bernardone, was at one of the great fairs of Champagne. He had left his pregnant wife Pica behind. When he arrived back in Assisi with his bales of cloth and merchandise, he found that she had given birth to a son. Much to his annoyance, she had baptized him Giovanni. The merchant, a strong-willed man, immediately changed his son's name to Francesco, the Frenchman—Francis.

If this were a mere whim, it was an extraordinarily drastic way in which to display it—more of the gesture one would expect from a poet or a sentimentalist, which Pietro Bernardone certainly was not—than from a hard-headed businessman, which is what he appears to have been. If it were not a mere whim, it was a deliberate and calculated and rather provocative move, for it can be imagined that the changing of the baptismal name of the son of one of the leading merchants of the community must have created a considerable stir in a small town like Assisi. At the very least it indicates that Pietro Bernardone was a great enthusiast for French ideas and that he wanted to flaunt this enthusiasm openly. There can be no doubt that it was he who later on brought up his son to speak French and to sing French songs, a notable habit that is often referred to as if it were extremely unusual.

There is a considerable mystery about the father of Saint Francis. He is cast by all the saint's biographers, without exception, as the villain of the piece, both harsh and avaricious—and yet, on any normal view of human relations, it was the father who behaved well and even overindulgently, spoiling his son, putting up with his extravagances, fitting him out as a knight with all the expense that that involved—until he was provoked almost beyond endurance; and it was the son Francis who behaved badly and indeed in an abominably insulting way. "Honor thy father and thy mother," says the Bible, which both Francis and his friars were so fond of quoting. Yet no one seems even to have reproached Francis for committing what was presumably a mortal sin [sic] in failing to honor his father; and even the Bishop of Assisi, a very worldly man and none too generous himself [sic],* supported the son against the father. Why? It is more usual, to say the least, for the established authorities to support men of substance of their own generation against extravagant, insolent, and rebellious young men than vice versa. And why, furthermore, was Pietro Bernardone so ill thought of in Assisi that, in the documents of the commune, drawn up at that period, his other son Angelo was always referred to as "the son of the Lady Pica" and never, though it would have been normal, as "the son of Pietro"?

What, in any case, was Pietro Bernardone's background? There is a late document that implies that he came from Lucca, and a still later one that attempts to find a noble origin for his wife Pica. These can both be discounted. There is a possibility that Pica was a nickname, that in fact she was a Picard from northern France (her grandson, one of Angelo's two boys, was also called Piccardo); but this is mere guesswork. What is certain is that, in the communal documents, she is always referred to as *domina,* but her husband is never given the honorary title of *dominus* despite his status as a leading merchant of Assisi and as a considerable landowner of various orchards and farms, both in the plain below Assisi and on the slopes of Monte Subasio.

* Bishop Guido's reputation as a deeply spiritual and caring person is noted by virtually all of Saint Francis's biographers.

For some reason he seems to have been extremely unpopular with the powers-that-were and to have been relegated almost to the status of a nonperson by Francis's biographers. He was, at the same time, clearly a great admirer of French ideas. Can this have been the cause of his unpopularity? I think it can and it must have been. It is important to know because clearly Pietro Bernardone was a very strong character, and his ideas, as in the case of all fathers with strong characters in close-knit families, directly formed his son's ideas—either in the sense that Francis accepted his father's views or in the opposite but equally important sense that he reacted against them. It will become clear that Francis was, even as a grown man, terrified of his father; and it took him twenty-five years of his life before he formally broke loose. That is a long and most important period in the life of a man who lived only to the age of forty-four or forty-five. And it is worthwhile to dig hard and wide and deep in the attempt to get to the roots of their relationship.

No striking tales have come down to us of Francis's childhood. His formal education was minimal. He learned "grammar" from the canons at the parish church of San Giorgio—reading and writing, at neither of which does he appear ever to have been very skilled, and the elements of Latin. At the age of fourteen, that is to say in 1195 or 1196, he started helping in his father's business, both buying and selling.

The family house of the Bernardones was probably just off the main square in Assisi, where the *mercatus* or market was held. It was normal for the *fondaco* of a merchant, the shop itself, to occupy the front part of the ground floor of the house where he and his family lived; the merchandise was displayed both inside the building and outside, in stalls on the street. At this stage in Italian history the merchant class, the bourgeoisie, was becoming increasingly powerful, and within the commune was on almost equal footing with the nobility. The nobles were gradually being forced by the economic and social changes of the period to abandon their isolated castles and fortresses in the outlying countryside and to come and live inside the walls of the cities and towns of Italy, submitting much against their will to the power—and the rules and regulations—of the urban *comune,* the commune. This was a gradual and bitter process; while it was occurring, and indeed long after it occurred, the nobles retained their pride of blood and their social prestige, even if they lost a considerable part of their actual power. They remained the knightly class, the *militares;* but the guilds of the merchants, the *mercatores,* were becoming the dominant and directing body; of these merchants the élite were the merchants who dealt in cloth and clothes. . . .

. . . traders in wool were known (at that time) as the propagandists of Cathari beliefs; Pietro Bernardone was a wool merchant and a declared admirer of France; and the Cathari Church had in his time spread down into the valley of Spoleto, in which Assisi stands.

I am not suggesting that Pietro Bernardone was a "Perfect" of this group. I am suggesting that he was either a "Believer" or an open sympathizer with Catharist teachings; that he belonged to a minority but to a powerful minority in Assisi, and that for this reason when the majority, the traditional believers in the traditional Church, established their position of dominance he became, despite his riches and influence, a highly unpopular man.

One need hardly delve into psychology to conclude that Francis both hated his father and longed for his approval; and that this relationship is the key to, at any rate, the first half of his life.

He was not perhaps a very intelligent or discriminating man; he probably did not distinguish too clearly between the aristocratic traditions and feudal panache that had dazzled him at the courts of Champagne and the strictly Catharist beliefs and practices. What I am suggesting is that he was a forceful personality who tried to impose all that he had learned or heard in France upon his son Francis; and that Francis, all his life, was to be influenced by this informal education he had received from his father—enjoying parts of it, detesting other parts, but always strongly reacting. As for his mother, *domina* Pica, all the evidence seems to show that she was a traditional Italian *mamma,* of the weak not the strong variety, doting on her *figliolo,* afraid of her husband's temper, and shocked by his views, conventionally accepting the Church and its teachings. One need hardly delve into psychology to conclude that Francis both hated his father and longed for his approval; and that this relationship is the key to, at any rate, the first half of his life.

Saint Francis and His Father: Another View

JOHN RUSKIN

One of Saint Francis's three great virtues being obedience, he begins his spiritual life by quarreling with his father. He, I suppose in modern terms I should say, "commercially invests" some of his father's goods in charity. His father objects to that investment; on which Saint Francis runs away, taking what he can find about the house along with him. His father follows to claim his property, but finds it is all gone, already; and that Saint Francis has made friends with the Bishop of Assisi. His father flies into an indecent passion and declares he will disinherit him; on which Saint Francis then and there takes all his clothes off, throws them frantically in his father's face, and says he has nothing more to do with clothes or father. The good bishop, in tears of admiration, embraces Saint Francis, and covers him with his own mantle.

I have read the picture [a Giotto painting] to you as . . . from the plain, common-sense, Protestant side. If you are content with that view of it, you may leave the chapel, and, so far as any study of history is concerned, Florence also; for you can never know anything either about Giotto, or her.

Yet do not be afraid of my rereading it to you from the mystic, nonsensical, and papistical side. I am going to read it to you—if after many and many a year of thought, I am able—as Giotto meant it; Giotto being, so far as we know, then the man of strongest brain and hand in Florence; the best friend of the best religious poet of the world [Dante]; and widely differing, as his friend did also, in his views of the world, from either Mr. Spurgeon or Pius IX.

The first duty of a child is to obey his father and mother, as the first duty of a citizen is to obey the laws of his state. And this duty is so strict that I believe the only limits to it are those fixed by Isaac and Iphigenia. On the other hand, the father and mother have also a fixed duty to the child—not to provoke it to wrath. I have never heard this text explained to fathers and mothers from the pulpit, which is curious. For it appears to me that God will expect the parents to understand their duty to their children, better even than children can be expected to know their duty to their parents.

31

But further. A *child's* duty is to obey its parents. It is never said anywhere in the Bible, and never was yet said in any good or wise book, that a man's, or woman's, is. *When,* precisely, a child becomes a man or a woman, it can no more be said than when it should first stand on its legs. But a time assuredly comes when it should. In great states, children are always trying to remain children, and the parents wanting to make men and women of them. In vile states, the children are always wanting to be men and women, and the parents to keep them children. It may be—and happy the house in which it is so—that the father's at least equal intellect, and older experience, may remain to the end of his life a law to his children, not of force, but of perfect guidance, with perfect love. Rarely it is so; not often possible. It is as natural for the old to be prejudiced as for the young to be presumptuous; and, in the change of centuries, each generation has something to judge of for itself.

But this scene, on which Giotto has dwelt with so great force, represents not the child's assertion of his independence, but his adoption of another Father.

You must not confuse the desire of this boy of Assisi to obey God rather than man with the desire of your young cockney hopeful to have a latchkey and a separate allowance. No point of duty has been more miserably warped and perverted by false priests, in all churches, than this duty of the young to choose whom they will serve. But the duty itself does not the less exist; and if there be any truth in Christianity at all, there will come, for all true disciples, a time when they have to take that saying to heart, "He that loveth father or mother more than me is not worthy of me."

That is the meaning of Saint Francis's renouncing his inheritance; and it is the beginning of Giotto's gospel of works. Unless this hardest of deeds be done first— this inheritance of mammon and the world cast away—all other deeds are useless.

"Loveth"—observe. There is no talk of disobeying fathers or mothers whom you do *not* love, or of running away from a home where you would rather not stay. But to leave the home which is your peace, and to be at enmity with those who are most dear to you—this, if there be meaning in Christ's words, one day or other will be demanded of his true followers.

And there *is* meaning in Christ's words. Whatever misuse may have been made of them—whatever false prophets—and heaven knows there have been many—have called the young children to them, not to bless, but to curse, the assured fact remains, that if you will obey God, there will come a moment when the voice of man will be raised, with all its holiest natural authority, against you. The friend and the wise adviser—the brother and the sister—the father and the master—the entire voice of your prudent and keen-sighted acquaintance—the entire weight of the scornful stupidity of the vulgar world—for *once,* they will be against you, all at once. You have to obey God rather than man. The human race, with all its wisdom and love, all its indignation and folly, on one side—God alone on the other. You have to choose.

That is the meaning of Saint Francis's renouncing his inheritance; and it is the beginning of Giotto's gospel of works. Unless this hardest of deeds be done first—this inheritance of mammon and the world cast away—all other deeds are useless. You cannot serve, cannot obey, God and mammon. No charities, no obediences, no self-denials, are of any use while you are still at heart in conformity with the world. You go to church because the world goes. You keep Sunday because your neighbors keep it. But you dress ridiculously because your neighbors ask it; and you dare not do a rough piece of work because your neighbors despise it. You must renounce your neighbor, in his riches and pride, and remember him in his distress. That is Saint Francis's "disobedience."

Dante on Saint Francis*

ADAPTED BY
MARION A. HABIG, O.F.M.

The Providence, which all things doth dispose
With such deep counsels that all mortal gaze
Is baffled ere to that great depth it goes—
That unto Christ, the Church might bend her
   ways,
As Bride of Him who, with a bitter cry,
Espoused her with the Blood we bless and praise,
And serve Him well in peace and loyalty,
With two high chiefs and blessed sons endowed,
That they on either side her guides might be.

The soul of one with love seraphic glowed,
The other by his wisdom on our earth
The light of cherubic distinction showed.[1]
Of one I'll speak, for, if we tell the worth
Of one, 'tis true of both, whiche'er we take;

To common end each labored from his birth.
Between Tupino and the streams that break
From mountain chosen by Ubaldo blest,
A lofty hill a fertile slope doth make.

Perugia's Sun-gate from that lofty crest
Feels heat and cold; Nocera's, Gualdo's pine
Behind it, by their heavy yoke opprest.
Where, on this slope, less steeply doth incline
The hill, was born into this world a sun,
As bright as orb that doth o'er Ganges shine.[2]
This place to name, let not a single one
Assisi call it—that were tame in sense—
As Orient its title now must run.

Such was his rise, nor was he far from thence,
When he began to make the wide earth share
Some comfort from his glorious excellence;
For he, a youth, his father's wrath did dare
For maid, for whom not one of all the crowd,
As she were death, would pleasure's gates unbar.
Before his father and the bishop, vowed
This youth a lasting marriage-pledge to her,[3]
And day by day more fervent love he showed.

Of her first Spouse bereaved, a thousand were,
And more, the years she lived, despised, obscure;
And, till he came, none did his suit prefer.
Nought it availed that she was found secure
With poor Amyclas when the voice was heard
Which made the world great terror-pangs endure.[4]
Nought it availed that she nor shrank nor feared,
So that, when Mary tarried yet below,
She on the Cross above with Christ appeared.

But lest I tell it too obscurely so,
By these two lovers, in my speech diffuse,
Thou Poverty and Francis mayest know.
Their concord and their looks of joy profuse,
The love, the wonder, and the aspect sweet,
Made men in holy meditation muse,
So that the holy Bernard bared his feet,
The first to start, and for this peace so tried,
That slow he thought his pace, though it was fleet.[5]

A wealth unknown, true good that doth abide!
Giles likewise bared his feet, Sylvester too,
To seek the Bridegroom—so they loved the Bride,
Then went that Father and that Master true
With her, his Bride, and then, his family,
Who round their loins the lowly girdle drew.
Nor was faint heart betrayed in downcast eye,
As being Pietro Bernardone's son,
By foolish men despised surprisingly.

---

* Dante's beautiful account of Saint Francis is not as well known as it deserves to be. It appears on Canto XI, lines 28 to 117, of *Paradise;* and Dante places the poetic narrative in the mouth of Saint Thomas Aquinas. Noteworthy is the fact that the famous bard was born less than four decades after the death of Il Poverello. The English version presented here has been adapted from Dean Plumptre's translation. We have made alterations that, in our opinion, clarify the meaning of these lines as well as improve their style and meter. M.A.H.

But, like a king, his stern intention
To Innocent he opened, who did give
The first seal to that new religion.[6]
Then, when the race, content as poor to live,
Grew after him, whose life, so high renowned,
In heaven's glory praises would receive,
With a new diadem once more was crowned
By Pope Honorius, who was inspired,
When he this Founder's purpose holy found.[7]

And after that, with martyr zeal untired,
He, in the presence of the Sultan proud,
Preached Christ, with those whom His example
    fired.[8]
And finding that this race no ripeness showed
For their conversion, not to toil in vain,
To Italy his further labors vowed.
On rugged rock 'twixt Tiber's, Arno's plain,
From Christ received the final seal's impress,
Which he two years did in his limbs sustain.

When it pleased Him, who chose him thus to bless,
To lead him up, the high reward to share
Which he had merited by lowliness.
Then to his brethren, each as rightful heir,
He gave in charge his Lady-love most dear,
And bade them love her with a steadfast care.
And from her breast, that soul so high and clear
Would fain depart and to its kingdom turn,
Nor for his body sought another bier.[9]

Notes

1 The "other" is the friend and contemporary of Saint Francis, Saint Dominic, the founder of the Order of Preachers.

2 Saint Francis of Assisi was born in 1181 (or 1182).

3 It was very probably in the spring of 1206 that Saint Francis renounced all earthly goods and returned to his father the very clothes he wore, in the court of Bishop Guido of Assisi.

4 The poet Lucan represents Caesar as expressing his admiration of the peaceful poverty of the fisherman Amyclas.

5 Bernard of Quintavalle, the first to become a follower of Saint Francis, joined him in the spring of 1208, two years after his perfect conversion.

6 Though some claim it was in the summer of 1210, it was very probably in the spring of 1209 that Francis, with his first eleven disciples, journeyed to Rome, received the verbal approbation of Pope Innocent III for his first, short, and simple Rule of the Order of Friars Minor, and pronounced his vows in accordance with that rule. During the year 1959, therefore, the Order of Friars Minor was celebrating its seven hundred and fiftieth anniversary. April 16, 1209, is the traditional and official date for the founding of the Order of Friars Minor.

7 In the bull *Solet annuere* of November 29, 1223, Pope Honorius III approved the final and present Rule of the Order of Friars Minor.

8 Saint Francis preached before Melek-el-Kamil, Sultan of Egypt, at Damietta, in the early part of September 1219.

9 At the Portiuncula Chapel of Our Lady of the Angels, in the valley below Assisi, Saint Francis died at sundown on October 3, 1226, about forty-five years old.

A Chronology of His Life

OMER ENGLEBERT

1181   *Summer or fall (?):* Born in Assisi. Baptized Giovanni di Pietro di Bernardone; renamed Francesco by father.

1198   *January 8:* Innocent III elected Pope.
Spring: Duke Conrad of Urslingen's Rocca fortress besieged, taken, and razed by people of Assisi, as he yields Duchy of Spoleto to Innocent III.

1199–1200   Civil war in Assisi; destruction of feudal nobles' castles; families of future Saint Clare and Brother Leonardo move to Perugia.

1202   *November:* War between Perugia and Assisi. Latter's army is defeated at Battle of Collestrada. Francis spends a year in prison in Perugia until ransomed by father as ill.

1204   Long illness.
End, or Spring, 1205 (?): Francis sets out for war in Apulia, with Walter de Brienne of the papal armies, but returns the next day, after a vision and message in Spoleto. Beginning of the gradual process of conversion.

1205   *June:* Walter de Brienne dies in southern Italy.
Fall and end: Message of the Crucifix of San Damiano. Conflict with father.

1206   *January or February:* Bishop's trial.
Spring: Francis in Gubbio, nursing victims of leprosy.
Summer, probably July: Returns to Assisi, assumes hermit's habit, and begins to repair San Damiano; end of

conversion process; beginning of Thomas of Celano's "years of conversion" chronology.

Summer, to January or early February: Repairs San Damiano, San Pietro, and Portiuncula.

1208 *February 24:* Francis hears Gospel of Saint Matthias Mass. Changes from hermit's habit to that of barefoot preacher; begins to preach.

April 16: Brothers Bernard and Peter Catanii join Francis. *April 23:* Brother Giles is received at the Portiuncula.

Spring: First Mission: Francis and Giles go to the Marches of Ancona.

Summer: Three more, including Philip, join them.

Fall and winter: Second Mission: All seven go to Poggio Bustone in the Valley of Rieti. After being assured of the remission of his sin and the future growth of the Order, Francis sends the six, plus a new seventh follower, on the third mission, two by two. Bernard and Giles go to Florence.

1209 *Early:* The eight return to the Portiuncula. Four more join them.

Spring: Francis writes brief rule and goes to Rome with his eleven first companions. There he obtains the approval of Pope Innocent III. On the way back, they stay a while at Orte, then settle at Rivo Torto.

September: German Emperor-elect Otto IV passes by Rivo Torto.

1209 OR The friars move to the Portiuncula.
1210 Possible beginning of Third Order.

1211 *Summer (?):* Francis goes to Dalmatia and returns.

1212 *March 18/19:* On Palm Sunday night, reception of Saint Clare at the Portiuncula.

May (?): After a few days at San Paolo and a few weeks at Panzo Benedictine convents, Clare moves to San Damiano.

1213 *May 8:* At San Leo, near San Marino, Count Orlando offers Mount La Verna to Francis as a hermitage.

1213/14 OR Francis travels to Spain and back.
1214/15 (?)

1215 *November:* Fourth Lateran General Council. Francis in Rome.

1216 *July 16:* Pope Innocent III dies in Perugia. *July 18:* Honorius III elected. French Archbishop Jacques de Vitry at Perugia.

Summer: Francis obtains the Portiuncula Indulgence from Pope Honorius in Perugia.

1217 *May 5:* Pentecost General Chapter (official gathering of all the friars) at the Portiuncula. First missions beyond the Alps and overseas. Giles leaves for Tunis, Elias for Syria, and Francis for France, but Cardinal Hugolin meets him in Florence and persuades him to stay in Italy.

1219 *May 26:* Chapter. First martyrs leave for Morocco. *June 24:* Francis sails from Ancona for Acre and Damietta.

Fall: Francis visits Sultan. *November 5:* Damietta taken by Crusaders.

1220 *January:* First martyrs killed in Morocco.

Early: Francis goes to Acre and Holy Land.

Spring or summer (?): Francis returns to Italy, landing at Venice. Cardinal Hugolin appointed protector of the order.

1220
(OR 1217, Francis resigns. Peter Catanii vicar.
1218) (?)

1221 *March:* Peter Catanii dies.
May 30: Chapter. First Rule. Elias vicar. Rule of Third Order approved by Honorius III.

1221/ Francis on a preaching tour in southern
1222 (?) Italy.

1222 *August 15:* Francis preaches in Bologna.

1223 *Early:* At Fonte Colombo Francis composes second rule. Chapter on *June 11* discusses it. *Fall:* Further discussion in Rome.

November 29: Pope Honorius III approves Rule of 1223.

December 24/25: Christmas Crib Midnight Mass at Greccio.

1224 *June 2:* Chapter sends mission to England.

End of July or early August (?): In Foligno, Elias is given message in vision that Francis has only two years to live.

August 15–September 29 (Assumption to Saint Michael's Day): Francis fasts at La Verna, receiving the stigmata about *September 14.*

October and early November: Francis returns to the Portiuncula via Borgo San Sepolchro, Monte Casale, and Città di Castello.

1224/ *December–February (?):* Riding on a
1225 donkey, he makes a preaching tour in Umbria and the Marches.

1225 *March (?):* While he is visiting Saint Clare at San Damiano, his eye sickness suddenly turns much worse. Almost blind, he has to stay there in a cell in or by the chaplain's house. At the insistence of Brother Elias, at last consents to receive medical care, but weather is too cold and treatment is postponed.

April–May (?): Still at San Damiano, undergoes treatment without improvement. Receives divine promise of eternal life and composes "Canticle of Brother Sun."

June (?): Adding to the "Canticle," reconciles feuding bishop and podesta (mayor) of Assisi. Summoned by a letter from Cardinal Hugolin, leaves San Damiano for Rieti Valley.

Early July (?): Welcomed in Rieti by Hugolin and papal court (there from *June 23 to February 6*). Goes to Fonte Colombo to undergo eye treatment urged by Hugolin, but has it postponed owing to absence of Brother Elias.

July–August (?): Doctor cauterizes the saint's temples at Fonte Colombo, without improvement.

September: Francis moves to San Fabiano near Rieti to be treated by other doctors, who pierce his ears. Restores the trampled vineyard of the poor priest.

1225/1226 *October–March (?):* In either Rieti or Fonte Colombo.

1226 *April:* Francis is in Siena for further treatment.

May or June (?): Returns to the Portiuncula via Cortona.

July–August: Because of summer heat, he is taken to Bagnara in the hills near Nocera.

Late August or early September: His condition growing worse, he is taken via Nottiano to the palace of the bishop in Assisi. Bishop Guido is absent on a pilgrimage to Monte Gargano.

September: Knowing that his death is imminent, Francis insists on being carried to the Portiuncula.

October 3: He dies there. Sunday, *October 4,* is buried in San Giorgio Church.

1227 *March 19:* His friend Hugolin becomes Pope Gregory IX.

1228 *July 16:* In Assisi Gregory IX canonizes Francis.

1230 *May 25:* Removal of the saint's remains to his new basilica, San Francesco.

His Values

A Gospel Way of Life

ROY M. GASNICK, O.F.M.

At a time when the Church had overidentified with the state, when bishops, abbots, even popes were more civil authorities than religious leaders, when Christians accepted feudal civilities and authority structures instead of the Gospel as the norm for religion, Francis of Assisi was touched by God to rebuild the Church, to be a witness to the truth and value of the Gospel itself. The Church, in her liturgy, says it this way:

O Lord Jesus Christ, who, when the world was growing cold, reproduced the sacred marks of your Passion in the body of the blessed Francis in order that your Love might also set our hearts afire. . . .

Though Francis was a witness to the whole of the Gospel, he tended to emphasize those aspects of it that had been least understood or least practiced.

Though Francis was a witness to the whole of the Gospel, he tended to emphasize those aspects of it that had been least understood or least practiced. Of these, the following are most prominent.

THE FATHERHOOD OF GOD God, for Francis, was no stern monarch to be obeyed in fear because he was continually counting up the numbers of transgressions against his laws. God was rather Someone personally close, a Father wanting to see his sons and daughters succeed, giving them every grace necessary for success, leaving the rest up to their own free will to accept or reject. As Francis so often said with the total trust of a son, *"Cast your care upon the Lord, and he will provide for you."*

THE HUMANITY OF CHRIST There can be no doubt of Francis's love affair with Christ. It was not the Christ of so many of the late medieval paintings—the *Pantocrator*, the judge at the last judgment. It was the Christ of Bethlehem who became a man because he loved man, and the Christ of the Last Supper who gave himself as food for spiritually starving man, and the Christ of Calvary, who died as a sacrifice so that man would be raised up from his own inhumanity. *"Observe, O man,"* said Francis, understanding full well the meaning of Christ, *"to what distinction the Lord has raised you in creating you and molding you according to the image of his beloved son bodily and according to his likeness spiritually."*

PENANCE-CONVERSION When one is overwhelmed at discovering that he has such a Father and such a Brother, no other response is possible except total conversion, a conversion that is more like a love affair—giving oneself totally to God—than a mournful rejection of one's former life. So it was with Francis. His conversion, his penance were things of great joy, for he had found a bride greater than any other, a bride who gave him every fulfillment, a bride who would never abandon him unless he lost his own love. Of his conversion, Francis wrote,

37

"That which seemed to me bitter was changed into sweetness of body and soul."

THE GOSPEL AS A WAY OF LIFE   After such a conversion, Francis could no longer live the minimum obligations for one to remain a Christian. He had to go *beyond* the law, go further than the law, go as far as assimilating the Christ-life in himself. The challenge of the Gospel, and the possibilities it opened up for man to rise above his own humanity and for the world to rise above its collective evil, struck so vibrant a chord in Francis's musical soul that he cried out, *"This is what I want; this is what I desire; this is what I long for with all my heart and soul."*

THE CONTINUING INCARNATION   For Francis, the Incarnation was not just the historical event of God becoming man. The Incarnation was *then*, but it is also *now*. Anyone who accepts the Gospel life accepts the commission from God continually to bring forth Christ in his own portion of the world. In a most unusual statement, Francis says, *"We are his mothers when we carry him about in our heart and person by means of love and a clean and sincere conscience, and we give birth to him by means of our holy actions, which should shine as an example to others."*

THE MISSION OF APOSTLESHIP   Francis looked around him. Almost all of Europe had been Christianized, but the Christians had become apathetic. The Muslim world was shut off; the Far East had not yet been reached. Missionary work—the challenge given by Christ to the Apostles to preach the Gospel to all nations—was all but dead. Francis founded a new order in the Church, an order of apostles whom he sent out two by two as Christ had done, to shake up apathetic Europe, to penetrate the Muslim religious militarism, to reach the Far East, to go to the ends of the earth. The age that needs apostleship the most is every age.

BROTHERHOOD   Perhaps the most touching phrase in Francis's testament is the one he uses to describe his first followers and the beginning of the Franciscan Order: *"And after that, the Lord gave me some brothers. . . ."* At a time when class distinction was rigidified, when even in the monastic rules second-class citizenship was afforded to the lay brothers, when there were masters and serfs, nobles and peasants, *majores* and *minores*, when suspicion and distrust were the order of the day even among friends, Francis clearly showed that, at least in his Order, real brotherhood was still possible. When he named his Order that of the Little Brothers, he clearly indicated that brotherhood was his, as well as Christ's, challenge to man's inhumanity to man.

MINORITY   If Francis saw his Order as one of brothers, he also saw it especially as one of "little" brothers. Minority, or littleness, contains something of the idea we use today when speaking of minority groups—poor, powerless, and voiceless. Littleness for Francis was a repudiation of the drive for power, prestige, and status. It was a desire to become like the *anawim* of the Bible—God's poor, helpless, and defenseless ones, the ones Christ said were blessed, for theirs is the kingdom of heaven. It was a desire to serve and not be served, a desire to be available, to help, to be concerned, share with, suffer with, rejoice with; a desire to overcome the most evil tendency in any man—the desire to lord it over another.

POVERTY   Wealth, affluence, engrossment with personal property and material goods—these were seen by Francis as deterrents to brotherhood and union with God. Those whose lives are dominated by money and what money can buy are more concerned with things than with people. This is one of the worst perversions of the natural order because it leads so quickly to the dehumanization of the individual. Persons are more important than property; people are more important than things. Francis's poverty was meant to witness exactly that.

PERSONALISM   G. K. Chesterton, perhaps, has the final word about Francis's personalism. "It is more true that he deliberately did not see the mob for the men. He honored all men; that is, he not only loved but also respected them all. What gave him his extraordinary personal power was this: that from the pope to the beggar, from the sultan to the ragged robber crawling out of the wood, there was never a man who looked into those brown burning eyes without being certain that Francis was really interested in *him;* in his own inner individual life from cradle to the grave; that he himself was being valued and taken seriously."

PRAYER   Prayer, especially contemplative prayer, was so important in Francis's life that at one point he was severely tempted to abandon his mission of apostleship to the world and retire to a contemplative life. His mission, God told him, was otherwise. But wherever Francis was, in a cave or the marketplace, on Mount Alvernia or in a cardinal's palace, alone, with the friars or at work, he was always at prayer: sometimes contemplative, sometimes spontaneous, sometimes in common with his brothers, sometimes the prayer of work.

ACCEPTANCE OF SUFFERING There is a mystique about suffering that unbelievers will never fathom. To them, suffering is an evil that must be avoided at all costs. Francis approached suffering with awe. He read the message clearly: Christ had to suffer in order to redeem and elevate man. Francis not only accepted suffering but also prayed for it as Saint Paul had done, "to fill up in my own flesh what is wanting to the sufferings of Christ for his body, which is the Church."

PEACE Francis was accepted as a peacemaker in the disputes between the *majores* and *minores* in Assisi, between the Christians and the Muslims, between the nobles and their serfs in the matter of war because he was a peaceful man himself. *"While you are proclaiming peace with your lips,"* he told his followers, *"be careful to have it even more fully in your heart. Nobody should be aroused to wrath or insult on your account. Everyone should rather be moved to peace, goodwill, and mercy as a result of your self-restraint."*

RESPECT FOR THE CHURCH The Church will always be subject to human weakness and even fallibility in other than essential doctrinal and moral areas. The human weaknesses in the Church of Francis's time were so vast that the Church was hardly a sign of God's presence among men. The Church was feared because of its political power; many of the clergy were living scandalous lives; and anticlericalism, with good reason, was rampant. God called Francis to "repair my Church, which you see is falling into ruin." Francis did so in the Christ-way and not the world-way: *"We have been sent as a help to the clergy toward the salvation of souls, so that what they are found less equal to may be supplied by us. . . . If you act like children of peace, you will win both clergy and people for the Lord, and the Lord regards that as more acceptable than winning the people only to the scandal of the clergy."*

FRANCISCAN WITNESS TODAY The world has changed many times over since Francis's time and yet, sadly, so many of the same conditions and problems have returned in our own time. Millions of words have been spilled out recommending how to solve these problems, how to change conditions, how to shake up the apathetic. So many of the words are clichés that fail to arouse; so many of those who speak cannot be heard because of the contradicting noise of what they do. The result has a devastating logic to it. In the words of Paul Simon:

And so you see I have come to doubt
All that I once held as true;
I stand alone without beliefs,
The only truth I know is you.

When Christ says, "You too are to be my witnesses," perhaps he is saying that the only truth the people of our time will know is the individual, the believer, the one concerned about others, the one who is loving, peaceful, and faithful. To say it another way, *You may be the only Gospel your neighbor will ever read.*

Prayer to Saint Francis

FRANCES FROST

Will there come a day
when the fox, at bay,
may find man's shoulder
his shelter, his boulder?

When will the deer
stand without fear
while man's hand touches
his russet haunches?

When will the snare
return to air
the bright-winged captive
to praise God and live?

Saint Francis, when will
man cease to kill
the shy, and that other—
his shyer brother?

Personalism: Francis's Own Revolution

G.K. CHESTERTON

I have said that Saint Francis deliberately did not see the woods for the trees. It is even more true that he deliberately did not see the mob for the men. What distinguishes this very genuine democrat from any mere demagogue is that he never either deceived or was deceived by the illusion of mass suggestion. Whatever his taste in monsters, he never saw before him a many-headed beast. He saw only the image of God multiplied but never monotonous. To him a man was always a man and did not disappear in a dense crowd any more than in a desert. He honored all men; that is, he not only loved but also respected them all. What gave him his extraordinary personal power was this: that from the pope to the beggar, from the sultan of Syria in his pavilion to the ragged robber crawling out of the wood, there was never a man who looked into those brown burning eyes without being certain that Francis Bernardone was really interested in *him;* in his own inner individual life from the cradle to the grave; that he himself was being valued and taken seriously, and not merely added to the spoils of some social policy or the names in some clerical document.

What gave him his extraordinary personal power was this: that from the pope to the beggar, from the sultan of Syria in his pavilion to the ragged robber crawling out of the wood, there was never a man who looked into those brown burning eyes without being certain that Francis Bernardone was really interested in him. . . .

Now for this particular moral and religious idea there is no external expression except courtesy. Exhortation does not express it, for it is not mere abstract enthusiasm; beneficence does not express it, for it is not mere pity. It can be conveyed only

by a certain grand manner that may be called good
manners. We may say if we like that Saint Francis,
in the bare and barren simplicity of his life, had
clung to one rag of luxury: the manners of a court.
But whereas in a court there is one king and a
hundred courtiers, in this story there was one cour-
tier, moving among a hundred kings, for he treated
the whole mob of men as a mob of kings. And this
was really and truly the only attitude that will appeal to that part of man to which he wished to
appeal. It cannot be done by giving gold or even
bread, for it is a proverb that any reveler may fling
largess in mere scorn. It cannot even be done by
giving time and attention, for any number of phi-
lanthropists and benevolent bureaucrats do such
work with a scorn far more cold and horrible in
their hearts. No plans or proposals or efficient re-
arrangements will give back to a broken man his
self-respect and sense of speaking with an equal.
One gesture will do it.

With that gesture Francis of Assisi moved among
men; and it was soon found to have something in
it of magic and to act, in a double sense, like a
charm. But it must always be conceived as a completely natural gesture; for indeed it was almost a
gesture of apology. He must be imagined as moving
thus swiftly through the world with a sort of impetuous politeness; almost like the movement of a
man who stumbles on one knee half in haste and
half in obeisance. The eager face under the brown
hood was that of a man always going somewhere, as
if he followed as well as watched the flight of the
birds. And this sense of motion is indeed the meaning of the whole revolution that he made; for the
work that has now to be described was of the nature of an earthquake or a volcano, an explosion
that drove outward with dynamic energy the forces
stored up by ten centuries in the monastic fortress
or arsenal and scattered all its riches recklessly to
the ends of the earth.

In a better sense than the antithesis commonly
conveys, it is true to say that what St. Benedict had
stored, St. Francis scattered; but in the world of
spiritual things what had been stored into the barns
like grain was scattered over the world as seed.
The servants of God who had been a besieged gar-
rison became a marching army; the ways of the
world were filled as with thunder with the trampling of their feet, and far ahead of that ever-
swelling host went a man singing, as simply he had
sung that morning in the winter woods, where he
walked alone.

The Nonuse of Power

MARIO VON GALLI, S.J.

. . . [Since] Christ was certainly no "lawgiver," and one does him no honor with that title, the Church had to assume a more consolidated form as it grew larger. That is in the very nature of the case. Deviation from the ideal model comes in when the forms are taken to be more important than the spirit, when one comes to believe that the forms are the spirit crystallized in a supratemporal pattern. To be sure, there are sacraments and offices in the Church that can be traced back to divine institution, however one may picture that in the concrete. To be sure, there is also a legitimate and necessary Church law. But in the process of concrete consolidation, there always remains room for adaptation to the signs of the time, for a closer approximation to the mature pattern of the Christian human being.

Now the astonishing thing is that of all the Rules of religious orders we possess, the Rule of Francis of Assisi is the least like a real Rule. This matter, which we have touched upon before, is a very timely issue in an age when there is so much talk about structural reforms in the Church and in religious orders. One need only read one of the countless commentaries on canon law to see how much is in flux there at the present time. To us it seems to be a revolutionary turn of events. Yet it was all there in the work of Francis of Assisi, who simply wanted to live the Gospel.

So far as we can tell, the first Rule he proposed to Innocent III (1209) was merely a patchwork of short scriptural passages. We no longer have this "patchwork," and recent scholarship has given up all attempts to reconstruct it. The important point is that Francis really did not want to go beyond the "rules of conduct" contained in Holy Scripture. That kept him from turning his Rule into a sacrosanct shrine, as almost all other religious orders have done to some extent. In his day it was not possible to carry this approach through to the end, but one might well ask whether it is not possible to do that today.

This first Rule of Francis was approved, at least orally, by the Pope. It was followed by three later Rules. The longer they were, the more the spiritual aspect retreated into the background and the more they came to resemble the second type of constitution mentioned above. So true is this that Hans Urs von Balthasar presents only *two* rules of Francis in the series on great church figures of which he was the editor (*Die grossen Ordensregeln*, 1961, in the series *Menschen der Kirche*). There we find the longer second rule of 1221, the first still extant, which was really closer to the spiritual side, and the last definitive rule of 1223 (considered the third rule, actually the fourth). Commenting on them, Laurentius Casutt calls attention to the fact that even the last rule of Francis is considerably different from all the other religious rules in the Church. A host of practical questions relating to conduct are not mentioned at all. So something of the founder's outlook still remains. As Casutt puts it: "Just as the Gospel could hardly be called a law book, so Francis did not want to leave a legal commentary to his friars. Laws need not necessarily stand in the way of the spirit, but they often do. The saint knew this. He knew even better that legal norms are superfluous to a large extent where a living, holy spirit is operative."

This observation itself brings Francis of Assisi closer to our age than any other reform-minded saint. Now I can quote the words of Jesuit Father Peter Lippert, for their meaning will be clear enough from what has been said above:

"The organizational principle which leads from Benedict through Dominic and Ignatius to the newer communities seems to have practically exhausted its inner possibilities. . . . The fundamental newness that is precisely the thing being sought today by countless souls . . . is to be found only along a completely different line: along the line of the original ideal of Francis. In other words: in the direction of a freely chosen lifestyle and freely chosen bonds of love; in the direction of a life that operates through spontaneous initiative of the self *rather than through great constructs of the will;* in the direction of a truly living and individual personality shaped by its own *inner laws and standards.* If God should someday deign to reveal the Order of the future to his Church . . . it will surely bear the stamp of Francis's soul and spirit."

Now let us get to a few specific matters. Today we talk a great deal about the transformation of existing structures, the need for democratization, the decentralization of authority, and the function of service. We deduce the need for such a transformation, which is also making headway in the

Church, from man's growing awareness of his own maturity and adulthood. This growing awareness is evident throughout the world, both in developed and in underdeveloped countries. It accords completely with man's dignity as a human being, as Father John Courtney Murray tried to explain over the course of many years. After much earnest debate Vatican II finally came to adopt his viewpoint in its declaration on religious freedom (*Dignitatis Humanae Personae*), for it grounds its argument on this ontological datum, thus going far beyond the traditional arguments based on tolerance. But Father Murray himself admits that this principle could not become operative in the practical order so long as the notion of human dignity was not alive in the consciousness of peoples and nations. This shift in awareness from a patriarchal outlook to a personal focus is a relatively new datum. It has been quite rightly called a revolutionary event in the history of the human spirit. Over the course of centuries it has worked itself out in many different areas, being mixed up with all sorts of deviations in the process. It has been operative in the realm of politics (e.g., the French Revolution) and in the realm of societal relationships (e.g., the revolutions of the working classes). Its impact reaches down to Marxism and to the student riots of today. It is a historical process that is now worldwide in scope.

The Franciscans were the first religious not to elect a "Father Abbot." The religious piety of Francis was deeply grounded on God the Father, but he could not find any place for the father image within his community of friars. There, all were brothers. . . .

But one may well be astonished to find this tendency, grounded solely on the religious soil of the Gospel, already operative in the work of Francis of Assisi. In the first (still extant) rule we find this maxim: "All the friars without exception are forbidden to wield power or authority, particularly over one another. . . . No one is to be called 'prior.' They are all to be known as Friars Minor without distinction, and they should be prepared to wash one another's feet." The Franciscans were the first religious not to elect a "Father Abbot." The

religious piety of Francis was deeply grounded on God the Father, but he could not find any place for the father image within his community of friars. There, all were brothers, with different functions of service to perform. Even the "minister general" could be deposed by his own fellow-friars, according to Francis. This could not happen ordinarily in the older orders, which were organized along strictly hierarchical lines (e.g., the Benedictines, the Cistercians, and the Carthusians). Even later the paternal image continued to play an important role for the Jesuits: e.g., when the duties of various superiors are described in their constitutions. But there is no direct or indirect suggestion of the father-son relationship when relations between superiors and subordinates are described in the Franciscan rule of 1221 or that of 1223 (the one solemnly approved by Pope Honorius III).

My feeling is that not enough attention has been paid to this fact. In an age when people's conceptual structures were still sociologically tied up with patriarchal models to a greater extent, it was an astonishing and indeed revolutionary departure. And it is readily apparent that it was not just a matter of terminology so far as Francis was concerned. He wanted to give expression to an attitude that was meant to differentiate clearly his community from other orders! And an attempt to explain it away psychologically, by saying that the encounters between young Francesco and his father destroyed his father image, falls apart in the light of his spirituality. Lacking a deep-rooted awareness of God as his Father, he would have had no grounds for his cosmic mysticism and his love of nature. But the father image was reserved for God alone. All others are brothers and sisters. The equality of all human beings is taken quite seriously. That is fine and good in terms of the Gospel. But in the sociological structures of the medieval period it could not be carried through with complete success.

The case is different today. This line of thought is wholly in accord with the outlook of modern man. When *Paris Match* polled a sampling of young people between eighteen and twenty-five, it found that 70 percent of them had a deep sense of responsibility for the world at large. As they saw it, the meaning of life was to be "useful to others." The common task, shared by all, is what holds the world together in their eyes. And this task is not so much to make scientific progress or to win mastery over the earth and nature, even though these

things are indispensable means to the real end, but the real end is the establishment of a fraternal community between all human beings.

Here is the source of the antiauthoritarian attitude evinced by young people. They see authority as a force that creates and maintains inequalities that go against man's dignity, which fails to recognize the equality of all human beings. They do not reject order and structure as such, insofar as these things are solidly grounded on reality; indeed they take these things for granted as necessary presuppositions. What they oppose is not authority as such, but authority that violates man's dignity. Real progress means using science, technology, and the communications media to make it possible for mankind to effectively recognize the dignity of every individual, and to allow each person to contribute his or her effort to the common good in a free and responsible way. When individuals are able to develop their sense of personal responsibility to the utmost, they will help to create the longed-for community among men. The reduction and/or abolition of coercive structures, along with the shouldering of greater personal responsibility, is the goal of young people. It is the thrust of evolutionary development in our time. The "establishment" comprises all those forces that will not dismantle coercive structures or build new structures because of their narrow, vested interests.

Young people enjoy a certain advantage, for they tend to underestimate the difficulties of any undertaking. They feel the upward rush of life and the great promise it contains. They tear down obstructions without a second thought, failing to realize that such obstructions may also serve as dams to protect the good things. They have not yet come to experience the truth of the parable of the wheat and the chaff, the close-knit intermingling of good and evil that does not allow for thorough weeding. That is certainly true of young people. On the other hand, prudent and cautious people often fail to see that a situation has changed, that unsuspected new possibilities, directions, and insights lie in front of them. So while we may not want to say yes too quickly to all the details and concrete embodiments of the new outlook on life, we should take serious note of the authenticity of the basic underlying tendency. It embodies the hope of the future. If a person blocks and frustrates it with overcautious restrictions, then he or she is a murderer of mankind—far more so than the treacherous moraines that lie at the edges of glaciers.

If a person has taken a stance against the revolutionary tendencies of the present day, then he should seriously contemplate the figure of Francis. Francis did not infringe upon any authority. On the contrary, he sought approval of his community from the Pope, and he asked a cardinal to be the protector of his order. So, one might say, he was not a revolutionary after all. But he was. In its *de facto* pattern, his community was a revolution. All were brothers; there was no father in it. There was no specified set of rules. The spirit was to create new forms as the situation called for them. Francis fashioned a *de facto* revolution without any polemics.

The priests of his day had grown quite corrupt. Some had grown hungry for power; others had become very worldly. Yet he respected them, chose not to preach without their permission, and respectfully kissed their hands in honor of their offices. Seemingly a naive thing to do; in fact, a very realistic approach.

One cannot validly counter this statement by saying that the father image soon showed up quite forcefully in the structures of the various Francis-

can communities, so that they were no longer distinguishable from other religious communities in their type of government. To be sure, the Conventuals used a great deal of gruesome paternal force in dealing with the Spirituals. But that sort of approach stands in dialectical contrast to the real core of the Franciscan approach, as borderline phenomena often do. One cannot pass judgment on the movement solely on that basis. Consider the case of celibacy lived for the sake of the kingdom of God. It is foolish to denigrate this kind of life by saying the person's aggressive drives, repressed by such a life, can easily flow over into a hunger for power. The fact is not to be denied. But if you seek a lifestyle without any risks, you will not accomplish much at all. It will be a flat existence. The point applies to the Franciscan approach as well.

Moreover, I must say that something of the pervading spirit of brotherhood continues to live on in the Franciscan communities of today, particularly among the Capuchins. It keeps superiors close to their brother religious in the community. That spirit is quite palpable to an outsider. The spirit of Francis, kept alive in the tone of the Rule, is stronger than the spirit of canon law—especially where the latter is merely a formal shell.

Let me get back to the main point. I think we can make this general statement. There are figures in history that bring to light the slumbering forces in a developing thrust. I am thinking, for example, of figures who stand at the dawn of a new era. The age in which they live feels, more intuitively than consciously, that some sort of hidden guiding image for it is being brought out into the open. It rejoices to see this, and becomes almost intoxicated with the insight. But reflective people and realists shake their heads over such utopian dreams. They are right to some extent, but not completely at all. True enough, the new forces have not yet grown to maturity. They are like blades of grass, not yet capable of casting a protective shadow or providing a nest for the birds of the air. So the figures submerge once again, flitting away like a dream. But the new forces continue to grow while older forces, which once held the field, die out. Now, in the hubbub of full-fledged transformation, we must turn our thoughts back to the figure that was there at the start of it all. For now it may be feasible for people to carry through; now it may help us to interpret correctly the "signs of the time."

Franciscan Eremitism

THOMAS MERTON

The First Rule of the Friars Minor, approved orally in 1209, does not specifically legislate for hermitages, but it mentions them in passing as taken for granted. "Let the brothers wherever they may be in hermitages or other places take heed not to make any place their own and maintain it against anybody else. And let whoever may approach them, whether friend or foe or thief or robber, be received kindly." Here we find not only the spirit we would expect from having read the lives and legends of Saint Francis but also the authentic tradition of the earlier itinerant hermit movement, which was nonmonastic and completely open to the world of the poor and the outcast. It is taken for granted that the hermit will meet with thieves and robbers, and he must not place himself above them or separate himself from them but must show himself to be their brother. The hermit is not just the man who, like Saint Arsenius, has fled entirely from men. He is not just the man of deep contemplative recollection; he is the vulnerable, open and loving brother of everyone—like Charles de Foucauld in our own time. He is a "Little Brother of the Poor."

The spirit of the eremitical life as seen by Saint Francis is therefore cleansed of every taint of selfishness and individualism. Solitude is surrounded by fraternal care and is therefore solidly established in the life of the order and of the Church.

The special statute or instruction composed by Saint Francis for those retiring to hermitages is well known. A hermitage is in fact a small community of three or four brothers, some living entirely in silence and contemplative solitude with others who take care of their needs as their "mothers." These "mothers" must also see that their "children" are not disturbed by outsiders. But the contemplatives should also from time to time take over the active duties and give their "mothers" a rest. It is a charming document that, however, does not give a very detailed picture of the life these hermits led.

The importance of the document lies in the spirit that it exhales—a spirit of simplicity and charity that pervades even the life of solitary contemplation. It has been observed that the genius of sanctity is notable for the way in which it easily reconciles things that seem at first sight irreconcilable. Here Saint Francis has completely reconciled the life of solitary prayer with warm and open fraternal love. Instead of detailing the austerities and penances the hermits must perform, the hours they must devote to prayer, and so on, the saint simply communicates the atmosphere of Love that is to form the ideal climate of prayer in the hermitage. The spirit of the eremitical life as seen by Saint Francis is therefore cleansed of any taint of selfishness and individualism. Solitude is surrounded by fraternal care and is therefore solidly established in the life of the order and of the Church. It is not an individualistic exploit in which the hermit by the power of his own asceticism gains a right to isolation in an elevation above others. On the contrary, the hermit is reminded above all that he is dependent on the charity and the goodwill of others. This is certainly another and very effective way of guaranteeing the sincerity of the hermit's life of prayer since it shows him how much he owes it to others to become a true man of God.

Meanwhile, we shall presently see that Franciscan eremitism had another aspect: it was open to the world and oriented to the apostolic life.

Saint Francis founded at least twenty mountain hermitages, and there is no need to remind the reader what outstanding importance his own solitary retreat at Mount Alvernia played in his life. He received the stigmata there in 1224. Franciscan mysticism is centered upon this solitary vision of the Crucified, and the love generated in this solitude is poured out on the world in preaching.

Blessed Giles of Assisi was essentially an itinerant hermit. On his return from the Holy Land in 1215 he was assigned in obedience to a hermitage by Saint Francis. In 1219 he went to Tunis vainly seeking martyrdom. From 1219 to about 1225 he lived at the Carceri in a small chapel surrounded by other caves. It is interesting that the Carceri, which had once been used by Benedictine hermits, became, after Mount Alvernia, the symbol of Franciscan solitude. It is thought that Saint Francis wrote part of the rule there. The mysticism of Blessed Giles developed in the hermitage of Cetona, and he also founded other hermitages himself.

With Blessed Giles we also find another emphasis. The hermitage is the stronghold of the pure Franciscan spirit, the primitive ideal of the holy founder, threatened by others too preoccupied, as some thought, with power and prestige. In the struggle to preserve the primitive spirit of poverty and utter Franciscan simplicity, the hermitages played the part that may be imagined. It is interesting, incidentally, that when Saint Bonaventure was made cardinal he received the news while he was washing dishes in a hermitage.

It is not hard to understand that in periods of reform the ideal of solitude has had an important part to play in renewal of the Franciscan life and apostolate. This is especially clear when we study Saint Leonard of Port Maurice and the Franciscan revival in Italy in the eighteenth century. Saint Leonard himself got his vocation while listening to the friars chant compline in the *ritiro* on the Palatine, and his promotion of the *ritiro* movement is both characteristic and important in his life as a reformer.

The *ritiro* movement went back perhaps to the sixteenth century. In addition to hermitages, which always existed and provided solitude for friars desiring a life of more intense prayer, specially fervent communities were formed to serve as models of observance. A *ritiro* must not in fact be confused with a hermitage. It was simply a community of picked volunteers who elected to live the Rule in its perfection with special emphasis on poverty, cloister, prayer, and all that could enhance the contemplative and ascetic side of the Franciscan life. However the *ritiri* were not unconnected with the eremitical strain in the Order, and the first *ritiro* founded by blessed Bonaventure of Barcelona had developed out of a hermitage.

Saint Leonard of Port Maurice began by reforming a *ritiro* (even a *ritiro* could eventually need to be reformed!) when he became Guardian of San Francesco al Monte in Florence. His emphasis here was not specifically on solitude and contemplation, but simply on the exact observance of the rules. The *ritiri* were not originally centers of eremitical life; they were meant to be houses of model regularity and fervor. To promote greater solitude, Saint Leonard of Port Maurice created the *solitudine*. The purpose of this more frankly eremitical type of community was the life of pure contemplation.

Saint Leonard described his purpose in these words:

By complete separation from the world to become able to give oneself to pure contemplation and then after the acquisition of greater fervor to return into the communities to apply oneself more avidly to the salvation of one's neighbor.

As always, in the Franciscan tradition, the idea of solitude is not self-sufficient. Solitude opens out to the world and bears fruit in preaching.

The character of the *solitudine* instituted by Saint Leonard is that of the reforms of that time. The strictness and austerity remind one of De Rancé and La Trappe. The cells were so small that when standing in the middle one could touch the ceiling and the two sides. The discipline was taken daily in common for half an hour. Fasting continued all the year round. Perpetual silence was observed, and the friars went barefoot. There were small hermitages attached to the convent, and to these one might retire for greater solitude and more prayer.

This rigorous and solitary life was not intended to be permanent. Most of the five retreatants in the community were men who were there for two months only. However, friars could remain in the *solitudine* for longer periods—even for years. Besides the retreatants, there was a superior (presidente) with a gatekeeper and a cook (the latter a tertiary).* There were also cells for religious of

* Third Order Secular Franciscans.

other orders who might want to come there to renew their fervor.

There is an obvious resemblance between the *solitudine* and the Carmelite "desert." It is a place of temporary eremitical retreat to which one withdraws in order to renew the spirit of prayer and fervor and from which one returns to the work of preaching with a more perfect charity and a message of more convincing hope. The emphasis is on the fact that in solitary prayer and meditation one gets deeper into the root of things, comes to see himself more clearly as he is in the eyes of God, realizes more perfectly the real nature of his need of grace and for the Holy Spirit, and comes to a more ardent love of Jesus crucified. With all this one is normally opened to the world of other men and made ready for the more complete gift of himself to the work of saving souls.

However, both the *ritiri* and the *solitudini* came under very heavy criticism. First they seemed to create a division within the Order. Secondly, it could be asked whether their spirit was too formal and rigorous to be called authentically Franciscan. It is certainly true that the rather forbidding austerity of the *solitudine* might be considered a little alien to the primitive Franciscan spirit of simplicity and evangelical freedom. The severe regulations contrast with the warm and tender spirit of Saint Francis's statute for hermits. But the solitary convents evidently had the effect that Saint Leonard desired, and the preaching of the saint when he emerged from his solitude was said to be characterized by a great tenderness, which, instead of frightening sinners, encouraged and strengthened them.

This very brief outline suggests a few conclusions. The eremitical spirit has always had a place in the Franciscan life, but it is not the spirit of monasticism or of total, definitive separation from the world. The eremitism of Saint Francis and his followers is deeply evangelical and remains always open to the world, while recognizing the need to maintain a certain distance and perspective, a freedom that keeps one from being submerged in active cares and devoured by the claims of exhausting work.

In all forms of the religious life we are asking ourselves, today, whether the accepted methods of renewing our fervor are quite adequate to present-day needs. Certainly the prescribed eight-day retreat has its value. But the new generation is asking itself seriously whether this rather formalistic exercise really produces any lasting fruit. Is it simply

a tightening of nuts and bolts on machinery that is obsolete? Modern religious who feel the need of silence generally seek it not merely for the purpose of self-scrutiny and ascetic castigation, but in order to recuperate spiritual powers that may have been gravely damaged by the noise and rush of a pressurized existence. This silence is not necessarily tight-lipped and absolute—the silence of men pacing the garden with puckered brows and ignoring each other—but the tranquillity of necessary leisure in which religious can relax in the peace of a friendly and restful solitude and once again become themselves. Today more than ever we need to recognize that the gift of solitude is not ordered to the acquisition of strange contemplative powers, but first of all to the recovery of one's deep self, and to the renewal of an authenticity that is twisted out of shape by the pretentious routines of a disordered togetherness. What the world asks of the priest today is that he should be first of all a *person* who can give himself because he has a self to give. And indeed, we cannot give Christ if we have not found him, and we cannot find him if we cannot find ourselves.

These considerations may be useful to those whose imaginations and hopes are still able to be stirred by the thought of solitude, and of its important place in every form of the religious and apostolic life, in every age, especially our own.

48

Saint Francis and Self-Achievement

ROMANO GUARDINI

Every truly perceptive person recognizes in his life one process that is full of wonder. That process brings to attention in a special manner the thought of providence. We may think of providence in terms of particular events; but these are supplementary, exterior. In a far more exalted sense, providence finds expression in the entire course of one's personal growth. A person matures according to his or her own nature and, by being himself or herself, becomes a guide and a liberator of others. By developing the innermost being, a person articulates the deepest sentiments of others. He becomes a word for those who are united with him in some special community of existence or mode of life. Providence, understood in this sense, is deeply rooted in man's being; complete autonomy and a most profound sense of destiny achieve an inexpressible union.

Saint Francis was such a man. In him, this union was achieved. In him, the purity of free personal growth became the liberating word and directive form for many.

I have followed Saint Francis in the land where he lived and in the traditions that have been handed down about him. I have striven for impartiality; as I have seen his figure, I shall present it. This will not be a disquisition on "Saint Francis and Our Times." I shall deal solely with him, and—in the only way consonant with the mystery that he is—without any distinct purpose in mind. If, however, he does find a place in our age, if that *communio* to which we referred unites him with us, then we ought to turn to him in great simplicity and apply to ourselves the word in him that is addressed to us. . . .

[Francis] was uncomely in appearance, small, in fact, and, according to the legend, ugly. We recall the passage from the *Fioretti*, where Fra Masseo, beautiful and well proportioned, cries out, "Why you? Why you? . . . Why do they all run after you? You are neither beautiful nor attractive."

Some see him as merely an unpretentiously joyous man, but this is one of those half-truths by which pious and not-so-pious literature has robbed this truly eminent figure of his greatness. He is regarded as a primitive Brother Jocund, simple as the birds in the trees. But that he certainly was not! True, he prized simplicity very highly, but that does not mean he was a simpleton. He set a distant goal for himself. No creative person is simple, for he is torn between what is and what is to be. Unborn things crowded in on the soul of Saint Francis, and he had to pay for them with all those deep sufferings that are the price of producing new life. He was faced with that question of the value of the creative man who is more than he really is, greater than himself and smaller. It is a question of value that consists in this: he who is simply a man, possessed of dignity and his own life, in a very singular way becomes an instrument, a channel, for something else, for the thing to be created. On this point much could still be said.

Many contrasts existed in him, and the important point is that he lived each of them entirely, that he did not try to efface any one of them. He acted on them all. This is a great task. He must have possessed invincible strength to conquer this situation and to give his life that lucidity that marks all his words and his works.

He was most understanding, and understanding means sympathy, "suffering with" others. From him comes the saying that a man knows only as much as he has suffered. Francis was endowed with an extremely fine sensibility. Many contrasts existed in him, and the important point is that he lived each of them entirely, that he did not try to efface any one of them. He acted on them all. This is a great task. He must have possessed an invincible strength to conquer this situation and to give his life that lucidity that marks all his words and his works.

Thus Francis matured.

In his soul burned an unquenchable desire for great things. He drew his chivalrous ideas of honor, of service to beauty and renown from the tales of his father, from the songs and stories of the troubadours. The ultimate, which for him was poverty, he was to express later by saying that he had espoused Lady Poverty, the most beauteous of all.

He knew that great things were in the offing. At Ponte San Giovanni, he was captured as a twenty-year-old by the Perugians. When the prisoners had languished in captivity for a year and all had lost courage, Francis experienced the triumph of a coming glory. Again and again he closed his narratives with unshakable faith: "You will see; one day the whole earth will honor me!" Later, as an escape from great anxiety of heart, he attached himself to the suite of a knight of Assisi who planned to join Walter of Brienne in southern Italy to fight for the Guelph * cause, and Francis imagined himself in a palace full of arms and splendor.

He was chivalrous—*cortese*. This word cannot be translated, because *courteous* has another meaning now. In its original sense, the word bespoke a form of life, that of noble behavior. With Francis this noble behavior assumed a deep, inner sweetness, giving it a bell-like character of clarity and beauty.

But accompanying this there was something more. This thoroughly chivalrous man never wished to be a lord. Although he belonged to the rising middle class, he leaned always toward the common folk, fought for their liberty and their rights. He lived at a time when the Guelph movement, the struggle of the citizenry for freedom and power, had gained the upper hand in Italy. At Legnano this young power had conquered the empire. Then came the counterattack under Henry VI. The Ghibellines gained strength, and Conrad, Duke of Spoleto, ruled over Assisi as a tyrant from the castle whose ruins even today are impressive. When Innocent III ascended the throne in 1198, Conrad considered his position untenable and submitted to the suzerainty of the Pope. Profiting by his absence, the citizens of Assisi stormed the castle —it is difficult to conceive how they could reduce it to ruins so rapidly—and with incredible speed surrounded the city with mighty walls. Francis was seventeen at the time, and no doubt he savored the passion for liberty to the depths of his being.

The citizenry became conscious of their power. They rose against the nobility, demanded freedom from socage, and partition of the estates. The nobility sought aid from their ancient enemy, Perugia, which declared war on Assisi. Francis remained faithful to the citizenry and fought with them as one of the *popolani,* the common folk, as one of the *minori,* the little people. We may see an omen of his future mission in the fact that he reckoned himself among them. After a year peace was concluded. A treaty followed. The rights of the

* The Guelphs supported the Pope in the medieval struggle for supremacy.

50

property owners and nobles were reestablished; socage was again imposed on the people. Ten more years passed in this fashion, when Francis stood up anew for the citizenry and helped to bring about a liberating agreement.

Something far deeper than the desire for liberty and social justice drove him to join the oppressed and suffering *minori*. This tendency revealed itself most clearly in his meetings with paupers. Even during the years when he gave his senses full rein and his life was one continuous, brilliant feast, if he happened to come upon a pauper, he was overwhelmed. It was not merely the sight of indigence, but something far more profound that called to him from the poor man. . . .

Francis's *cortesia* must have sparkled with beauty. Walking the streets of Assisi one evening, I imagined I heard the tumult of youthful spirits, as singing and laughing they set the quiet night ringing. But Francis became so immersed in this life that he fell sick, and for a time he lay at death's door.

This experience affected him deeply. The old, carefree self-assurance left him. Gradually he convalesced, but the disquiet remained. One day—it was spring—he rose and went out through the gate to commune with nature, hoping in this way to find himself again. He followed a secret oscillation that determined his entire life; one pole lay in the city, the other in nature. He sought the life-giving powers of the earth to renew his strength. He sought them now, but there was no response. The void that had opened in him remained; in fact, it grew deeper. He did not understand himself any longer. Neither did his parents nor his friends understand him. Francis took the only step left to him. Again he threw himself into his former life.

Soon a new plan engaged his attention, the journey to Walter of Brienne in Apulia. Expectation and impatience tormented him. He garbed himself so splendidly that the whole city spoke of it—only to give everything to a poor knight shortly before the departure date. Again and again he repeated, "I know that one day I will be a great prince." He set out, but on the way, at Spoleto, a fever prostrated him. And then a dream shattered the attraction of worldly knighthood.

"Where are you going?" a voice asked.

"To Apulia, to become a knight."

"Now tell me, Francis, which of the two would be of greater advantage to you, the master or the servant?"

"The master!"

"Why then do you leave the master for the sake of the servant, the prince for the vassal?"

Francis turned back. The entire city mocked him. His father grew furious at being thus compromised. And again Francis immersed himself in the old life.

But the void in his soul deepened. A time of painful searching began. He found a sympathetic friend. Some conjecture that it was the later Elias of Cortona, the man who, in opposition to Francis and with the cooperation of Cardinal Hugolin, gave a moderate tendency to the Order. If it were he, then this meeting was a symbol of tragic proportions.

Francis carried his misery out into nature, by lonely paths into a cave near Assisi. He wanted to know what he should do, what was expected of him, what moved and urged him on so mysteriously.

One day he invited his friends to dinner. They made him king of the feast. At the end of the meal the group stormed through the night, their song and tumult echoing in the streets. The year was 1205; he had attained his twenty-third year. The *Legenda Trium Sociorum* [*Legend of the Three Companions*] says that he walked in the midst of his companions, carrying the sceptre of his joyous kingship in his hand. Yet he moved more slowly, lagged behind them, became pensive. Then suddenly it happened. God touched his heart: "Behold, on the instant the Lord visited him, and such great sweetness filled his heart that he could neither move nor speak, and could feel or perceive nothing but that sweetness."

The companions noticed that he was no longer with them; they returned "and saw with amazement how he had changed into a completely different person. . . ."

Of all this and much else we ought to speak. But one trait of Saint Francis, without which his image would be false, still must be mentioned. Hitherto, reference frequently has been made to the strong contrasts that existed side by side in him. Possibly his greatness is revealed best in the fact that he did not try to reconcile these contrasts, but carried out entirely those on one side as well as those on the other. His foundation was so deep, his life so genuine, that the contrarieties, far from remaining merely opposing entities, merged into a living union. For this reason he merits credence. For this reason he is worthy of trust, because he so clearly experienced the powers that everywhere exist side by side and in opposition to one another.

Poor Man of God

DAN MAUK

Francis of Assisi is most easily remembered as a soul so full of love for God that his worldly cares were few and seldom. He was a gentle man, a man of great tenderness—so much tenderness that Thomas of Celano, the first biographer of Francis, describes how the Poverello once preached to the birds:

My brothers, birds, you should praise your Creator very much and always love him: He gave feathers to clothe you, wings so that you can fly, and whatever else was necessary for you. God made you noble among his creatures, and he gave you a home in the purity of the air; though you neither sow nor reap, he nevertheless protects and governs you without any solicitude on your part.

And it is said that the birds rejoiced at his words.

In *The Little Flowers,* we read that Francis tamed the fierce wolf of Gubbio; it "lowered its head and lay down at the saint's feet, as though it had become a lamb." But if we look further, we will see that Francis was more than just a lover of God's animals, a man to be remembered in bird-bath figures.

Francis Bernardone was a man who fully embraced the Gospels and found in the Word of God a way of life and a clear direction to follow, so much that he began a written Rule for his followers by saying: "The Rule and life of the Friars Minor is this, namely, to observe the Holy Gospel of our Lord Jesus Christ." Francis realized that the "Rule" for Christian life had already been written and now only needed to be joyfully and seriously followed. The words of Matthew's Gospel moved him to action and a lifelong commitment—"If thou wilt be perfect, go, sell what thou hast and give to the poor, and thou shalt have treasure in heaven, and come, follow me" (19:21); and Francis repeated these words to those who came to follow him.

For his wealth, and for his spouse, he chose Lady Poverty, because, like Jesus, he had a Father in heaven who was his only treasure. It has been said that there was no one so desirous of gold as Francis was desirous of poverty, and no one so solicitous in guarding his treasure as he was solicitous in guarding this pearl of the Gospel. How great was his compassion for the poor, again described by Celano:

. . . the soul of Francis melted toward the poor, and to those to whom he could not extend a helping hand, he at least showed his affection. Whatever he saw in anyone of want, whatever of penury, he transferred in his mind, by a quick change, to Christ. Thus in all of the poor he saw the Son of the poor lady, and he bore naked in his heart Him whom she bore naked in her arms.

Francis was a peacemaker in the true sense of the Gospels. For him, war, violence, and destruction had no place in the hearts of the children of God. In the Rule he wrote for the Third Order,* the laity who chose to follow him, he declared that they were "not to take up lethal weapons, or bear them about, against anybody." So warmed by God's love, Francis's heart was light and soaring—so much that he could walk through the woods praising God by rubbing two sticks as a violin. Francis, the man and character in Kazantzakis's novel *St. Francis,* could say, "When a person believes in God, there is no such thing as a mute piece of wood, or pain unaccompanied by exultation, or ordinary life without miracles." Two sticks for a violin are all one needs if deep within the chambers of the heart there already lodges music so profound.

* Secular Franciscans.

If we are to capture the essence of the man called Francis, the animating force behind him, it would be an injustice to focus in on merely one aspect of his life: his love for poverty, his simplicity and joy, his life of prayer, etc. To see the whole of Francis is to see a man of God—one who saw how well bound together are the body and the world, the soul and God. When Francis knelt before the cross in the Church of San Damiano and heard the words of the crucified Christ, "Go, Francis, and repair my house," there took place in his heart a complete change that left him ever after burning with love for the Crucified One. In the years that followed, his joy and light-heartedness were also accompanied by times of deep and dark suffering. He knew well the "dark night of the spirit," suffering many physical illnesses, seeing his quickly expanding order of brothers often falling into mediocrity and corruption. He was a man who had attained mystical heights, planted deeply in suffering. But so in love with God was Francis, so filled with the Spirit, that even in the midst of darkness he would compose his famous poem and prayer, "The Canticle of Brother Sun." Accordingly, he calls on all creatures, the sun, the moon, the stars, even suffering and death itself, to pour out their praise to God.

Today, while scientists guide and direct the great technology overcoming the earth, and politicians and governmental authorities and wealthy corporations dangle the world over the delicate fringes of destruction, we are able to look to Francis as a great witness, teacher, and guide.

Today, while scientists guide and direct the great technology overcoming the earth, and politicians, governmental authorities, and wealthy corporations dangle the world over the delicate fringes of destruction, we are able to look to Francis as a great witness, teacher, and guide. We can share in that greatness and power that made Francis exuberant with joy, true joy, if we are courageous enough to become little ones, and join him in his prayer—

May the power of your love, O Lord, fiery and sweet as honey, wean my heart from all that is under heaven, so that I may die for love of your love, you who were so good as to die for love of my love.

The Leper

PHILIP SCHARPER

One day Francis was out riding in the fields near Assisi. He was a young man in his early twenties. Suddenly out from the side of the road stepped a leper. Francis recoiled in horror at the stench, the crumbling ulcerous flesh, and he was tempted to dig his spurs into the flanks of his horse and gallop swiftly away.

Where would Francis find his lepers today? The lepers were the social outcasts of that time. Where are the social outcasts, who are the social outcasts in New York, Chicago, in Los Angeles, in Rome or in London and in the other cities of the world? That is where you would find Francis.

But no, he fought down his squeamishness and his pride. He slowly climbed down out of the saddle, walked over to the leper, took his hand and kissed it. He had won a battle with himself. He was beginning to have some sense of the presence of God in all His creatures. He was beginning to feel a kind of brotherhood with all created things under the Fatherhood of God, with the leper as much as with the lamb and the birds and the flowers. In fact, he was beginning to see the image of Christ more in the poor and the afflicted. It was as though in looking at the leper he saw the broken and bleeding body of Christ his brother.

Long afterward, looking back over the years, Francis saw this as a turning point in his life. In his testament, the will that he wrote shortly before he died, he says, "When I was young, I was nauseated at the sight of lepers and then God sent me amongst them, and what had previously nauseated me now became a source of sweetness."

Where would Francis find his lepers today? The lepers were the social outcasts of that time. Where are the social outcasts? Who are the social outcasts in New York, in Chicago, in Los Angeles, in Rome or in London and in other cities of the world? That is where you would find Francis.

Francis's kissing of the leper was not just another of those flamboyant gestures which characterized his younger days. If, in the words of St. Paul, every person is a living temple of the living God, then to shun and despise the lepers, as Francis himself had once done, was a sacrilege—a sacrilege even greater than to let a temple of stone and wood fall into ruin, as had this church of John the Baptist, Francis's patron saint. His life was now divided between the service of lepers—disfigured temples of flesh and blood—and lonely prayer in abandoned churches, where the only other sounds were bird song and the whispering of the wind.

Lenin Was Right

LIAM BROPHY

Just now the towns and cities east of the Iron Curtain are festooned with portraits of Lenin to commemorate the twenty-fifth anniversary of his death. The jubilation, like labor in those silent parts, is mainly forced. Lack of due appreciation for the greatness of the father of Sovietism might land a Czech or Hungarian in a Siberian concentration camp, for it seems that even fourteen million slaves have not sufficed to help the USSR catch up with the United States in production. And yet, such is the irony of history, were Lenin himself conducting Russian and world affairs from the Kremlin today, it is more probable that St. Francis of Assisi would be feted through a free world. For it has been verified that Lenin on his deathbed admitted to a Hungarian priest, who had been a former classmate, that his method of emancipating the proletariat had been tragically wrong. "I have been mistaken," he said. "It was necessary, I suppose, to liberate the multitude of oppressed people; but our method has provoked other oppressions, frightful massacres. You know that my most awful nightmare is to feel myself drowning in an ocean of the blood of countless victims. *To save our Russia, what we needed (but it is too late now) was ten Francises of Assisi. Ten Francises of Assisi, and we should have saved Russia.*"

No social theorist ever made of himself a *corpus vile* with the seraphic ardor with which Saint Francis of Assisi identified himself with the poorest of the poor. No man, said Bishop Jacques Bossuet, was ever such a desperate lover of poverty as he. Is he not remembered in all ages by the endearing term *Il Poverello*—the poor little one? Poet as he

was, the well of Italian poetry undefiled, he personified his beloved Poverty, so that *La Donna Povertà* was to become the shining inspiration of his brown-robed knights for all future generations. The Art Department of the Propaganda and Agitation Administration in the USSR had not been able to force its poets into glorifying the proletariat ideal with such lyricism to command the loyalty of free men.

Lenin was right. To convert the world to just ways of thinking and win freedom for the oppressed, the seraphic approach of the Franciscan spirit would have more than sufficed. Lenin had chosen the Marxian approach, which was its dark opposite, and the result has filled the world with wars and endless woe. How opposite the approaches are can be best judged by contrasting Saint Francis and Karl Marx and their ideologies of love and hatred.

The world into which Saint Francis was born in c. 1182 resembled our own in the general feeling of disintegration that haunted men with a vague uneasiness, and in the growing prestige of the merchant classes. Medieval unity and universality were breaking up, and the social framework, which men had come to regard as a fixed boundary to personal ambition, was splitting. The Holy Roman Empire was entering the stage wherein it was to merit the Voltairian jibe. The free cities in Germany and the city-states in Italy were asserting their autonomy. In spite of reforms by the Church during and after the time of Pope Gregory VII, insidious and violent heresies were spreading among the masses. Most of them, like the Fraticelli,* were advocating communist rule and the overthrow of clerical authority, and were putting their crude ideas into operation by force. Money was being used as a means of exchange in place of the barter of agricultural produce. Industries were springing up through the concentration on specialized work by the various guilds and corporations.

"To save our Russia, what we needed (but it is too late now) was ten Francises of Assisi. Ten Francises of Assisi, and we should have saved Russia."

The rapid disintegration of the old feudal framework of society, with the rise of the monied classes

* Heretical Franciscans who left their order in the late fourteenth century.

54

and the merchant princes, forerunners of our modern barons of big business, filled the masses with distaste for their lot, dissatisfaction that the new tide in the affairs of men did not float them to leisure and prosperity, and led to sporadic revolts against all authority. Heretical movements, such as the Humiliati,* were winning supporters among the dispossessed, the disgruntled, and the really unfortunate outcasts of society in the same manner as communism today.

Painters have depicted the Poverello outlined against the dawnlight of the Renaissance whose daystar and singing herald he was. But it should not be forgotten that the social and political background of his life was as full of menace, proportionately, as our own. If serenity did return to Europe, it was because this great peacemaker tamed the war lust that was ravaging and terrorizing whole nations—a fact recorded with significant symbolism in the legend of the taming of the wolf of Gubbio.

Francis was a man sent from God to bring peace to the world and to exalt holy poverty. His formula was the simple and stupendous one of love. Love radiated from this Seraph of Assisi so that even our troubled and tormented age still feels the life-giving warmth of it, and thrills, in spite of terrorism and *Nervenkriegen* (war of nerves), to the exquisite sensibilities of so great a lover. For he was a great lover of his fellow-men, and love, lifted to levels of sanctity, had given him a sure clairvoyance of the human heart. The life of the saint, as recorded by Thomas of Celano, and the incidents related in the *Legends of the Three Companions* and the idyllic *Fioretti* reveal him as a man who had an infinite capacity for taking pains in the cause of charity, a genius in love. God set the seal of his approval on such love by appearing to him on Mount Alvernia in the appropriate form of a seraph, and by imprinting on his hands and feet and side the wounds of Christ's Passion.

Karl Marx built up his plans for social reform within the walls of the British Museum. He was before all else a theorizer. It is recorded of him that he kept his hands white and free from all stain of manual labor. If he desired the good of the proletariat, he showed no inclination to study their conditions as one of themselves. At no time did he come out into the light of things to let human nature be his teacher. *Das Kapital* is a tedious weav-

ing of brain-spun theories. Marx conspicuously lacked a sense of humor and, what is akin, an intuition for the poetry of life. He conjured up his rigid system of dialectic materialism without even glancing for a moment into the fantastic depths of the human heart and its vexing vagaries that set the formulas of calculators at naught. He never knew its capacity for holiness and heroism. He ignored its fatal flaw of Original Sin.

So it was that he came to expect too much and too little from man. He believed that men could be made perfect in a classless society by altering their environment. If every man had enough, he reasoned, all social ills would disappear, and war be but the rumor of thunder beyond the hills. He had not the insight of Cardinal Newman, who wrote: "Quarry the granite rocks with razors or moor the vessel with a thread of silk; then may you hope with such keen and delicate instruments as human knowledge and human reason to contend against these giants, the passion and the pride of man."

Hatred was the driving force that Marx proposed to bring this communistic utopia of a classless society into being. That hatred is to be directed not merely against the evils of capitalism, but against the capitalist class itself, in which were included the multitude of those who defend the things of the spirit. "Love men, hate their errors" was Saint Augustine's wise dictum. But of that wisdom Marx knew nothing. And, when this consuming hatred should have produced the reign of the proletariat in a classless society, it was to disappear, for, said Marx, every man would have sufficient of the world's goods to satisfy him, and there would be no usurping class left to hate. What a childish concept of the human heart is here! Hatred of all emotions is the most difficult to control, as any

* A medieval order that consisted of laymen who lived at home, cared for the poor, and met on Sunday to hear one of the brothers speak.

witness of mob riots will testify, and it certainly cannot be turned off with the abrupt finality of a tap once its end is achieved. And whereas love is creative and enriches the life of the lover a hundredfold, hatred is essentially destructive and corrosive. The end of hatred is despair and death. While love can exalt man to the very heart of the Mystical Rose, as Dante sang, hatred rots the heart within a man.

Joy is one of the chief fruits of love, and this is especially true of seraphic love. Franciscan joy has become proverbial. Gloom, melancholy, and *la noia* (boredom) the seraphic saint regarded as marks of the devil's disciples. He who was the gentlest of saints would reprimand any of his brethren whom he saw with a rueful countenance. He reminded them of the counsel of Saint Paul to "rejoice in the Lord always."

One of the chief characteristics of communism is its utter joylessness. It was not "born out of joyful superabundance of creative forces," said Nicholas Berdyaev, who witnessed its violent birth, "but from profound unhappiness. . . . It resembles the animation produced by an injection of camphor, rather than the springtime of national life."

Love, which has need of eternity and looks through death on God, holds death to be but an incident in the ascent of the spirit to endless and perfect possession. Saint Francis cried out, "Welcome, Sister Death," as the breath left his frail body, and his beloved larks flocked around to sing his requiem. The Marxists have denied personal immortality. After all, they have nothing to live for hereafter. But they shun discussion on death. Engels referred to "the tedium of personal survival." No Communist loves his system so well as to wish to live eternally in a state of beatific boredom, chanting the "International" through sempiternal years.

Who, on contemplating the modern world, will deny that Lenin spoke wisely in his last hours? This loveless, joyless, war-menaced world needs another Saint Francis. The fruits of Franciscan spirituality are the exact specifics for its ills. The hearts of earnest and thinking people are everywhere lifted up in expectation of the saint whom it shall please God to send us for liberation. If Saint Francis may not walk among us as he walked the Umbrian valleys seven centuries ago, the saint that is to come will bear remarkable resemblance to the loving, laughing seraph who bade the worshipers through the world to unite under the sign of *Pax et Bonum*—Peace and Good.

We Seem to Think

PETER MAURIN

Saint Francis thought
that to choose to be poor
is just as good
as if one should marry
the most beautiful girl in the world.
We seem to think
that poor people
are social nuisances
and not the Ambassadors of God.
We seem to think
that Lady Poverty
is an ugly girl
and not the beautiful girl
that Saint Francis of Assisi
says she is.
And because we think so,
we refuse to feed the poor
with our superfluous goods
and let the politicians
feed the poor
by going around
like pickpockets,
robbing Peter
to pay Paul,
and feeding the poor
by soaking the rich.

The Lady Poverty

EVELYN UNDERHILL

I met her on the Umbrian hills,
    Her hair unbound, her feet unshod;
As one whom secret glory fills
    She walked, alone with God.

I met her in the city street;
    Oh, changed was all her aspect then!
With heavy eyes and weary feet
    She walked, alone with men.

Francis and Christ

OSCAR WILDE

There is something so unique about Christ. Of course just as there are false dawns before the dawn itself, and winter days so full of sudden sunlight that they will cheat the wise crocus into squandering its gold before its time, and make some foolish bird call to its mate to build on barren boughs, so there were Christians before Christ. For that we should be grateful. The unfortunate thing is that there have been none since. I make one exception, Saint Francis of Assisi. But then God had given him at his birth the soul of a poet, and he himself when quite young had in mystical marriage taken Poverty as his bride; and with the soul of a poet and the body of a beggar he found the way to perfection not difficult. He understood Christ, and so he became like him. We do not require the *Liber Conformitatum* [Book of Conformities] to teach us that the life of Saint Francis was the true *Imitatio Christi* [Imitation of Christ], a poem compared to which the book of that name is merely prose. . . . Indeed, that is the charm about Christ, when all is said. He is just like a work of art himself. He does not really teach one anything, but by being brought into his presence one becomes something. And everybody is predestined to his presence. Once at least in his life each man walks with Christ to Emmaus.*

* A village outside Jerusalem where Jesus appeared to two disciples the evening of his Resurrection (Luke 24:13).

The Cuckoo at Lavernia

WILLIAM WORDSWORTH

Oft have I heard the Nightingale and Thrush
Blending as in a common English grove
Their love-songs; but, where'er my feet might
    roam,
Whate'er assemblages of new and old,
Strange and familiar, might beguile the way,
A gratulation from that vagrant Voice
Was wanting;—and most happily till now.

  For see, Lavernia! mark the far-famed Pile,
High on the brink of that precipitous rock,
Implanted like a Fortress, as in truth
It is, a Christian Fortress, garrisoned
In faith and hope, and dutiful obedience,
By a few Monks, a stern society,
Dead to the world and scorning earth-born joys.
Nay—though the hopes that drew, the fears that
    drove
St. Francis, far from Man's resort, to abide
Among these sterile heights of Apennine,
Bound him, nor, since he raised yon House, have
    ceased
To bind his spiritual Progeny, with rules
Stringent as flesh can tolerate and live;
His milder Genius (thanks to the good God
That made us) over those severe restraints
Of mind, that dread heart-freezing discipline,
Doth sometimes here predominate, and works
By unsought means for gracious purposes;
For earth through heaven, for heaven, by changeful
    earth,
Illustrated, and mutually endeared.

  Rapt though he were above the power of sense,
Familiarly, yet out of the cleansed heart
Of that once sinful being overflowed
On sun, moon, stars, the nether elements,
And every shape of creature they sustain,
Divine affections; and with beast and bird,
(Stilled from afar—such marvel story tells—
By casual outbreak of his passionate words,
And from their own pursuits in field or grove
Drawn to his side by look or act of love
Humane, the virtue of his innocent life)
He wont to hold companionship so free,

So pure, so fraught with knowledge and delight
As to be likened in his followers' minds
To that which our first Parents, ere the fall
From their high state darkened the Earth with fear,
Held with all Kinds in Eden's blissful bowers. . . .

The Ungloomy Ascetic

G.K. CHESTERTON

The whole point about Saint Francis of Assisi is that he certainly was ascetical, and he certainly was not gloomy. As soon as ever he had been unhorsed by the glorious humiliation of his vision of dependence on the divine love, he flung himself into fasting and vigil exactly as he had flung himself furiously into battle. He had wheeled his charger clean round, but there was no halt or check in the thundering impetuosity of his charge. There was nothing negative about it; it was not a regimen or a stoical simplicity of life. It was not self-denial merely in the sense of self-control. It was as positive as a passion; it had all the air of being as positive as a pleasure. He devoured fasting as a man devours food. He plunged after poverty as men have dug madly for gold.

The whole point about Saint Francis of Assisi is that he certainly was ascetical, and he certainly was not gloomy.

And it is precisely the positive and passionate quality of this part of his personality that is a challenge to the modern mind in the whole problem of the pursuit of pleasure. There undeniably is the historical fact; and there attached to it is another moral fact almost as undeniable. It is certain that he held on this heroic or unnatural course from the moment when he went forth in his hair shirt into the winter woods to the moment when he desired even in his death-agony to lie bare upon the bare ground, to prove that he had and that he was nothing. And we can say, with almost as deep a certainty, that the stars that passed upon that gaunt and wasted corpse stark upon the rocky floor had, for once, in all their shining cycles round the world of laboring humanity, looked down upon a happy man.

Saint Francis and Man

CONSTANTINE KOSER, O.F.M.

What we fear about life with God and the excuse we make for running away from it is alienation, crushing verticalism, and repression of man and his world. But it is the very life with God, intense and sublime as we find it in Saint Francis, which disproves the fears and refutes the excuses. Life with God makes us more human and makes us find the true depths, the greatest depth, of love of man.

In the love of God and of Christ—Son of God, Man, Child, Crucified, Eucharistic Bread—Francis found the basis of his respectful and courteous love of Mary, the Virgin Mother of Jesus. In life with God he encountered the angels and saints in a deep-rooted, gentlemanly love. In life with God he met the Church; not the abstract Church, but the concrete: the Pope, the bishops, the priests, the friars, the nuns, the laity.

Francis encounters all men in God, and lists them by categories, which themselves give eloquent testimony of the breadth of his love: ". . . all children, big and small, the poor and the needy, kings and princes, laborers and farmers, servants and masters; . . . all virgins and other women, married or unmarried; . . . all lay folk, men and women, infants and adolescents, young and old, the healthy and the sick, the little and the great, all peoples, tribes, families, and languages, all nations and men everywhere, present and to come. . . ."

Out of the bottomless lake of the love of God flowed the stream of the Poverello's warmth, understanding, and tender compassion toward his companions, toward those who suffer, toward those who believe, toward those who are still far from God, toward all men.

The Poverello's attitude toward man takes its roots from the Gospel and also from his own experiences in his own times. Yet, seven and a half centuries later, it seems to be more than modern; it seems stimulating and revolutionary! It will never grow old.

Especially revealing is the way Francis faced the old but ever-new problem of obedience and authority. If we read his writings and ponder the episodes of his life, we come to realize that, while he considered obedience a virtue limited only by the conscience's relationship with God, his principal preoccupation was with the exercise of authority. He wished it to respect the person, to be full of understanding and constructive love, to preserve the liberty of the subject, to seek means of establishing coresponsibility and collaboration without resorting to force or harshness.

Being himself a strong and independent personality, as few others have ever been, Francis always esteemed the value of the person, with its rights and singular endowments. His whole life, his whole spirituality reveal profound and loving respect for the human element in everything.

Being himself a strong and independent personality, as few others have ever been, Francis always esteemed the value of the person, with its rights and singular endowments. His whole life, his whole spirituality reveal profound and loving respect for the human element in everything.

Francis was also a group-oriented person. We see him, before his "conversion," a happy-go-lucky and stimulating companion at festivals, an encouraging and comforting friend in prison. After becoming "converted" he attracted, without wanting to, his companions; together with them he began a very singular kind of common life, built upon spontaneity, respect, mutual attention, with flourishes of loving courtesy, and with reciprocal love as the binding force of the whole brotherhood.

This is the way he expressed it in his rule: "Wherever the friars meet one another, they should show that they are members of the same family. And they should have no hesitation in making known their needs to one another. For if a mother loves and cares for her child in the flesh, a friar should certainly love and care for his spiritual brother all the more tenderly. If a friar falls ill, the others are bound to look after him as they would like to be looked after themselves."

To look out for the rights of "the other," and not of oneself; to take care that each one has room for his own life, for his person, and that each can find security and a welcome in his brother: for Francis this is the one and only basis for societies and groups. This is the one and only basis he desired for his Order. This is Gospel teaching learned and lived intensely by Saint Francis.

A great lesson for all men, but particularly for Franciscans. So evident is the lesson that even "outsiders" can see it in Francis and love him for it. We must understand that fraternal life springs from life with God. He who walks ever forward on this road will become a man of today, of any "today," no matter how far in the future it lies.

Within the context of brotherly love for men in God, Francis lived out the tensions between solitude and community in life with God. He felt the tensions. The enticement of contemplative life in solitude always tempted him to abandon the apostolic impulse. It was ever a relief to shake the clinging dust of the road from his bare feet as he returned to his life of contemplation. He loved above all else to be alone with God and a few of his brothers in solitude. This always shines forth in his writings and in all the testimonies about him.

Nevertheless, we shall never find any reference in which Saint Francis displays a negative attitude toward life in brotherhood with all men, nor any suspicion that life among men constitutes an obstacle to life with God. He knows that if his life with God suffers from his life with men, it is because he, Francis, has not attained the proper degree of either. And so he flees to the broad spaces of solitude to fill himself with God in order to return and mingle again with men, all men.

The Poverello never knew brotherhood as a merely natural, simple, horizontal relationship. Brotherhood for him originates in life with God and always has an ecclesial aspect. His catholicity, that is, his adhesion to a concrete Church, which he accepted as being founded by Christ, knew no bounds. His relationship to the Church always colored his relationships with men. In fact, we might say that his relationships with men *were* an aspect of his relationship with the Church.

He accepted and loved the Church just as he found her. Not that he closed his eyes to defects, to stain, to degeneracy in the Church; on the contrary, perhaps no one was ever more sensitive to these things than Francis. Seeing them, he set out to reform them by love, not by ranting and raving, as did so many other "reformers." And his love did succeed in working profound improvements in the Church.

Francis, so far as we know, never manifested any conscious theological ideas concerning the people of God or of the Mystical Body of Christ. Nor do we ever hear of his preaching the doctrines of sanctifying grace and incorporation into Christ. He had heard about them, of course, but in the same vague way as most people of his day. What he learned, however, he practiced so intensely that he simply passed beyond the level of theological teaching in his day, and became a *living* doctrine, a "thoroughly catholic man."

Here again there is a powerful lesson for our times. We have to live our present knowledge of the Church as Francis lived his. We have to improve the image of the Church by our lives until all men see what the Church really is: a splendid revelation of God and Christ to all men. We have to make our own ecclesial lives an invitation to all men for the life with God.

We find the Poverello's prayer life situated at the exact point where the private and ecclesial aspects of personal and group relationships converge. When we say "personal" prayer we usually mean "nonofficial," "nonliturgical" prayer. This is mere terminology, but many times it leads us into the error of forgetting that prayer is not prayer unless it is personal. Even official, liturgical prayer must be *our* prayer, or it is not prayer at all, at least so far as we are concerned. Francis agreed wholeheartedly with the ancient maxim: "Match your heart with your voice."

Prayer in common, using preestablished formulas, becomes a genuine expression of the soul only after so much personal prayer in the sense of individual communication with God. Still, to pray as God wills us to pray, we cannot eliminate "the others" from our prayer; we cannot expect a "private audience" with God.

In Saint Francis we see intense cultivation of private prayer, but at the same time strong love of official, liturgical, communitarian prayer. He understood that this kind of prayer with its prearranged formulas cannot be true prayer without the nourishment of personal prayer. For this reason he was careful not to overload the day with prescribed common prayers, leaving much time for reflection, meditation, intimate and spontaneous conversation with God. Because he lived intensely with God, he felt no difficulty with the preestablished formulas of the Church, but simply integrated them easily into the mainstream of his interior life.

With his respect for, and sensitivity to, genuine values, Francis avoided the pitfalls of devotionalism while cultivating his favorite devotions. He never forgot to give priority to "the spirit of prayer and devotion." His criterion was never the number nor the length of the "devotion," but *devotion,* which of course means profound dedication to God.

His intense love of prayer never conflicted with his deep-seated respect for work; but at the same time he warned that "the friars . . . should work in a spirit of faith and devotion and avoid idleness, which is the enemy of the soul, without however extinguishing the spirit of prayer and devotion to which every temporal consideration must be subordinate." Excellent advice today and always.

With his ecclesial leanings and his love for all men, the Poverello always felt himself impelled to work for the good of souls. He never saw any conflict, however, between apostolate and prayer, although he certainly experienced difficulties trying to harmonize the two. Always attentive to the appeal of "the spirit of prayer and devotion," he would return to his beloved solitude to cleanse his soul of any dust that it might have acquired on the highways of the apostolate. Then his zeal for souls would drive him out again to face the apostolic combat with renewed and invigorated love.

The difficulties he met never made him abandon the apostolate for the contemplative life, but he knew he had to make the contemplation stimulate the apostolate. He knew that all true life with God included love and labor for souls, and the difficulties of reconciling the two originate in the one who feels the difficulties. To overcome them one must not choose between contemplation and apostolate but must rise to the level of life with God in which these difficulties cease.

Monks Versus Slippery Fishes

G.K. CHESTERTON

There is undoubtedly a sense in which two is company and three is none; there is also another sense in which three is company and four is none, as is proved by the procession of historic and fictitious figures moving three deep, the famous trios such as the Three Musketeers or the Three Soldiers of Kipling. But there is yet another and a different sense in which four is company and three is none if we use the word *company* in the vaguer sense of a crowd or a mass. With the fourth man enters the shadow of a mob; the group is no longer one of three individuals conceived only individually.

That shadow of the fourth man fell across the little hermitage of the Portiuncula when a man named Giles, apparently a poor workman, was invited by Saint Francis to enter. He mingled without difficulty with the merchant and the canon who had already become the companions of Francis; but with his coming an invisible line was crossed; for it must have been felt by this time that the growth of that small group had become potentially infinite, or at least that its outline had become permanently indefinite. It may have been in the time of that transition that Francis had another of his dreams full of voices; but now the voices were a clamor of the tongues of all nations, Frenchmen and Italians and English and Spanish and Germans, telling of the glory of God, each in his own tongue, a new Pentecost and a happier Babel.

Before describing the first steps he took to regularize the growing group, it is well to have a rough grasp of what he conceived that group to be. He did not call his followers monks; and it is not clear, at this time at least, that he even thought of them as monks. He called them by a name that is generally rendered in English as Friars Minor; but we shall be much closer to the atmosphere of his own mind if we render it almost literally as the Little Brothers. Presumably he was already resolved, indeed, that they should take the three vows of poverty, chastity, and obedience, which had always been the marks of a monk. But it would seem that he was not so much afraid of the idea of a monk as of the idea of an abbot. He was afraid that the great spiritual magistracies, which had given even to their holiest possessors at least a sort of impersonal and corporate pride, would import an element of pomposity that would spoil his extremely and almost extravagantly simple version of the life of humility.

But the supreme difference between his discipline and the discipline of the old monastic system was concerned, of course, with the idea that the monks were to become migratory and almost nomadic instead of stationary. They were to mingle with the world; and to this the more old-fashioned monk would naturally reply by asking how they were to mingle with the world without becoming entangled with the world. It was a much more real question than a loose religiosity is likely to realize; but St. Francis had his answer to it, of his own individual sort; and the interest of the problem is in that highly individual answer.

The good Bishop of Assisi expressed a sort of horror at the hard life that the Little Brothers lived at

"Makes one stop and think."

the Portiuncula, without comforts, without possessions, eating anything they could get and sleeping anyhow on the ground. St. Francis answered him with that curious and almost stunning shrewdness that the unworldly can sometimes wield like a club of stone. He said, "If we had any possessions, we should need weapons and laws to defend them." That sentence is the clue to the whole policy that he pursued. It rested upon a real piece of logic; and about that he was never anything but logical. He was ready to own himself wrong about anything else; but he was quite certain he was right about this particular rule. He was only once seen angry; and that was when there was talk of an exception to the rule.

His argument was this: that the dedicated man might go anywhere among any kind of men, even the worst kind of men, so long as there was nothing by which they could hold him. If he had any ties or needs like ordinary men, he would become like ordinary men. St. Francis was the last man in the world to think any the worse of ordinary men for being ordinary. They had more affection and admiration from him than they are ever likely to have again. But for his own particular purpose of stirring up the world to a new spiritual enthusiasm, he saw with a logical clarity that was quite the reverse of fanatical or sentimental, that friars must not become like ordinary men; that the salt must not lose its savor even to turn into human nature's daily food. And the difference between a friar and an ordinary man was really that a friar was freer than an ordinary man. It was necessary that he should be free from the cloister; but it was even more important that he should be free from the world.

It is perfectly sound common sense to say that there is a sense in which the ordinary man cannot be free from the world, or rather ought not to be free from the world. The feudal world in particular was one labyrinthine system of dependence, but it was not only the feudal world that went to make up the medieval world nor the medieval world that went to make up the whole world; and the whole world is full of this fact. Family life as much as feudal life is in its nature a system of dependence. Modern trade unions as much as medieval guilds are interdependent among themselves even in order to be independent of others. In medieval as in modern life, even where these limitations do exist for the sake of liberty, they have in them a considerable element of luck. They are partly the result of circumstances sometimes the almost unavoidable result of circumstances.

So the twelfth century had been the age of vows; and there was something of relative freedom in that feudal gesture of the vow, for no man asks vows from slaves any more than from spades. Still, in practice, a man rode to war in support of the ancient house of the Column or behind the Great Dog of the Stairway largely because he had been born in a certain city or countryside. But no man need obey little Francis in the old brown habit unless he chose. Even in his relations with his chosen leader he was in one sense relatively free, compared with the world around him. He was obedient but not dependent. And he was as free as the wind; he was almost wildly free in his relation to that world around him. The world around him was, as has been noted, a network of feudal and family and other forms of dependence.

The whole idea of Saint Francis was that the Little Brothers should be like little fishes who could go freely in and out of that net. They could do so precisely because they were small fishes and in that sense even slippery fishes.

The whole idea of St. Francis was that the Little Brothers should be like little fishes who could go freely in and out of that net. They could do so precisely because they were small fishes and in that sense even slippery fishes. There was nothing that the world could hold them by, for the world catches us mostly by the fringes of our garments, the futile externals of our lives.

The Great Lay Adventure of the Late Middle Ages

JOHN O'CONNOR, S.M.

A further attempt to give the layman a distinct place in the religious state was made in the thirteenth century by the movement of Francis of Assisi. This lay movement too met the needs of the times by bringing the Gospel of Christ in all simplicity to the newly formed villages and towns. Francis wanted his lay religious to give their services in hospitals, in harvesting with the peasants in the fields, and in ministering to the needs of the poor. The essence of Christianity was to present Christ the crucified to everyone of the faithful through preaching and through the ordinary affairs of daily life.

But Francis did not adopt the ways of the clergy; he continued to think and act as a layman patterning his life with the mature views of the single layman's state.

The disciples of Francis—laymen and priests—did more than any other group at that period to build the faith and make it strong. Even during Francis's lifetime, however, certain Church authorities tried to make the movement distinctly clerical, going so far as to have Francis and his early disciples made deacons. But Francis did not adopt the ways of the

clergy; he continued to think and act as a layman patterning his life quite in line with the mature views of the single layman's state. The first two Ministers General after Francis were laymen, but soon a Minister General of the Order proclaimed that book learning was required of all those who would hold office in the Order. Certainly it can be said that, at least partially, as a result of becoming clericalized, the Order lost its ability to move the masses—the peasants, the laborers, and the ordinary working people.

A Third Order: Secular Franciscans

RUDOLF HARVEY, O.F.M.

Franciscanism was from the beginning a lay movement of the humble and the highborn within a class-conscious Church. Its inspiration and recruitment came from outside the clerical superstructure. In its mobility it avoided the monastic precedent that marked the classic and conventional form of religious vocation.

Poverty and evangelism were twin objectives through which these lay pioneers could invigorate society because their grass roots were not suffocated by churchly marble. Men followed the uncompli-

cated Francis who said what he thought and did what he said. His words and sermons left no smell of brimstone in the air. He had never to weigh the balance between freedom and law because in his own life love sufficed to give liberty the direction it needed.

When others sought more minute regulations he would simply confront them with the plain words of the Gospel. However much hard-breathing partisans of discipline criticized his administration, they could never suspect the integrity of his motives. One who so conspicuously possessed the immutable dignity of a saint was in their midst.

Under the human warmth of his personality the ancient religion was thawed at its roots and the sap flowed again. For the faith of one nation, and then of all Europe, a winter of the spirit had ended and a fresh spring had begun. He was the bridge between feudalism and democracy, between the few and the many, the wealthy and the hungry, the powerful and the defenseless. He was the dawn of a new world, as his tertiary Dante called him.

If there is little surface sameness between the times of Saint Francis and our own, there is a basic similarity of outlook in religious practice and psychology. The Second Vatican Council regretted a spirit of legalism, triumphalism, and juridicism in the Church and called for its removal. Seven centuries ago Francis asked for the same thing and got it.

The Franciscan commitment to the world of our time and the needs of our day is exemplified by a story told of Francis's companion Brother Giles

who said the cricket has more sense than people have. "People sing 'La, la!' (There, there!), but crickets sing 'Ca, ca!' (Here, here!)." It is not up there in some other world, but here in this one that we should do good.

History shows, what men on the scene could not have known, that Francis was standing at the direct center of the most meaningful events of his time and was causing many of them. He was a pebble God dropped into the Western pond whose concentric and widening ripples would touch and irrigate shores of philosophy and theology, literature and the fine arts. Neither prelate nor artist, he revived and invigorated both religion and art. Neither statesman nor economist, he changed both government and economics.

Like all men with a sense of destiny, Francis knew he was exercising a fulcrum on the future. "All the world will follow me," he used to say. But unlike most men who have this power, he was not inflated by it. In the humility of truth, he acknowledged it as God's gift to the world through him. There were no tangled motives of pride in any of his acts.

Before his day, the rules of religious orders were a portfolio policy for a patterned sanctity. His own free spirit prevented him from saddling and hindering the liberty of his followers. He was no Savonarola rasping at society, sandpapering souls to a smoothness consistent with the veneer of piety he wished them to acquire. His actions were never part of a finely calculated and ceremonious sanctity, symbols in an algebra of piety and morality, but

spontaneous and wholehearted deeds of love, open-handed gifts devotedly laid on the altar.

Feudalism lasted a thousand years. The Crusades sapped its strength. The Third Order of Saint Francis dealt it its deathblow.

Feudalism lasted a thousand years. The Crusades sapped its strength. The Third Order of Saint Francis dealt it its deathblow. At a time and place in which feuds and vendettas were as common as olive trees and few men went abroad unarmed, his Secular Franciscans were forbidden to fight or carry weapons. They were to live within their means, shun vanities and luxuries, give their excess to the poor, and swear no oath, not even one of fealty.

They were a peace corps. Civil wars cannot be fought without ammunition. In forbidding arms and the fealty oath, Francis broke the back of feudalism.

He would have welcomed this social revolution, but certainly he never planned it. He did not regard the Third Order as a battlefront in a war against worldliness. His thoughts were not cast in military terms; spiritual spoils and theological stratagems were alien to his mind. The Third Order came about inevitably and almost spontaneously, the way a branch happens to a tree.

The great net of Francis's personality, daily thrown farther from Assisi, was gathering increasingly larger hauls of followers. From Assisi first and

then from the adjacent towns, they came singly and in families, and finally by whole parishes and cities.

The Franciscan Movement was not a project because no one projected it, but it was a larger enterprise than the founding of a new religious order. It was the founding of a whole new social order, the creation throughout the Italian peninsula and soon afterward through Middle Europe, of a vast magnetic field to which a multitude and variety of good men and the higher human movements of art and literature soon began to flow.

Think of all the grand ventures planned and begun since his time that are now only footnotes to history. Some were movements that never really moved, their human juices leached out of them by egoism or their impetus slackened by the friction of routine. Some were outdistanced by time, like the military monastic orders that outlived their usefulness. Others, once launched with high motives, foundered in shallowness. Yet his Third Order is today an international society larger, busier, and more productive than it ever was in all the seven hundred years of its existence.

After Pope Gregory IX called the first fraternities "communities of penitents," the Third Order came to be known as the Order of Penance. Men and women, married and single, diocesan priests and religious sisters became members. There is no certain date or place of its official founding, but there are records of Francis's resolve to institute it.

One such, reported by Thomas of Celano, occurred after Francis's celebrated sermon to the birds at Bevagna. He and Brother Masseo were about to preach in the Alviano marketplace at twilight. The audience strained to hear their words above the chatter of the swallows. "My sisters," said Francis, scolding the birds, "it is now *my* turn to speak. Be quiet while I preach the word of God!" The swallows obeyed.

"Because of this miracle," writes Thomas of Celano, "and because of the inspiring sermon that followed it, the townsfolk decided to become his disciples. 'Be not too hasty,' said Francis, 'I will ordain for you what you should do to be saved.' And from that time on he considered establishing a third order."

Successive chapter headings such as these in Celano's first *Life of Saint Francis* explain his attraction: "On his eager desire to undergo martyrdom," they read; "On his sermon to the birds and the way the creatures obeyed him"; "On his preaching at Ascoli and how the sick were cured by things which he had touched although he was not there"; "How he healed the lame man at Toscanella and the paralytic at Narni"; "How he restored the sight of the blind woman and healed a crippled woman at Gubbio"; "How he freed one of the friars from epilepsy or from the devil and how he freed the possessed woman at the town of San Gemini"; "How he drove out a devil at Città di Castello."

Here was Galilee all over again. Francis, like his Master, had compassion on the multitude and fitted the new Rule to the circumstances of each postulant. A Secular Franciscan who was a pastor was told by Francis to remain in his parish and donate his sur-

plus tithes to the poor. In Poggibonsi the merchant Luchesio and his wife Bona Donna took the Third Order habit, dispensed their goods to the poor, and dedicated their lives to the corporal works of mercy. . . .

In time the roll of Secular Franciscans would lengthen with names of the great and the humble: King Louis of France and Queen Elizabeth of Hungary; Novellone, the saintly shoemaker; Blessed Peter of Siena, the combmaker; Matt Talbot of Dublin, the day laborer. There would be artists such as Michelangelo, Rafaelo Sanzo, and Murillo; musicians such as Gounod and Palestrina, poets such as Jacopone da Todi, Metrarch, and Francis Thompson; statesmen such as Windhorst and Saint Thomas More; and scientists such as Ampere and Faraday.

Seven centuries before the Second Vatican Council pleaded for lay involvement, Francis had begun this movement, which in our own day prompts the Salvation Army to venerate him as patron and even Communists to muster their sparse reverence to salute "the liberator of the medieval proletariat." When a Berlin journalist was asked to characterize Chancellor Dollfuss of Austria, he dubbed him "Francis of Assisi with a cigar" and gave the public a picture they could identify.

Today's Secular Franciscan is an admired citizen, but when the Order began, its members automatically incurred the wrath of the public authorities. Their presence was a mute and mighty contradiction of state policy. Refusing military conscription in the aggressive wars of the times, they were regarded as subversive and subjected to special taxes and public harassment. On December 16, 1221, Pope Honorius III ordered the Bishop of Rimini to protect them, and Gregory IX threatened their persecutors with canonical penalties.

The twelve chapters of the Third Order Rule of 1228 forbid any breach of the peace, prescribe the prompt payment of all personal debts and the drafting of a will within three months after reception into the Order to obviate dissension among heirs of the Secular Franciscan.

Francis was twelve years old when the thirteenth century began. The watershed between the Dark Ages and the Medieval Renaissance, a new birth, which he heralded and which his Third Order largely caused, was artistic and literary as well as spiritual. The Franciscans Dante and Giotto were his spiritual sons sharing and imparting through their genius of words and colors his vision of the world as a happy home for men and beasts provided and lavishly furnished by their Creator.

His Best Friend

Clare

MURRAY BODO, O.F.M.

She followed him because she loved the treasure. She heard him speak of what he had found, and a passage in her own heart opened up. They had found the same treasure in different caves, and they would share it with whomever they met in that sacred place below the surface of life. She was Clare and he was Francis, and together they would show the world its hidden heart.

Clare was only eleven that day in the Piazza del Comune when she saw this young man gone "mad." He, the rich son of Pietro Bernardone, was making his way across the piazza, unkempt and haggard, begging food from the cursing citizens. Her young eyes were transfixed at this incredible sight, and she did not understand what he was doing. She, with her child's mind, thought he was funny and began to giggle, trying at the same time to wriggle free of her mother's firm grip. She wanted to run after him and join in all the mocking "fun" the grown-ups seemed to be having.

The following year, when she was twelve, a strange scene was enacted between Francis and his father in the cathedral courtyard. Later she heard her parents talking in low voices about Francis, the wild twenty-four-year-old son of Bernardone, and of how he had renounced his father before Guido, the Bishop of Assisi. She wondered what "renounced" meant and why the bishop was there. But this time she didn't laugh. She sensed in her parents' voices a terrible seriousness. What Francis had done was something evil, something good children never do, and that night her sleep was filled with nightmares of beggars and bishops and fathers red with anger. Francis had already begun to haunt her.

By the time she was fourteen, he had become something of a celebrity, if still an oddity, a name on the lips of everyone in Assisi. He had repaired the crumbling Churches of San Damiano, San Pietro, and Our Lady of the Angels (the Portiuncula) with stones he had begged in the city. He lived with and nursed the lepers on the plain below Assisi, and he had changed his hermit's garb for that of a barefoot preacher.

And then she heard him preach. The words were simple and unadorned, but they touched her like a deep and purifying shaft of light. Her whole being seemed bathed in a light that came from somewhere inside her own heart.

What it was that Francis had opened up she did not know. It was not merely a fascination with Francis himself that drew her, but his words and something inside the words—the treasure, a secret, powerful force that came, she was sure, from God himself.

Her soul thirsted for more, and she longed to hear Francis whenever he preached to the people. But she was still in her teens and did not have the freedom to come and go as she pleased. She would, however, find a way. She would find a way because what was happening inside her came from God. She saw in Francis someone who must be experiencing what she felt in her own heart. . . .

She was in love! With God? With Francis? With both of them? With love? How did you sort it all out? Or should you? She was to learn over and over again the difference between loving and being in love, but this was the first time, and it was all too much for her.

She threw open the shutters of her bedroom and leaned out in the morning freshness, her gaze resting on the façade of the Church of San Rufino, the patron of Assisi. She and Francis had been baptized in that church, and she had made her first communion there. Her father's palazzo was adjacent to the church, so she had grown up, as it were, in the courtyard of the Church of San Rufino. And now during this Lent of her eighteenth year, Francis had been preaching from its pulpit.

What he said inflamed her heart as nothing ever had before, but so did Francis himself. He seemed always to be looking only at her and to be speaking to her alone. At first this had disarmed her as she sat next to her parents in the first pew and looked into his penetrating brown eyes. How small he would look as he mounted the pulpit, and how large he would grow with every word that struck her heart.

And then their long talks together, the flame burning bright in her soul. Francis must have

69

known how she felt about him, must have wondered how he as going to handle what was happening inside this young, impressionable girl with the golden hair. Oh, how she missed him just thinking about him this Palm Sunday morning!

The sun had not yet climbed to the top of Mount Subasio, but the light of dawn had preceded it into her little square, and she kept her eyes on San Rufino. Shortly the town would begin to wake with the clatter of shutters, and bells would ring in the sun of another day. And she would go to Palm Sunday services for the last time with her family.

For Francis and Bishop Guido had finally decided that this would be the day of her leaving the world to follow Jesus Christ as a spiritual daughter of Francis Bernardone. She would be the first woman to believe and follow the dream of poverty and littleness that God had given Francis for the rebuilding of his kingdom.

And this very night it would all happen. Clare was so in love that the coming of night seemed an eternity away. These last hours would be the longest of her life, for just below the city in the little Chapel of Saint Mary of the Angels someone divine and someone human were waiting for her. She was in love, her heart rushing to begin loving. . . .

By her vows of poverty, chastity, and obedience, Clare was wed forever to her Lord and Savior Jesus Christ. But in that solemn ceremony when Francis himself took her hair into his hands, cut through her curls, and watched them fall onto the dirt floor of the chapel, something else happened as well: she was wed in mind and heart to Francis.

Even externally she became like him. In a ritual that mirrored Francis's own stripping of himself before the Bishop of Assisi, Clare placed her satin dress into the hands of the brothers and put on a rough woolen habit. She secured it about the waist with an ordinary rope more beautiful to her than the jeweled belt she had worn in her father's house. And with naked feet she stepped into a pair of wooden sandals that shone like golden slippers in the candlelight from Mary's tiny altar. Now they were one, she and Francis, alike in everything from the dream they shared to the very clothes they wore.

She would hold fast to the total poverty of this ecstatic moment till the end of her days. Now she and Francis shared everything that mattered to her in life. What greater union could there possibly be than union in the Lord? Clare viewed that moment of consecration in the Portiuncula as a sacrament of her union with her Lord and with Francis. He was now bound to her and she to him by

their common consecration to the Lord. She was as much a part of his life as were his own brothers—perhaps more so because she was a woman and he a man. In some transcendent yet tangible way they were building a new Eden in which men and women walked in the cool of the evening hand in hand with God.

They had both stood naked and innocent before God and man: Francis when he stripped himself in front of the crowd gathered before Bishop Guido and she when she placed her lovely dress into the brothers' open palms. Now there was nothing worldly between her and Francis; the Lord was there, and they would walk at either side of him forever.

The Lord stood between them, but he was transparent. They saw each other even more clearly through the radiance of his glorified body. His presence made their union more real to her because it was beyond space and time and yet grounded in the most tangible of all realities, the human heart and mind, the human soul and body. What woman or man could ask for more here where all is not yet perfect, here where evil is still a reality to be reckoned with, here where the cross is still the only chariot to heaven?

Those who observed Clare and Francis with purely human eyes would think they walked separately the road to God, that they were distant and removed from each other. But if they had eyes of the spirit, they would see two hearts inseparably joined, two souls united in God. Whoever saw one would see the other more really than anyone with earthly vision would ever believe. That was the mystery of spiritual love, and Clare and Francis were proof of its existence. She wondered how many would have eyes to see. . . .

"A place for me." That is how she viewed the Church of San Damiano. Once she was there, she could live apart from Francis and still be a part of his life. Before coming to San Damiano she felt so alone. Francis had his brothers, and wherever they were, he had a place to call home. The brotherhood *was* his home. She needed something like that, too.

Immediately after Francis had received her into the order he took her to the Benedictine nuns of San Paolo near Bastia. A few days later she moved to another Benedictine convent, San Angelo di Panzo on the slopes of Mount Subasio. There she was joined by her sister Agnes, a girl of fifteen, who like Clare had run away from her home to give her life to God.

But Clare was not a Benedictine, and she felt alone and removed from the brothers. So she asked Francis for a home where she could live the new way of life he had given her. And Francis understood.

He begged the Church of San Damiano from the Bishop of Assisi and gave it to Clare and Agnes so they would have a place on this earth where they could live the perfect poverty of Jesus Christ. Soon Clare and Agnes were joined by Pacifica, Benvenuta, Cecilia, and Philippa. Clare was at peace, for now there was a sisterhood that was a home.

San Damiano was the small chapel where Francis had heard the voice of Christ from the crucifix: "Francis, go and repair my house which, as you see, is entirely in ruins." Francis had done as the Lord had commanded. He restored this little church, prophesying as he did so that some day this would be the home of the Poor Ladies of the Lord.

How this fact filled Clare with joy! The home Francis had given her was the very place where his own call from God had begun. How well he had understood her request. This church was so much a part of him. Here he had worked in the sweat of his brow, begging stones in Assisi and mortaring them into place. Here in his fear he had hidden from his father's wrath, and here he had learned in prayer how to overcome fear and face his father.

In choosing this particular place he had given her a large part of himself. Yes, he had understood what she was asking. It was truly a place for her. . . .

Though Clare loved the Lord with her whole heart, Francis was also a part of that love. Sorting that out was not difficult because the two had always been associated in her mind. She had never loved God in the abstract but rather as she saw him incarnate in Francis. She had found God in Francis. Wherever one was, there was the other also. And she never thought this feeling divided her love.

Their love began there, the three of them: Francis, Clare, and the Lord.

Over the years Clare grew in the conviction that God was present to her in every person she met, and it all began with Francis in their little Eden of Assisi. That is why she loved Assisi so. Their love began there, the three of them: Francis, Clare, and the Lord.

Francis and Clare: The Good Companions

PHYLLIS McGINLEY

. . . I have deliberately mixed the genders in giving examples of saintly friendships. For, contrary to the sour view taken by saint-loathers, the affection of my favorite heroes and heroines as often as not wreathes itself around someone of the opposite sex. No doubt about it, there are masculine and feminine principles native to the race, and even among the saints one principle complements the other when there is work to be accomplished or simple human needs to be reckoned with. As Frédéric Ozanam * has remarked in another connection, "It appears that nothing great can be done in the Church without a woman having a share in it." I would go further. I would say that some of the greatest saints of both sexes seem to soar higher and more daringly feather to feather with the man or the woman who accompanies the flight. . . .

[Such is the case with] the famous friendship of Clare and Francis of Assisi. It is not easy to follow them accurately, since hagiographers of the period have so hung them with pious stories that they nearly smother under wreaths of artificial flowers. It is unlikely, for example, that Clare any more than Francis was God-haunted from youth. She belonged to a family important and imposing in Assisi, an arrogant household of lords and knights. (Francis came much lower in the social scale, since his father was a merchant, even though an affluent one.) No doubt, since she is supposed to have been very pretty, she was as full of small prides and vanities as any other girl of her age and station. All we really know about her before she put on the Franciscan habit and founded the Poor Clares is that she had suitors whom she refused; that when her family grew annoyed at her obstinacy in not choosing one whom they particularly favored, she went to her aunt, a certain Sister Bona, for comfort; and that Sister Bona, probably as a special treat, took her to hear the odd Little Poor Man preach. One suspects it was the substitute in those days for taking her to a matinee or for a day's shopping in town. After all, Francis's dramatic con-

* French Catholic historian and scholar who helped found the Society of Saint Vincent de Paul.

version and his eccentricities were prime gossip in Assisi just then.

Bona, however, did more than merely entertain Clare with the town's sensation. She also took her, as it were, backstage—to meet the friar himself at the Portiuncula, where his group lived in such lively and joyous poverty. Clare was eighteen at the time and probably longing for something remarkable to happen to her. What happened, of course, was Francis.

Whether she caught fire at the beginning—whether it was spiritual love at first sight—we have no way of knowing. The only thing biographers truly agree on is that the meetings, chaperoned by Bona but always clandestine (for to her grand relatives Francis must have seemed no better than a mad and mendicant clown) went on for about a year; and at some time during the year Clare decided the vocation of Francis must be her own. Then came the celebrated elopement. Late at night on Palm Sunday Clare let herself out of her house by the little "door of death"—the side door that in many homes was opened only to carry out the dead—and headed for the Portiuncula. She had dressed herself like a bride, complete to veil and all her jewels, a romantic Italianate touch both saints had evidently planned in advance as a symbolic flourish. Francis met her at the chapel, took off the bridal clothes, cut her hair, and dressed her in the same sort of rough, undyed cloak he himself wore.

Clare was eighteen at the time and probably longing for something remarkable to happen to her. What happened, of course, was Francis.

Since she patently could not stay on with the friars, she went first to a Benedictine convent nearby and eventually to another refuge, and was at last able to found her own order, which maintained as nearly as was possible to women of that day the same rule of total poverty Francis had insisted on for his own community. (Many of the earlier stories say that Clare's family rode out angrily to drag her back from sanctuary, and it is certainly possible they strenuously objected to her runaway adventure. But since her mother and two of her sisters eventually joined her community, it certainly looks as if the objections did not last as long or were not as aggressive as the tales contend.)

In any event she found her final haven at San Damiano, not far from Francis's house, and Clare was never to leave it again except to visit the Portiuncula from time to time; and even that pleasure was at length denied her by a puritanical Pope who could not understand the remarkable relationship between the two shining saints.

Unworldly innocents! Clare had imagined herself wandering about the country, free as Francis, to do good deeds and speak ecstatic words. Such an ideal in the twelfth century was about as capable of coming true as was Francis's dream of converting the Sultan in one interview. So she stayed enclosed like other nuns of her era. But the two friends were faithful to the end—"Do not believe," said Francis, "that I do not love her with a perfect love"—and between them they invigorated not only Italy but also Christian Europe. They kindled, as Remy de Gourmont has said, "a new poetry, a new art, a renewed religion."

The Lady Clare

JOAN MOWAT ERIKSON

But why, we may ask in retrospect, had Saint Francis persuaded Clare in the first place that he needed her to carry out his particular mission to the world? St. Benedict had created an order of women, a sister organization to his monastic order. But Benedict may well have been motivated to do so because of his devotion to his own sister Scholastica. Saint Francis knew the Benedictine nuns near Assisi and committed Clare to their charge after she had made her vows in his presence. The involvement of women in his work seems to have been of great importance to him, and Clare may have sensed this need. We can only surmise what her motivations may have been in giving up her privileged life to assume one of dedicated poverty under Saint Francis's rule. Yet their story indicates that she understood him and his work perhaps more truly than anyone else.

> *The involvement of women in his work seems to have been of great importance to him.*

Medieval noblewomen were placed in a unique position by the changing social mores of their times. Where the martial spirit had dominated and indeed had been vital to survival during the constant warring that prevailed, a new era, more attuned to social and mercantile concerns, was dawning. The itinerant, competitive, often brutal lives that men were still forced to live as fighters laid the burden almost wholly on women of representing the aesthetic, the warmly solicitous, the more gracious aspects of life to balance the scale and make possible a creative style of living. Courtly ladies in the castles of the nobility, surrounded by knights, who knew only fighting and were free of all family ties, became idealized representations of all feminine virtue and beauty. They sensed the need, knew their powers, and responded according to their own ideals of conduct. It is possible that Clare, daughter of a noble house, was aware of the role that she and her cloistered ladies played in the lives of mendicant friars, lives given to constant wandering, with no place as their physical home.

Saint Clare speaks of Francis as "after God, the charioteer of her soul." This is the heroic, chivalric language of medieval imagery. But she used other images that are more childlike and suggest that Francis combined for her not only the attributes of a loving father but also those of a nourishing mother, being a source of both spiritual and sensual sustenance.

How Saint Clare Ate a Meal with Saint Francis and His Friars

THE FIORETTI

When Saint Francis was staying in Assisi, he often visited Saint Clare and consoled her with holy advice. And as she had a very great desire to eat a meal with him once, she asked him several times to give her that consolation. But Saint Francis always refused to grant her that favor.

So it happened that his companions, perceiving Saint Clare's desire, said to Saint Francis: "Father, it seems to us that this strictness is not according to divine charity—that you do not grant the request of Sister Clare, a virgin so holy and dear to God, in such a little thing as eating with you, especially considering that she gave up the riches and pomp of the world as a result of your preaching. So you should not only let her eat a meal with you once, but if she were to ask an even greater favor of you, you should grant it to your little spiritual plant."

Saint Francis answered: "So you think I should grant this wish of hers?"

And the companions said: "Yes, Father, for she deserves this favor and consolation."

Then Saint Francis replied: "Since it seems so to you, I agree. But in order to give her greater pleasure, I want this meal to be at Saint Mary of the Angels, for she has been cloistered at San Damiano for a long time and she will enjoy seeing once more for a while the place of Saint Mary where she was shorn and made a spouse of the Lord Jesus Christ. So we will eat there together, in the name of the Lord."

He therefore set a day when Saint Clare would go out of the monastery with one sister companion, escorted also by his companions.

And she came to Saint Mary of the Angels. And first she reverently and humbly greeted the Blessed Virgin Mary before her altar, where she had been shorn and received the veil. And then they devoutly showed her around the place until it was mealtime. Meanwhile Saint Francis had the table prepared on the bare ground, as was his custom.

And when it was time to eat, Saint Francis and Saint Clare sat down together, and one of his companions with St. Clare's companion, and all his other companions were grouped around that humble table. But at the first course Saint Francis began to speak about God in such a sweet and holy and profound and divine and marvelous way that he himself and Saint Clare and her companion and all the others who were at that poor little table were rapt in God by the overabundance of divine grace that descended upon them.

And while they were sitting there, in a rapture, with their eyes and hands raised to heaven, it seemed to the men of Assisi and Bettona and the entire district that the Church of Saint Mary of the Angels and the whole place and the forest, which was at that time around the place, were all aflame, and that an immense fire was burning over all of them. Consequently the men of Assisi ran down there in great haste to save the place and put out the fire, as they firmly believed that everything was burning up.

But when they reached the place, they saw that nothing was on fire. Entering the place, they found Saint Francis with Saint Clare and all the companions sitting around that very humble table, rapt in God by contemplation and invested with power from on high. Then they knew for sure that it had been a heavenly and not a material fire that God had miraculously shown them to symbolize the fire of divine love that was burning in the souls of those holy friars and nuns. So they withdrew, with great consolation in their hearts and with holy edification.

Later, after a long while, when Saint Francis and Saint Clare and the others came back to themselves, they felt so refreshed by spiritual food that they paid little or no attention to the material food. And when that blessed meal was over, Saint Clare, well accompanied, returned to San Damiano.

Feminine and Franciscan

SISTER MARY SERAPHIM,
P.C.P.A.

Francis Bernardone, deemed a religious fanatic in his early thirties, had deliberately fostered a clandestine friendship with the eighteen-year-old daughter of a rich Assisian family. Into the volatile mixture of the deep human attraction that sprang up between them dipped the torch of the Spirit of God. The white-hot flame that was ignited seared them both, even unto sanctity.

Ever since, the world has probed the mystery of their friendship, seeking to discover the humanness in it and at the same time secretly hoping to find an even greater manifestation of the divine. Francis and Clare have not been disappointing. The purity of their mutual affection, founded as it was on unshakable loyalty and fidelity to their Lord, was never tarnished by the inherent weakness of our human condition but rather burnished by it to a fine luster.

When did Clare and Francis first meet? Although both grew up in the same enclosed city-state of Assisi, it is unlikely that they met as children, for Clare was of the nobility while Francis Bernardone was the son of a merchant. But by the time Francis had begun to gather a few brethren, Clare must have been quite familiar with his disturbing career. When Francis preached of his unique happiness, his fiery words touched the soul of Clare and kindled a like vision. She pursued it with all the directness of her nature.

Francis was consumed with a vision of total love for Christ and total surrender to his demands. As a result everything else in the world became only secondary means to be used or discarded according to whether or not they served his overmastering purpose. Of all the multitude of things that teemed on the earth, one became supremely desirable because it appeared as the straightest road to his goal. Poverty, of which the Middle Ages knew an abundance, became the mystical bride of his heart. In her company, Francis found freedom, joy, peace.

When Francis installed Clare and her first companions in the ruinous little convent of San Damiano, she knew she had discovered the purpose for which she was created. In her lyrical joy, Clare developed a marvelous synthesis of the freedom of the original Franciscan spirit with the concentrated spiritual activity of the strictly cloistered life. She was audacious enough to defend her ideal of perfect poverty before prelates and princes. Yet Clare did so with a charm and simplicity that never brought her total submission to the Church into question. Though it required a lifetime to accomplish her end, she valiantly maintained her right to the "Privilege of Most High Poverty" without surrendering one iota. The Church crowned her tenacity with a proclamation of heroic sanctity only two years after her death.

"It frequently happens that a woman attains to greatness in the natural or supernatural order because she has built her life upon the ideals of the man she admires," Father Lothar Hardick points out. "Her capacity for sacrifice and persistent effort, her loyalty and trust, allow her to reach the heights of heroism, once the man has shown her the way. This is particularly true of Clare. It is impossible to think of her apart from Francis" (Ignatius Brady, O.F.M., ed. *Life and Writings of Saint Clare of Assisi* [St. Bonaventure, N.Y.: The Franciscan Institute, 1953], pp. 117–18).

Pope Alexander IV wrote wonderingly of this woman who had sought only to serve her God in total love: "On earth this light was enclosed within walls, and yet its rays were seen far beyond; she lived in a strict monastic circle, and yet her light was diffused in the whole world; she restricted herself within, yet she was manifested to those outside. Clare hid herself; and her life is known to all; Clare was silent, yet the fame of her was everywhere heard; she remained in her cell, yet she was preaching to the city" (Bull of Canonization).

Her unique contribution to the Church was made possible, not in spite of the fact that she was a woman, but precisely because of it. She cultivated a specifically feminine approach to the Franciscan ideal and therefore one that is valid for Franciscan women the world over.

Clare has been characterized as "the new woman in the valley of Spoleto." Her unique contribution to the Church was made possible, not in spite of the fact that she was a woman, but precisely *because* of it. She cultivated a specifically feminine approach to the Franciscan ideal and therefore one that is valid for Franciscan women the world over. Commentaries on Franciscanism have until now been written almost entirely by men in the First Order, and it is not surprising that they have largely passed over the feminine expressions possible in the interpretation of the charisma of Saint Francis. Yet if we read Thomas of Celano's *Legends* correctly, we soon perceive that for Francis, at least, Clare and her sisters attained to a more perfect spiritual interpretation of his ideals than some of his brethren.

The Poor Ladies were not intended to replace the brotherhood but rather to be a visible incarnation of the more intangible elements of their own vocation. Similarly the friars have always been regarded by the cloistered branch as their visible emissaries to the world whom they are bound to uphold by their hidden life of prayer and sacrifice.

Clare's interpretation of the Franciscan ideal evolved in a more enduring form than that of the brethren. Although the apostolate of the friars has (and necessarily so) changed with the needs of succeeding centuries, the Clares' mission of contemplative adoration of the Crucified has remained essentially unchanged. The poverty they embrace can be realistically lived within the confines of their monastery whether in the thirteenth, sixteenth, or twentieth century. This does not imply that the present-day Poor Clares are alienated from their social environment. Rather it should demonstrate the perennial contemporaneity of their spirit.

For example, who was chosen during this last half of our century as patroness of television? Some modern saint who utilized the latest devices of technology for the furtherance of the apostolate? Surprisingly, no! It was Saint Clare of Assisi, a medieval nun whose modernity of spirit made her a "natural" for the choice. The specific incident in her life that qualified her for the selection is the well-known miracle of her Christmas Eve vision. Left alone in her cell, confined to a sick bed, Clare enjoyed participating in all the splendors of the Christmas services being celebrated in the Church of San Francesco, many miles from her convent. This extraordinary "live transmission" of a distant event was only one of such favors Clare experienced. However, we believe that the fundamental reason for proclaiming her as TV's patroness is her joyous and optimistic spirit that makes her so thoroughly compatible with the more exalted ideals that the entertainment world sincerely professes (on paper at least).

From the first community of Poor Ladies, a multitude of monasteries trace their spiritual origin, and what was first spoken of Saint Clare remains true today for her daughters. Most thinking men will admit that the presence in modern society of monasteries of Poor Clares preaches a more efficacious sermon on the overmastering rights of a sovereign God than any psychedelic fantasy. At the same time, the cloister walls stir hearts to wonder what kind of God this must be who can call young women, century after century, to be his alone. The happiness and peace that radiate from these hidden sanctuaries are proverbial. Even the hippies

and dropouts from our society instinctively know that the values that they (usually obscurely) are seeking, are lived, and lived genuinely and joyously, behind these strange enclosures.

In 1960, 786 monasteries of Poor Clares dotted the world, with a total of 17,699 twentieth-century women within their walls. In the United States, there were 502 nuns in 27 monasteries. Since then, their number has not declined, and as the nuns continue in the flaming example of their founder to incarnate the spirit of poverty and freedom through total surrender to love, their numbers increase with impressive steadiness. Their message and their spirit remain astonishingly relevant in the world of the 1970s. They proclaim peace, freedom, and joy to a world that craves these values without knowing where to find them. The Poor Clare, in her simple garb and unpretentious manner, shouts to the skies that life has meaning, and such a meaning that one life span is insufficient to exhaust it. On the threshold of tomorrow they stand, their faces mirroring the light of eternity while they cradle with their maternal prayers the future children of the kingdom.

These women following the light footfalls of a medieval nun who was simply alight with love—a hidden flame glowing beside the ardent Poverello but so like him that their names are inseparably linked in history. Their spirit is only one: the pure essence of the Gospel life, the glad tidings of Love.

Song of Francis, Clare, and the Brothers

DONOVAN

Father of all things, Mother of light,
Soothe and ease our human plight.
Mary in mercy, Jesus in joy,
Please will you help us win the fight.

There's a shape in the sky beckoning me,
There's a sound in the wild wind calling,
There's a song to be sung for glory,
And I feel that it's coming our way.

There's a pain on the land weakening me,
There's a sign in the city of sorrow,
There's a shadow of darkness accumulating,
And a fear that it's coming our way.

There's a love for all men sleeping within,
There's a friend of a friend awakening,
There's a jubilant joy bursting to be,
And I feel that it's coming our way.

Father of all things, Mother of light,
Soothe and ease our human plight.
Mary in mercy, Jesus in joy,
Please will you help us win the fight.

His Universe

Kind Men and Beasts

PHYLLIS McGINLEY

It is one of the ironies of this ironic age that man, so hard on his own kind, so ready to wipe out his own works and marvels, grows constantly more sympathetic toward his brothers, the beasts. In a century that contains Dachau and the hundred-megaton bomb, we have invented vast game sanctuaries for elephants or warthogs, and we tirelessly protect the whooping crane. In my own village I am constrained by law from trapping the gray squirrel, which, with nothing in his favor except cheeky good looks, yearly raids my walnut tree and mutilates my attic. If so much as a sparrow falls, the Humane Society rushes a specialist to its rescue. Now that science has discovered the genial dolphin with its high I.Q. and plans to teach it to talk, the Peaceable Kingdom seems very near at hand. It is as if man and beast were preparing to lie down together in the teeth of the approaching storm, as lion and gazelle close ranks when a forest fire menaces or water holes run dry.

Francis sometimes seems the only saint that people everywhere recognize and accept, if often for the wrong reasons. His statue, inane as a greeting card, stands in thousands of suburban gardens where he is halfway confused with Pan, or even Peter Pan.

Consideration for animals is a singularly modern phenomenon. In earlier centuries, Saladin * might love his charger, or a medieval lady pamper her hound. But the general run of humanity thought their dumb brothers expendable, outside the fold of compassion. Only the Christian saints behaved differently—walked, as saints always do, ahead of their times. Long before Game Reservations and the SPCA were dreamed of, holy men were being tender in a less self-conscious way than we to every-

* Sultan of Egypt and Syria, 1174–93.

thing that stirred in woods or jungles or the air. . . .

For two millennia, and long before it was fashionable, saints have been making friends of the beasts. It is one of the tenderest chapters in Christianity and not well-enough remembered. I have already mentioned Francis of Assisi, who named the birds his sisters and cherished the mice tormenting him in his cell. Francis sometimes seems the only saint that people everywhere recognize and accept, if often for the wrong reasons. His statue, inane as a greeting card, stands in thousands of suburban gardens where he is halfway confused with Pan, or even Peter Pan. The real Francis, stern to himself, a preacher, an organizer, above all a reformer, is quite a different person from the meek little dreamer of legend. But of course part of the legendary Francis is real, as myths always are. For Francis, like his Master, so loved the world that the meanest inhabitant in it called upon his pity.

Some of the stories about Francis may sound apocryphal, like the tale of the grasshopper that on a winter midnight came to help him sing his office, leaving its tiny tracks in the snow to shame monks who had been too slothful to assist. Still, his heart truly brimmed over with such affection it had to scatter like rain onto animals as well as men. He particularly loved the crested lark, dressed like a good religious in a brown habit and hood, and the story goes that on the evening of his death a cloud of larks wheeled over his house and grievingly sang their farewells. (An equally touching if even less likely story is told about Blessed Gandulf of Binasco, one of Francis's own friars. When Binasco's body was being enshrined, the swallows he had once scolded for chattering too loudly while he preached flew into the church during the night, then "parted into two groups and sang, in alternating choirs, a *Te Deum* of their own.")

The flight of Francis's larks may have been coincidence, yet they mourned with reason, since they were losing a great friend. He felt so strongly for the mistreated animals of his day, for the snared birds and beaten horses and hungry dogs, that he went to the burghers, to the governors, finally to the emperor, begging for a law against their abuse. He demanded that farmers be forced to treat their cattle humanely and give them an extra treat on

Christmas Day. He wanted towns and corporations to take time off from levying taxes and scatter crumbs, instead, on the frozen roads. He pleaded for hostels where strays could be fed and housed, and he raged against the caging of larks. Like his plan to stop the Crusades by a personal interview with the Sultan, these schemes came to little. But in Assisi to this day, at the time of the Angelus, they feed his birds in the market place. . . .

If in our age there are saints living and working among us—and I have no doubt there are—they will be living and working much like their old exemplars. They will be poor, for they must spend all they have on derelicts and needy neighbors. They will be busier than any business person—rescuing slum dwellers, saving lives in jungle hospitals, teaching trades to Bolivian Indians, helping the migrant workers in California orchards. But when they are at home, wherever home may be (a shed, a tenement, a tent, an Andean hut), they will be sharing quarters with some beast that needs tending. They will be feeding hungry kittens or splinting the leg of an injured seagull or—who knows?—teaching catechism to some garrulous dolphin. For while the old needs remain, there will always be some good person to ease them. The patterns of compassion do not change.

Saint Francis and the Animals

PAUL GALLICO

Of all the men who have made an impact upon the world and the human heart, next to Jesus, time has least diminished Francis of Assisi.

If one thinks of oneself standing for a moment poised between two worlds, his and ours, and looks back upon him with modern eyes, his life becomes even more meaningful, nostalgic, and hopelessly desirable.

For everything in modern times is exaggerated and intensified until living has become a fever and the throat begins to feel raw and the tongue swollen with the thirst for peace, serenity, and a return to dignity. One comes to Francis as to a cooling draught. . . .

Once you have accepted a man as a saint, it is difficult to return to the contemplation of him as a man, for custom, time, and canonization throw an aura about him. And yet, so many of the qualities of Francis and the things he did that were accounted saintly, were manly too, so warm and earthily human and mortal that one thinks one loves him for this manliness only to find then that they approach the divine because of the manner in which they were used to enrich the world. We are all endowed in some measure with similar traits and capabilities, but only Francis used them to send up a lifelong song to his Creator.

For instance, through his existence one encounters with a kind of pleased astonishment the constant evidence of his gentle courtesy.

I do not know why one should *not* look for courtesy in a saint, but it does seem foreign to the sometimes chill and austere presence one comes to associate with the holy. One remembers thunderers, sufferers, fanatics, martyrs, mystics, zealots, and benefactors of mankind, but not so many of exquisite courtesy.

Yet the root of courtesy is love. Good manners are founded upon the ardent desire not to offend one's fellows and the experience of genuine regret at having done so. One feels that the engaging politeness of Francis stemmed from his sincerity and the depth of affection he entertained, not only for humans but for every object animate and even inanimate that shared living space with him on earth.

Francis had a relationship to everything: to man, beasts of the fields and forests, the birds, the fish, trees, flowers, even stones, the sun, the moon, the wind and the stars, fire and water, rain and snow, storms, the earth, summer, winter, and the tender elegy of springtime. With all of these he dealt courteously and admitted them to the circle of his immediate family, for a man who believes in and loves his Creator with his whole heart must also dignify and love all of His creations.

Many of the legends regarding Francis, his feeling for his surroundings and the living things that populated the countryside, can be misleading unless one remembers this matter of courtesy toward and fellow feeling for one's lesser neighbors.

There is, for instance, the story of the fisherman who presented Francis with a carp that had just been drawn from the lake. His poet's delight in the silvery beauty of the fish was mingled with pity for its gasping struggles. He returned it to the waters whence it had come. Thankfully, says the tale, the fish followed his boat to the other side of the lake and was waiting for the saint when he returned.

It is not the legend of the grateful fish that is important, but the release. Do we ever experience the deep sense of kinship entertained by Francis for the other inhabitants of our planet? Have we so much as a moment to spare to try to love, understand, or pity what we destroy?

Francis did not preach a sermon demanding that all fish be returned to the sea, or for that matter that we refrain from catching them. But toward that particular one that had swum into his ken he behaved like a friend and a gentleman. There is nothing that Francis ever said or did to indicate that a man need be ashamed or feel guilty because of eating a lamb cutlet, provided he loves the living lamb, or that it is wrong to bring down a pheasant with a fowling piece, if one is capable of humbleness in the presence of such a beauty awing.

Francis accepted and lived with the hunter, the fisherman, the farmer, the butcher. He neither humanized nor sentimentalized animals. But he did feel for them, admitting them to their rights of kinship with him and giving them the same courtesy that he bestowed on his fellows.

Francis accepted and lived with the hunter, the fisherman, the farmer, the butcher. He neither humanized nor sentimentalized animals. But he did feel for them, admitting them to their rights of kinship with him and giving them the same courtesy that he bestowed upon his fellows.

And if he were sorry for their difficulties in a predatory world, he was also keenly aware of the many beauties and blessings with which they had been endowed. What reaches one's heart is the touching simplicity with which he admitted every living thing to the equality of gratitude toward its Maker.

We admire the sincerity that led him to preach to the birds to remind them to praise and thank Him who had endowed them with such lovely plumage, abundant food, and graceful power of flight. And it is the gesture of addressing them as fellow creatures that is the wonder of this particular story and not the legendary account of their response at the finish of the sermon. For it is no

miracle at all that our animal brethren almost invariably react to true courtesy, kindness, and consideration. It is simply that there was and still is so little of it practiced in good faith that when it is tried and found to work, it smacks of the marvel. Francis must have thought it the most natural thing in the world for the beasts to have responded in kind to his politeness and consideration.

We find him experiencing no surprise at the taming of the wolf of Gubbio since he had never believed the beast to be either savage or evil, any more than he believed the bandits he occasionally encountered and turned from their paths to be vicious. The man who can wholeheartedly believe that all things are created by God and that God does not create evil, is freed from many burdens, and one of them is fear.

Many of us are capable of loving a pet, weeping over a run-over dog, or shedding tears over a dead bird, but for the most part we are mourning only the loss of an extension of our own egos. Old dog Tray is always to us what we think he ought to be and rarely what he actually is. Seldom is he or any of his kind admitted to friendship or a place on the hearth because he is after all a relative in the large family of the children of the Creator.

Francis had pets: a lamb, a pheasant, a rabbit, a cicada, a dog, a wolf, but upon honest and unsentimental terms. For he was as polite and considerate to an earthworm, a slug, a bird, a beetle, or a mole, as amusedly tolerant and, withal, understanding and warmly loving as one would be to one's brother and sister. Indeed, they were his brothers and sisters. He called them so, not with the pious emptiness the words have come to connote in modern times, but with the deep conviction of the kinship.

It is told of him that he would stoop to remove an earthworm from his path so as not to crush it. One feels that with Francis it was a personal as well as symbolic courtesy to something living he happened to encounter.

There appears to be a touch of the child's world of fancy in this, but it is really an intensely practical way of life aboard an overpopulated planet, and what is more, it has the great advantage of beauty over ugliness. Looking back to the daily joy and happiness that Francis managed to crowd into the forty-four years of his life, it is not at all difficult to understand that it is better to be kind than unkind and to be generous and accommodating instead of rude and possessive. This is not childish. It is one of the most adult discoveries ever made.

And one notes with equal satisfaction that Francis expected a full return of courtesies, and what is more, he got it. For in that state of Nature that exists in the faith that all is divinely created with love and delight in beauty (and who shall say that a maggot, a spider, a rat, or a hippopotamus is not beautiful in the eyes of God?), there must be give as well as take.

Thus there is no difficulty in understanding his request to the noisy swallows wheeling, looping, twittering in the late afternoon sky, drowning out Francis's attempt to preach, with their chatter —"My brothers and sisters, the swallows, it is now time for me to speak. You have been speaking enough all the time. Give me leave to be heard."

It is recorded that the swallows piped down.

In the same spirit was his request to Brother Fire in the shape of a red-hot iron physicians were about to use to cauterize his temples in an attempt to cure his growing blindness late in life: "Brother Fire, who art nobler and more useful than most other creatures, I have always been good to you and always will be so for the love of him who created you. Now show yourself gentle and courteous with me and do not burn me more than I can stand."

One can only long for a world in which Brother Fire indeed responds in kind to such a gentle and persuasive plea, for when it was over, Francis said to the physicians—"If that is not enough burning, then burn it again, for I have not felt the least pain."

These are the pictures that uplift the spirit and enchant the heart, a worn and sightless man who through faith and simplicity has found the key to communicating with the universe. . . .

Creation and Mysticism

P. POURRAT

The mystics of the twelfth century, it will be remembered, made use of creatures in order to rise to the state in which they could contemplate the Creator, but they regarded them from a metaphysical standpoint. The sensible world was a discourse of the Word of God; every creature was an expression, in word or phrase, of that sublime discourse. The mission of man was to discover the thought of the Word that lay hidden beneath the symbolism of sensible realities.

The attitude of Saint Francis of Assisi with regard to creatures is very different. He does not look upon them as symbols, but as living realities. The creatures of God form an immense family; they spring from the same heavenly Father and are nourished by the same providence. All show forth the wisdom, the power, and the goodness of the Creator, and all praise him after their kind. The fatherhood of God, spreading over all creation, was deeply realized by St. Francis, who looked upon every being as, in a measure, of the same family as himself. He loved them with a fraternal love.

He used, as Thomas of Celano tells us, to call them brethren.

This view, arising from faith and the natural kindness of his soul, inclined Francis to be almost as compassionate toward animals as he was toward men. He purchased the lambs that were being taken to the butcher in order to save their lives. He fed the bees in winter that they might not perish. Thousands of anecdotes of this kind are told of him by his biographers.

The animals seemed to understand the affection that Francis had for them. They submitted to him and carried out his commands. Swallows would stop singing so as not to disturb his preaching. Fire, at his bidding, gave him no pain when one day the doctor found it necessary to cauterize his face. The Saint of Assisi possessed something of the power of Adam, in the earthly paradise, over created beings.

Like the first man before the Fall, Francis was easily uplifted toward God by the consideration of creatures; he used to contemplate the Creator in each one of them with inexpressible joy. The beauty of the flowers enraptured him, for in them he saw a reflection of divine beauty. Fire reminded him of the brightness of eternal light; moreover, his affection for it was so great that he would never put it out, even when it burned his clothing. He would walk on stones with the greatest respect, for the love of Christ who is the rock upon which we have been exalted (Psalms 21:7). He especially loved water, which is chaste, and symbolizes the purification of the soul. Francis understood, in the highest degree, the mission given to man, of praising God in the name of all creation. The "Canticle of Brother Sun," is a magnificent expression of his soul in this regard. He addressed himself to creatures as though they had the gift of reason and invited them to glorify the Lord.

One day when he was traveling in the valley of Spoleto he saw a great number of birds gathered together in one place. Urged by his love of animals, Francis approached them, and, as they did not fly away, he began to preach to them:

"My brethren the birds," he said, "you ought greatly to praise your Creator and always to love him, who has given you feathers to clothe you and all else that you need. God has made you the most noble of his creatures; he has given you the air as a dwelling-place, and although you neither sow nor reap, he protects and guides you so that you lack nothing."

When the sermon was ended the birds began to lift up their heads and spread their wings and open their beaks, at the same time looking at Francis as though approving of his words. The saint reproached himself for not having preached sooner to the birds, which had listened with so much respect to the divine word.

This holy sentiment regarding nature was one of the strongest experienced by Francis. He translated it into song in that wonderful "Canticle of Brother Sun," which was composed by him two years before his death, when he was ill at St. Damian (Cf. Part VII, His Song).

The seraphic friar of Assisi used to be raised without effort toward God, even to the extent of ecstasy, by the contemplation of creation.

With no other saint, not even Saint Francis de Sales, is there this mystical love of nature to such a degree. The seraphic friar of Assisi used to be raised without effort toward God, even to the extent of ecstasy, by the contemplation of creation. No one is better able than he to make us understand what must have been the relations of man in a state of innocence with the created beings.

Saint Francis and the Birds

ROY McFADDEN

Hearing him, the birds came in a crowd,
Wing upon wing, from stone and blade and twig,
From tilted leaf and thorn and lumbering cloud,
Falling from hill, soaring from meadowland,

Wing upon widening wing, until the air
Wrinkled with sound and ran like watery sand
Round the sky's gleaming bowl. Then, like a
    flower
They swung, hill-blue and tremulous, each wing
A petal palpitating in a shower
Of words, till he beneath felt the stale crust
Of self crinkle and crumble and his words
Assume an independence, pure and cold,
Cageless, immaculate, one with the birds
Fattening their throats in song. Identity
Lost, he stood in swollen ecstasy.

A Patron Saint for Ecologists

LYNN WHITE, JR.

The new theology of Saint Francis, enunciated eight hundred years ago but only now finding ready takers, may be the world's only salvation. That is the opinion expressed by Lynn White, Jr., professor of medieval history at the University of California, Los Angeles, in a keynote address before the American Association for the Advancement of Science.

Drawing a word picture of the by-products of Western science and technology—among them smog, pollution, threat of genetic change from the bomb —that have gotten out of control and that threaten ecologic disaster, Professor White told the assembled scientists: "I personally doubt that disastrous ecologic backlash can be avoided simply by applying to our problems more science and more technology. No creature other than man," he declares, "has ever managed to foul its nest in such short order."

Then Professor White gave a statement that may one day prove to be world-shaking: "The remedy must . . . be essentially religious."

I propose Francis of Assisi as a patron saint for ecologists.

Professor White indicts Judaeo-Christian theology for much of the mess we are in. According to that theology "Christianity not only established a dualism of man and nature but also insisted that it is God's will that man exploit nature for his own ends."

Professor White states: "What we do about ecology depends on our ideas of the man-nature relationship. More science and more technology are not going to get us out of the present ecologic crisis until we find a new religion or rethink our old one."

"The present increasing disruption of the global environment," White told the scientists, "is the product of a dynamic technology and science that were originating in the same Western medieval world against which Saint Francis was rebelling in

so original a way. Their growth cannot be understood historically, apart from distinctive attitudes toward nature that are deeply grounded in Christian dogma. . . . No new set of basic values has been accepted in our society to displace those of Christianity. Hence we shall continue to have a worsening ecologic crisis until we reject the Christian axiom that nature has no reason for existence save to serve man. . . .

"Possibly we should ponder the greatest radical

in Christian history since Christ, St. Francis of Assisi.

"The greatest spiritual revolutionary in Western history, Saint Francis proposed what he thought was an alternative Christian view of nature and man's relation to it: he tried to substitute the idea of the equality of all creatures including man, for the idea of man's limitless rule over creation. He failed. Both our present science and our present technology are so tinctured with orthodox Christian arrogance toward nature that no solution for our ecologic crisis can be expected from them alone. Since the roots of our trouble are so largely religious, the remedy must also be essentially religious, whether we call it that or not. We must rethink and refeel our nature and destiny. The profoundly religious, but heretical, sense of the primitive Franciscans for the spiritual autonomy of all parts of nature may point a direction. . . .

"I propose Francis of Assisi as a patron saint for ecologists." *

* Pope John Paul II announced on April 6, 1980 (Easter Sunday) that he had proclaimed Saint Francis Patron Saint of Ecology.

The Sermon of Francis

HENRY WADSWORTH LONGFELLOW

Up soared the lark into the air,
A shaft of song, a wingéd prayer,
As if a soul, released from pain,
Were flying back to heaven again.

Saint Francis heard; it was to him
An emblem of the Seraphim;
The upward motion of the fire,
The light, the heat, the heart's desire.

Around Assisi's convent gate
The birds, God's poor who cannot wait,
From moor and mere and darksome wood
Came flocking for the dole of food.

"O brother birds," Saint Francis said,
"Ye come to me and ask for bread,
But not with bread alone today
Shall ye be fed and sent away.

"Ye shall be fed, ye happy birds,
With manna of celestial words;
Not mine, though mine they seem to be,
Not mine, though they be spoken through me.

"O doubly are ye bound to praise
The great Creator in your lays;
He giveth you your plumes of down,
Your crimson hoods, your cloaks of brown.

"He giveth you your wings to fly
And breathe a purer air on high,
And careth for you everywhere,
Who for yourselves so little care!"

With flutter of swift wings and songs
Together rose the feathered throngs,
And singing scattered far apart;
Deep peace was in Saint Francis' heart.

He knew not if the brotherhood
His homily had understood;
He only knew that to one ear
The meaning of his words was clear.

The Minstrel of God

CLEMENT WOOD

O sweet strange minstrel of the joyous singing,
When the torn lands lay bleeding in the dark
With dripping sword and ripping lancehead
    bringing
Death to harsher life, like Sister Lark
You trilled your melodies at the ear of heaven,
A halo of harmony above the pain,
Until the world, from which your soul was
    driven,
Woke to a little loveliness again.
Minstrel of God, you knew that they spoke ill
Who called the One you loved a Man of Sorrow:
Others had made His golden singing still;
And you could see a lightening tomorrow
   When song and the sweet salvation of mirth
   Should rule again over the reddened earth.

The noisy swallows quieted at your teaching;
The shrill grasshopper gave you heart to sing;
The falcon was your Angelus; your preaching
Went most to souls that heard you on the wing.
Even the wolf, his steel jaws hot from plunder,
Tamed at your soft whispering, as he
Brought his harsh and hungry nature under
Your love sway. Brother Wind and Sister Sea,
Moon and Brother Sun, with these you spoke,
Granting kind greeting to the Brother Fire
Who healed your body. To this varied folk
You had a word to lift their longing higher.
   Only one beast hid snarling in his den:
   You could not tame the wild lost tribe called
   men.

Prayer Against Hunters

MARION DOYLE

Little brown brother of the Umbrian hills,
  Childlike and pure, you surely are the one
To hear a plea of pity for the ills
  Man visits on all helpless things that run
  Or creep and fly beneath the stars and sun.

Guard them, I pray, from human lust and
    greed—
  The beautiful, the saucy and the shy—
And teach mankind to know wild creatures' need
  Of confidence when human feet go by;
A heart that almost bursts the walls of flesh,
  The frozen terror in a small bright eye,
  Are plea enough for their immunity.

A Little Litany to Saint Francis

PHILIP MURRAY

Saint Francis of the mountain cave and wattle hut,
  of the willow roofs and rush mats,
  of the rock and fountain,
  of the wheat field and the burning mountain,
  of the crossways and the lonely island,
  of the earthworm and the hungry robins,
  of the tame falcon that woke you for Matins,
  of the swallows of Alviano,
  of the sparrows of Bevagna,
  of the vineyards of Rieti,
    Teach us humility.

Saint Francis of the pheasant and turtle dove,
  of the cicada in the olive grove,
  of the wild rabbit at Greccio,
  of the fierce wolf at Gubbio,
  of the fireflies by the river,
  of the fishes in the lake,
  of poplar and pine,
  of cypress and oak,
  of bush and berry,
  of the honey bee,
    Teach us simplicity.

Saint Francis, poet and folk singer,
  of our Brother Sun, our Sister Moon,
  of our Sister Water, our Brother Fire,
  of our Brother Wind and all weather,
  of our Sister Earth, her fruits and flowers,
  of our Sister Death, and the larks at
    Portiuncula singing when you died,
      Pray for us,

                                    AMEN

His Passion

The Crucified One

P. POURRAT

The love of Christ crucified, above all, filled his soul. It was not simply a love, but a compassion for the suffering Jesus, a veritable participation in his pain. Not long after his conversion, Francis felt himself pierced through with the love of the divine Crucified One, in the Church of Saint Damian, then in ruin. While he prayed before a crucifix he heard the voice of Jesus saying to him: "Go, Francis, and repair my house; thou seest clearly that it is fallen in ruins." At the moment that he gave his servant a mission, Jesus imprinted his wounds deeply on his soul. From that day Francis was not able to think of the passion without weeping. "He filled the highways with lamentations," says Thomas of Celano, "and refused all consolation in meditating on the wounds of Christ." He would occasionally withdraw into the woods and desert places in order to lament by himself over the sufferings of Jesus.

"One day," as is related by the companions of Francis, "he was walking alone near the Church of Saint Mary of the Portiuncula weeping and lamenting aloud. A holy man heard him and thought he was suffering. Seized with pity he asked him why he wept. Francis answered: 'I bewail the passion of my Lord Jesus Christ, and I ought not to feel ashamed to go throughout the world thus weeping.'" The man then began to weep with him. It was often noticed that when he had just been praying his eyes were filled with blood because he had wept so much and so bitterly. "Not content with shedding tears, he used to deprive himself of food at the memory of the passion of the Lord."

He taught his followers this prayer with the intention of making them do unceasing honor to the passion of the Savior: "We adore thee, O Christ, in all the churches of the whole world, and we bless thee because by thy holy Cross thou hast redeemed the world."

Francis had so constant a memory of the passion present in his heart that it might be thought that he desired to participate actually in the pains of Christ. The *Fioretti* attribute the following prayer to him, which expresses the sentiment of his soul in this regard toward the end of his life, a little while before the apparition of the stigmata:

"O my Lord Jesus Christ, two graces do I beseech thee to grant me before I die: the first that, during my lifetime, I may feel in my soul and in my body, so far as may be possible, that pain which thou, sweet Lord, didst suffer in the hour of thy most bitter passion; the second is that I may feel in my heart, so far as may be possible, that exceeding love whereby thou, Son of God, wast enkindled, to bear willingly such passion for us sinners."

Francis of Assisi bequeathed to his order, as a precious heritage, a special devotion to the passion of Jesus; a devotion that very soon spread and became general throughout the Church.

His prayer was heard by the impression of the stigmata of Christ in his flesh. "About two years before his death," his companions tell us, "at the approach of the Feast of the Exaltation of the Holy Cross, he was praying one morning on the slope of Mount Alvernia. He was uplifted to God by desire and by seraphic ardor and felt himself transformed by a tender compassion for him who, in the excess of his charity, willed to be crucified. A six-winged seraph then appeared to him, bearing between his wings the form, of great beauty, of One Crucified, having the hands and feet stretched on the cross, and clearly a figure of our Lord Jesus. Two wings were folded so as to hide his head; two others veiled the rest of his body, and the other two were extended to sustain the flight of the seraph. When the vision had disappeared, a wonderful ardor of love rested in Francis's soul; and, more wonderful still, in his body there appeared the impression of the stigmata of our Lord Jesus Christ. The man of God hid them as much as possible until his death, not wishing to make public the mystery of the Lord; but he was not able so to conceal them from his companions, at least from those that were most familiar. But after his happy departure from this world all the breth-

ren who were then present and many of the laity saw his body gloriously marked with the stigmata of Christ."

Francis of Assisi bequeathed to his Order, as a precious heritage, a special devotion to the passion of Jesus; a devotion that very soon spread and became general throughout the Church.

Crisis in the Order

JOHN R. MOORMAN

. . . In the ten years or so that had elapsed since the coming of the first disciples, the little brotherhood had grown into a great religious order, and the machinery that had proved adequate in the early days, when almost every question was decided by Francis personally, was now proving itself hopelessly inadequate. There was, for example, no means of testing the vocations of those who came to join the Order, no training, no novitiate. Again, the type of life envisaged by St. Francis, while suitable enough for a small band of friends, was quite unsuitable for a large order numbering many thousands of friars. Many of the brethren had never seen St. Francis and had only a vague idea of what he stood for or of what his wishes were.

Above all, there was no proper rule. The only rule was that of 1210, a few texts from the Scriptures strung together with some simple regulations to govern the lives of the brethren. To this a few additions had been made but without any official sanction, and the whole thing was growing more haphazard and chaotic. And still the Order grew.

Francis felt himself losing grip. While he could act as the most inspiring of leaders to a small group of enthusiasts, he was not a great administrator, nor could he direct the affairs of a great religious order. He depended far too much upon direct personal influence and upon the hour-to-hour guidance of the Holy Spirit. He could not plan ahead because he was never certain where God would lead him, and he could not hope to hold together large numbers of men whom he had never seen and of whose devotion and zeal he had no evidence. . . .

The remaining six years of Francis's life (1220–26) were a sad time for him. Absolutely certain of his vocation and of the particular form it had taken, and longing to get others to accept the same standards of humility and poverty, he was obliged to see more and more departures from the original Rule and intention of the Order, while strong-minded men who failed to share in his ideals got more and more power into their own hands. Francis bore it all with such patience and humility as he could command, but that it was a very sore trial to him is shown by his occasional outbursts, both vocal and physical. Once he cried out: "Who are they who snatch my Order and my brethren out of my hands? If I come to the General Chapter, I'll show them what they will get." And when he once arrived at the Portiuncula and found the friars building a stone building, which was entirely against his wishes, he climbed up on to the roof and began hurling the tiles to the ground with his own hands.

In all this we see a very different Francis from the man whom we met in the stories of the early days. There is here something stern and even violent, a man moved by powerful emotions who could act with sudden passion and rebuke with severity. And yet, though Francis was very deeply moved, and sometimes very angry, in the midst of it all his humility is ever breaking through. "There is no prelate in the whole world," he once said with remarkable insight, "who is so much feared as the Lord would make me to be feared, if I so wished it, by my brethren. But," he added, "the Lord has granted me this grace that I wish to be content with all, as he that is least in the Order." Humility was the greatest of all virtues, but it needed great humility to see your own child whom you had borne and cherished, taken into the hands of others who, without knowing it, were undoing much of what you had been trying to do. To arrive, tired and hungry, at a house of the friars and be turned away with curses and blows and left outside in the wet and cold, and to accept this with humility and gladness was a sign of perfect joy; it was far more difficult to count it perfect joy when you stood up before the friars and implored them to stand firm by the high standards of poverty and humility and simplicity, and they only mocked and sneered and ignored what you said. Yet Francis was trying to learn this lesson, for he once said:

Suppose that, being set over the brethren, I go to the chapter and preach to them and admonish them, and at the end they speak against me, saying, "An unlettered and contemptible man will not do for us; therefore we will not have thee to reign over us because thou art uneloquent, simple, and ignorant"; and finally I am expelled with obloquy and despised by them all. I tell thee that

unless I heard these words with unchanged looks, with unchanged gladness of mind, and with unchanged purpose of sanctity, I should by no means be a Little Brother.

Francis was indeed passing through the furnace, but he had not altogether surrendered his power yet. There was still work to be done, still a battle to be fought for the Lady Poverty and for the ideals of humility and simplicity for which he had always striven. He was not going to desert his love in this hour of peril, however powerful and influential might be the forces against him.

The burning problem in these years was the Rule. Here was a great religious Order with some five or ten thousand members; and yet the only rule was a simple document that Francis had drawn up when the whole brotherhood consisted of only twelve members and when they had scarcely begun their apostolate.

So Francis spent the winter of 1220–21 in composing a new Rule, which was offered to the General Chapter in the following spring and which remained for two years the unofficial Rule of the Order. This document was intended as a compromise and, as so often happens with compromises, it pleased nobody. No one can suppose that it really represents the wishes of Saint Francis, for it contains a number of concessions the earlier Rule would never have sanctioned. It relaxes the earlier standard of the single tunic by allowing a friar now to have two habits, one with a hood and one without. It allows the friars to possess books for the purpose of saying the Office, and it makes various allowances for a man who found it difficult to give all his goods to the poor on joining the Order. In some ways, therefore, this new Rule was meant as an offer to the more liberal, relaxing party. But as a peace offering it failed, and Francis knew that further concessions would be demanded before they had done with him.

Francis was indeed passing through the furnace, but he had not altogether surrendered his power yet.

In 1221 Francis lost one of his best friends, Peter Catanii, who had succeeded him as Minister General and who had helped him in the writing of the latest Rule. His place as the head of the Order was taken by Brother Elias, the man who has had to bear most of the blame for the departure of the Order from its primitive purity. Elias was a great admirer of Saint Francis, but he was also ambitious, both for the Order and for himself. Of humble origin, he found himself on terms of intimacy with those who held the highest positions in the Church, and to some extent his head was turned by success. In spite of his devotion to the saint it is doubtful whether he ever really understood what Francis was striving for; and, like Ugolino and others, he was anxious to use the immense forces that Francis had generated in order to promote the work of the Church. His appointment as Minister General in 1221 was something of a disaster, for it meant that the relaxing party was now in power and Francis's own will became more and more disregarded.

The first thing was to supersede the Rule of 1221, which those in power regarded as too harsh. So Francis was bidden to write another, and he retired to the wooded hills of Fonte Colombo in the valley of Rieti with a handful of friends to make one more attempt to solve the problem of how to satisfy the relaxing party and yet be true to his conscience and his ideals. The misery he endured as he walked through the woods, or sat and meditated in his cave, must have been almost more than he could bear. At last he completed his task

and presented it to Honorius III and Cardinal Ugolino. But they found it unacceptable and prevailed on Francis to make certain vital alterations such as the omission of the clause that formed the very basis of the Franciscan way of life: "When the brothers go about the world, they are to carry nothing with them."

Pious pilgrims in Franciscan Italy point to Fonte Colombo as the "Sinai" of the Order. But the document that proceeded from that hermitage expresses but a poor shadow of the real wishes of Saint Francis. "If any man shall come to join the brothers, let him sell all his goods and take care to give everything to the poor." So Francis had written in the earliest Rule, and so they had done—Francis, and Bernard, and Sylvester, and the rest of them. But now, thirteen years later, this clear demand has been whittled down and the postulant is told that "if he cannot do this then his goodwill shall be enough." Again in the primitive Rule the friar is allowed but one tunic with the cord and breeches. This had been enough for the early friars who had borne the cold and discomfort rather than disobey what they regarded as a divine command. But in 1221 a second habit had been permitted, and by 1223 this was increased to include a *caparone* or large cape and sandals.

As soon as the text was complete it was taken to the Pope, who confirmed it and sealed it with a Papal Bull on November 25, 1223. The Rule of the Order of Friars Minor was now officially sanctioned; but what the struggle had meant to the sensitive mind and conscience of Saint Francis, who can say?

The Wounds of Christ

OMER ENGLEBERT

The summit of Alvernia is an uneven plateau, supported by titanic rocks and covered with pines and beeches, where even today legions of familiar birds are loud in their song. A hermitage was built there for the saint by Count Orlando of Chiusi, and also a little oratory, which was dedicated in the late sixteenth century to Saint Mary of the Angels. From this vantage point the eye takes in an immense panorama. On a clear day one may catch a glimpse of the Adriatic from La Penna, the summit of the mountain, nearly an hour's walk from the shrine.

As soon as Count Orlando learned of the arrival of Francis and his companions, he came from his castle to welcome them and bring them some provisions. Francis asked him to build him a hut "cell" under a large beech tree a stone's throw from the hermitage. When it was done, Orlando said to his guests: "Dear brothers, I do not mean to have you want for anything on this mountain wilderness, so that you may not be hindered in your spiritual exercises. So I say to you once and for all, feel perfectly free to come to me for anything you need. And if you do not come, I shall be very displeased."

Then he departed with his retinue.

The day was at its close. On Mount Alvernia the late afternoons of summer are of surpassing beauty. Nature, which has lain prostrate under the burning sun, seems to take on new life. A thousand voices awaken in the branches of trees and in the clefts of the moss-covered rocks, forming a sweet and melancholy symphony, while for hours the sun still illumines the distant peaks of the Apennines with its iridescent afterglow, filling the heart of the laggard contemplative with what a Franciscan poet terms "the nostalgia of the everlasting hills."

Francis bade his companions to be seated and instructed them how friars in hermitages should comport themselves, counseling them not to abuse the generosity of Count Orlando, but to remain ever true to Lady Poverty. Speaking to them also of his end, which he saw approaching, he said to them: "Because I see that I am drawing near to death, I wish to dwell here in solitude and bewail my sins before God. So if any lay people come here, you are to receive them yourselves, for I do not want to see anyone except Brother Leo."

He then blessed them and retired into his hut of branches. From time to time, he would come out and sit down under the beautiful beech to admire the magnificent scenery.

One day when he was thus engaged, his eyes fixed on the gigantic cliffs huddled there before him, towering above the great chasms, he wondered what could have caused such an upheaval in the earth's surface. Then as he prayed, it was revealed to him that these huge crevices had been opened at that moment when the rocks on Mount Calvary, according to the Gospel, were rent. From that time onward, Alvernia was for him a witness and constant reminder of Christ's Passion. His love for the crucified Savior increased, his prayer became continuous, and God now favored him with extraordinary mystical graces.

"With the best intentions," continues the chronicler, and with that biographer's indiscretion for which posterity will ever be grateful, "Brother Leo diligently spied on his spiritual father."

Sometimes he would hear him lamenting over his Order: "Lord," he would say, weeping, "what will become of this poor little family that you have entrusted to me, when I am gone?" But more often he surprised him in loving colloquy, or crying out for very love, or rapt in ecstasy. Thus it was, we are told, that he saw Francis lifted up several yards above the ground, sometimes even to the top of the great beech. Then he would silently draw near, and when the feet of the ecstatic were within reach, he would embrace them, saying, "Lord, be merciful to me, a sinner. And by the merits of this blessed father, may I find grace in Your sight!"

Meanwhile the Assumption drew near in which Francis had decided to begin a Lent that would last until the feast of Saint Michael the Archangel. Resolved to keep his too curious observer away, he enjoined Brother Leo to station himself at the door of the hermitage, saying, "When I call you, you are to come."

Then going some distance away, he called to him in a loud voice. Brother Leo came running. "Son," said Francis, "I am still not far enough away. We must find a place where you cannot hear me."

Finally they found the right spot. On the mountainside, hollowed out in the stone, there was a sort of ledge overhanging a chasm some 120 feet deep. The friars had to place a log as a bridge over the chasm to reach this ledge and erect on it a little hut of reeds. When this was done, their father dismissed them, saying:

"Return to the hermitage, for with God's grace, I desire to live here in absolute silence and not be disturbed by anyone. You, Brother Leo, may come only twice a day, the first time to bring me bread and water, then about midnight to recite matins with me. But before crossing the bridge, you are to take care to announce yourself by saying: *"Domine, labia mea aperies"* (Lord, open my lips). And if I answer *"Et os meum annuntiabit laudem tuam"* (And my mouth will proclaim your praise), you are to pass over. But if I do not, you are to go back at once."

When the Feast of the Assumption came, Francis commenced his great fast.

We are approaching the truly seraphic period in the life of the Poverello—days when, as if lost in God, his soul consummated its final alliance with and conformity to the very soul of Christ.

As the history of mystical phenomena offers nothing similar, and no one has ever been able to claim that he has drawn aside the veil from such mysteries, it is here especially that historians must limit themselves to reproducing the statements of authoritative witnesses. For us these are principally Brother Leo, the saint's confessor; St. Bonaventure, the seraphic doctor; the unknown author of the *Fioretti* (which contains the *Considerations on the Most Holy Stigmata*)—himself dependent in part on the *Actus beati Francisci* [*Acts of Blessed Francis*] and Thomas of Celano, and in part on the tradition of the friars residing at Alvernia.

They report that at this time the Poverello's fervor and austerities were redoubled, that he suffered dreadful pain, and was horribly tormented by the Evil One. "Oh," he would sometimes say to Brother Leo, "if the brothers only knew what I have to endure from the devil, there is not one of them who would not have compassion and pity for me."

Nevertheless, in the midst of this painful purification, God still sometimes sensibly visited his heart. Thus it was—to console him and give him a foretaste of heaven—that He sent him an angelic musician. Once and only once, the celestial spirit passed the bow over his viol, but "the melody that came forth was so beautiful," declared the saint later, "that I almost swooned; and if the angel had drawn his bow a second time, I know that my soul would have left my body, so boundless and unbearable was my joy."

Francis also enjoyed the friendship of a falcon that nested near his cell. Every night before matins, this affectionate creature would beat its wings against the walls of the hut. But if the saint were too ill or too tired, the compassionate bird would let him rest and not waken him until later.

Likewise Brother Leo, no less charitable, did not insist when the saint did not reply to his *Domine, labia mea aperies.* Once, though, he crossed the bridge anyway.

Not finding Francis in the hut, he started out in the moonlight to look for him in the woods. He found him in ecstasy, conversing with someone invisible. "Who are you?" the saint was saying, "and who am I, your miserable and useless servant?" Leo also saw a ball of fire descend from heaven and return almost immediately.

Seized with awe at this supernatural spectacle, and fearing lest his curiosity might lead Saint Fran-

cis to dispense with his services, the indiscreet friar attempted to flee, but the rustling of the leaves betrayed him.

"Who is there?" cried Francis.

"It is I, Father: Brother Leo."

"Didn't I forbid you, dear little sheep, to spy on me this way? Tell me under obedience, did you see or hear anything?"

Brother Leo confessed what he had seen and heard and asked for some explanation. The saint admitted to his friend that our Lord had just appeared to him, and he told Leo that something wonderful was going to happen soon on the mountain.

What was this wonderful thing? As was his habit, Francis wanted to consult the Gospels about it. In the hermitage chapel, where Brother Leo said mass, he asked his friend to open the missal three times at random, and each time it opened at the story of the Passion. "By this sign," writes Saint Bonaventure, "the saint understood that, having imitated Christ in his life, he was also to imitate him in the sufferings that preceded His death. So, filled with courage, despite his ruined health and physical exhaustion, he made ready for martyrdom."

His hands and feet appeared as though pierced with nails, with round black heads on the palm of the hands and on the feet, and with bent points extruding from the back of the hands and the soles of the feet. In addition, there was a wound in the right side, as if made by a lance, from which blood frequently flowed....

The feast of the Exaltation of the Cross had come. It commemorated the victory that had permitted Heraclius to regain the Savior's Cross from the infidels; and no feast was more popular at that time among Christians, who were continually being called on to take the cross in the Crusades. It was probably on this day, September 14, 1224, that the miracle of the stigmata took place.

In that hour that precedes sunrise, kneeling before his hut, Francis prayed, his face turned toward the east. "O Lord," he pleaded, "I beg of You two graces before I die—to experience in myself in all possible fullness the pains of your cruel Passion, and to feel for you the same love that made you sacrifice yourself for us."

For a long time he prayed, his heart aflame with love and pity. Then "suddenly," writes Saint Bonaventure, "from the heights of heaven a seraph with six wings of flame flew swiftly down." He bore the likeness of a man nailed to a cross. Two of his wings covered his face, with two others he flew and the last two covered his body. "It was Christ himself, who had assumed this form to manifest himself to the Saint. He fixed his gaze upon Francis, then left him, after imprinting the miraculous stigmata" of the Crucifixion on his flesh.

"From that moment," continues the seraphic doctor, "Francis was marked with the wounds of the divine Redeemer. His hands and feet appeared as though pierced with nails, with round, black heads on the palm of the hands and on the feet, and with bent points extruding from the back of the hands and the soles of the feet. In addition, there was a wound in the right side, as if made by a lance, from which blood frequently flowed, moistening his drawers and tunic."

There had been no witnesses to the prodigy, and although it had left visible marks, the saint's first thought was to keep it secret; then, after much hesitation, he decided to ask counsel of his companions. "So he asked them in veiled words if they thought that certain extraordinary graces ought to be kept secret or revealed."

Brother Illuminato, who well deserved his name, remarks Saint Bonaventure, divining that something out of the common order had occurred, spoke up:

"Brother Francis, it might be wrong for you to keep for yourself that which God has given you to edify your neighbor."

Timidly, then, the saint told what had happened; but without showing his wounds, which he always took care afterwards to cover up with bandages. He even formed the habit of keeping his bandaged hands in the sleeves of his habit.

However, as the stigmata never disappeared, a number of persons were able to see them. Among them were Brother Leo, whom Francis took as his nurse and who regularly bathed the oozing wound in the side; Brother Rufino and several others who gave sworn testimony about them; and all those present at the death of the saint or who were able to venerate him in his coffin, especially "Brother" Jacopa and her sons, and Sister Clare and her daughters. In addition, Pope Alexander IV, who in a sermon heard by Saint Bonaventure, averred that while Francis was still alive he had seen the miraculous marks with his own eyes.

Some rationalist scholars have indeed attempted

to impugn their existence, although the presence of "nails embedded in the flesh" proved most vexing to them. But their opinion bears no weight; and while waiting for them to furnish proof, we may refer to the judgment of the Holy See, which, by a favor not granted to any other saint and by the advice of Saint Robert Bellarmine, extended to the whole Church the annual observance of the feast of the Stigmata of Saint Francis at the time of Pope Paul V (1605–21); and although the changes made in 1960 reduced this feast to a commemoration, the feast is still observed by the Franciscan Order, to which it was granted by Pope Benedict XI (1303–04).

Franciscus Christificatus

FRANCIS THOMPSON

Thief that has leaped Heaven's star-spiked wall!
Christ's exultant bacchanal!
Wine-smears on thy hand and foot
Of the Vine that struck its root
Deep in Virgin soul, and was
Trained against the reared Cross:
Nay, thy very side its stain
Hath, to make it redly plain
How in the wassail quaffed full part
That flown vintager, thy heart.
Christ in blood stamps Himself afresh
On thy Veronical-veil of flesh.

Lovers, looking with amaze on
Each other, would be that they gaze on:
So for man's love God would be
Man, and man for His love He:
What God in Christ, man has in thee.
God gazed on man and grew embodied,
Thou, on Him gazing, turn'st engodded!
But though he held thy brow-spread tent
His little Heaven above Him bent,
The scept'ring reed suffices thee,
Which smote Him into sovereignty.

Thou who thoughtest thee too low
For His priest, thou shalt not so
'Scape Him and unpriested go!
In thy hand thou wouldst not hold Him,
In thy flesh thou shalt enfold Him;
Bread wouldst not change into Him . . . ah see!
How He doth change Himself to thee!

The Voice of Saint Francis of Assisi

VACHEL LINDSAY

I saw Saint Francis by a stream
Washing his wounds that bled.
The aspens quivered overhead.
The silver doves flew round.

Weeping and sore dismayed
"Peace, peace," Saint Francis prayed.

But the soft doves quickly fled.
Carrion crows flew round.
An earthquake rocked the ground.

"War, war," the west wind said.

His Song

The Making of "The Canticle of Brother Sun": I

FREDERICK OZANAM

A heart so filled with passion could not disburden itself by preaching alone. Preaching is limited to prose, and prose, however eloquent, is after all only the language of reason. When Reason has expressed precisely and clearly the truth she has conceived, she is content, but Love is not so easily satisfied; she must reproduce the beauties by which she is touched in language that thrills and delights. Love is restless; nothing satisfies her, but on the other hand nothing daunts her. She amplifies speech; she gives it poetic flight; she adorns it with rhythm and melody as with two wings. Saint Francis saw that the Church honored Poetry by giving her the first place in her worship, and admitting her to the very choir of her basilicas and even to the foot of the altar, while eloquence must remain in the pulpit, nearer the door and the crowd. He himself had proved the powerlessness of ordinary speech to express all which stirred his soul. When the name of the Savior Christ came to his lips he could not proceed, his voice would alter, according to the apt description of Saint Bonaventure, as if he had heard a melody within him whose notes he wished to recall. But this melody by which he was haunted ended by bursting forth into a new song, and this is what the historians record:

When the name of the Savior Christ came to his lips he could not proceed . . . as if he had heard a melody within him whose notes he wished to recall. But this melody by which he was haunted ended by bursting into a new song. . . .

In the eighteenth year of his penitence, the servant of God, after a forty nights' vigil, had an ecstasy, after which he ordered Brother Leo to take a pen and write. Then he intoned the "Canticle of the Sun" and, after he had improvised it, he charged Brother Pacifico, who had been a poet in his worldly life, to fit the words to a more regular rhythm, and he ordered the brothers to learn them by heart, so that they might recite them every day. The words of the "Canticle" are these:

Here beginneth the praise of created things that the blessed Francis made to the praise and glory of God when he lay sick at St. Damian's.

O highest, almighty, excellent Lord,
Thine be the praise, the glory, the honor,
  and all benediction.
To thee, O Highest, alone they belong,
And to name thee no man is worthy.

Be thou blessed, O Lord, with all things created,
Especially my Lord and Brother the Sun,
For by his dawning thou lightenest our darkness;
Beautiful is he and radiant with mighty splendor:
Of thee, O Most High, he beareth the token.

Praised be thou, O Lord, for Sister Moon and the Stars,
For that thou madest them clear, precious, and lovely.
Praised be thou, O Lord, for our Brother the Wind,
For air and cloud and sunshine and every weather
Whereby thou givest thy creatures their sustenance.

Praised be thou, O Lord, for Sister Water,
Our helpmate, lowly and precious and pure.

Praised be thou, O Lord, for our Brother the Fire,
Whereby thou sheddest Thy light on darkness,
For he is comely and pleasant and mighty and strong.

Praised be thou, O Lord, for our Sister the Earth,
That as a Mother sustaineth and feedeth us,
And after its kind bringeth forth fruit
And grass and many-colored flowers.

A few days afterward a great dispute arose between the Bishop of Assisi and the magistrates of the city. The bishop fulminated against the interdict, and the magistrates placed the prelate beyond the pale of the law and forbade all association with him and his followers. The saint, distressed by such strife, lamented that there was no one who would intervene to establish peace. He then added to his "Canticle" the following verse:

Praised be thou, O Lord, for them that for thy love forgive,
And undergo tribulation and weakness.
Blessed are they that shall in peace sustain,
For by thee, O Most High, they shall be crowned.

Then he ordered his followers to go boldly to seek the principal men of the town and to beg them to make their way to the bishop, and on arriving there to sing in chorus the new verse. The disciples obeyed and, at the chanting of his words, to which God seemed to lend a secret virtue, the adversaries embraced each other in their penitence and asked pardon.

Then, having been taken to Foligno to restore his failing health by the change of air, he experienced some alleviation of his sufferings. Soon, however, it was revealed to him that he would suffer for two years more, and after that he would enter into everlasting rest. Intoxicated with joy, he composed the following verse with which he ended the "Canticle":

Blessed be thou, O Lord, for our Sister, Bodily Death,
From which may no man that liveth escape;
Woe unto them that shall die in deadly sin;
Blessed they that shall conform to thy most holy will,
For them the second death harmeth not.
Praise and bless our Lord and thank him.
And serve him with all lowliness.

The "Canticle of Brother Sun" is quoted for the first time by Bartholomew of Pisa, in a book written in 1385, 160 years after the death of the saint, and yet no one can dispute its authenticity. This fashion of composing little by little, according to the inspiration of the heart and the need of the moment, is after the manner of great poets such as Dante and Camoëns, who carried with them into exile and into far countries the work they had conceived, and added to it day by day phrases inflamed by passionate grief or hope.

The poem of St. Francis is quite short, and yet his whole soul is poured out in it: his brotherly love for the creatures, the charity that inspired this humble and retiring spirit in times of public strife; that infinite love that, after having sought God in nature and having served him through suffering humanity, had no further aspiration than to find him in death. Through that canticle we gain a glimpse of the earthly paradise of Umbria, where the sky is so golden and the ground so carpeted with flowers. The language possesses all the spontaneity of primitive speech, and its crude rhythm is that of a poesy in an early stage of development that yet is pleasing to indulgent ears. Sometimes rhyme is replaced by assonance; sometimes it occurs only in the middle and at the end of the verse. The fastidious will have some difficulty in discovering the regular laws of a lyrical composition. It is only a cry, but it is the first cry of a nascent poesy that will develop and make itself heard through the whole world.

The Making of "The Canticle of Brother Sun": II

ELOI LECLERC, O.F.M.

Almost twenty years had passed since Francis's conversion to the evangelical life. They were years during which he constantly meditated on the "advent of gentleness" and the passion of the Most High Son of God, and strove daily to walk in the footsteps of the Lord. Now, on Mount Alvernia, he had just received in his flesh the stigmata that completed his likeness to the crucified Christ. Bleed-

ing from every wound, exhausted by fasting and illness, blind and almost brought to his final agony, Francis was simply "identified with Christ in redemptive suffering," to use the language of Claudel. Suffering filled his body; his suffering of soul was perhaps even more intense. The evangelical values of pure simplicity, poverty, and peace that were, in his eyes, so essential to the revelation of divine love, had been shunted aside in a Christendom engrossed by power and ruled by the idea of the Crusades. They were even questioned at times by his own followers. It was eventide in Francis's life, but he still had not experienced the full peace that evening should bring.

It was then that the decisive event took place. Francis descended from Mount Alvernia, almost at the end of his strength, and stopped at the monastery of San Damiano, where Clare and her sisters were living. It was there that he had first heard Christ speaking to him, inviting him to restore the house that was falling into ruins. Clare settled Francis in a house adjacent to the convent, where he remained in constant pain. "For forty days or more, blessed Francis could not bear the light of the sun during the day or the light of the fire at night. . . . His eyes caused him so much pain that he could neither lie down nor sleep, so to speak."

Then, "one night, as he was thinking of all the tribulations he was enduring, he felt sorry for him-

self and said interiorly: 'Lord, help me in my infirmities so that I may have the strength to bear them patiently.'" Celano gives us to understand that a conflict was raging in Francis's soul and that he was praying that he might overcome the temptation of discouragement:

As he prayed thus in agony and suddenly he heard a voice in spirit: "Tell me, Brother: if, in compensation for your sufferings and tribulations you were given an immense and precious treasure: the whole mass of earth changed into pure gold, pebbles into precious stones, and the water of the rivers into perfume, would you not regard the pebbles and the waters as nothing compared to such a treasure? Would you not rejoice?" Blessed Francis answered: "Lord, it would be a very great, very precious, and inestimable treasure beyond all else that one can love and desire!" "Well, Brother," the voice said, "be glad and joyful in the midst of your infirmities and tribulations: as of now, live in peace as if you were already sharing my kingdom."

A supernatural joy immediately filled Francis's soul, the joy that comes from the certainty of possessing the kingdom. Now he knew for sure that the road he had been following—the road of suffering with Christ—was indeed the road that "leads to the land of the living." At this moment it was as if a glorious sun had risen in his soul. In the morning he called his companions together and, unable to contain his joy, sang to them the "Canticle of Brother Sun," which he had just composed.

The "Canticle" springs from existential depths. It is the end result and surely the supreme expression of a whole life.

In the light of this account it seems impossible to understand the "Canticle" *properly* unless we directly relate it to Francis's innermost experience, his bitter suffering, his heroic patience, his daily struggle for evangelical values, and his supernatural joy, or, in a word, to his life of intimacy with Christ. The "Canticle" springs from existential depths. It is the end result and surely the supreme expression of a whole life.

At first sight, there is something rather surprising in all this. Here is a man whose diseased eyes cannot bear the light nor any longer enjoy the sight of creatures, a man who is interested only in the splendors of the kingdom. Yet, in order to express his joy, this man sings of matter: matter that burns and emits a brilliant light—the sun and the fire; matter that nourishes—the air, the water, and the earth, "our mother." And he does so in terms strangely reminiscent of ancient pagan hymns in which men gave thanks for the sun's mastery and for the earth's maternal fruitfulness. His language is the ancient language typical of the sacred, the language of the cosmic hierophants, and he uses it with the spontaneity, directness, and warmth that

We would indeed have every reason to be surprised, were it not that these cosmic realities, given the manner in which they are celebrated and the rich affective and oneiric freight they unconsciously carry, constitute a kind of language expressive of an inner experience of the sacred. "To manifest the 'sacred' *on* the 'cosmos' and to manifest it *in* the 'psyche' are the same thing. . . . Cosmos and Psyche are the two poles of the same 'expressivity';

mark a man's words when he speaks his mother tongue. Moreover, in the entire "Canticle" there is not a single reference or slightest allusion to the supernatural mystery of Christ and his kingdom! It is only material things that are used to celebrate the glory of the Most High.

I express myself in expressing the world; I explore my own sacrality in deciphering that of the world." On reading this statement from Paul Ricoeur's *The Symbolism of Evil*, we saw in it the key to a reading of Francis's "Canticle" in terms of the interiority it reflects.

106

Il Cantico del Sole

THE ORIGINAL ITALIAN

Altissimu, omnipotente, bonsignore,
    tue sono le laude
    la gloria elhonore
    et omne benedictione.

Ad te solo, Altissimo, se Konfano
    et nullu homo enne dignu
    te mentovare.

Laudato sie, misignore, cum tucte le tue creature,
    spetialmente messor lo frate sole,
    loquale iorno et allumini noi par loi.

Et ellu ebellu eradiante cum grande splendore:
    de te, Altissimo, porta significatione.

Laudato si, misignore, per sora luna ele stelle:
    in celu lai formate clarite
    et pretiose et belle.

Laudate si, misignore, per frate vento,
    et per aere et nubilo
    et sereno et omne tempo
    per loquale a le tue creature
    dai sustentamento.

Laudato si, misignore, per sor aqua,
    laquale e multo utile et humile
    et pretiosa et casta.

Laudato si, misignore, per frate focu,
    per loquale ennalumini la nocte:
    edello ebello et iocundo
    et robustoso et forte.

Laudato si, misignore, per sora nostra matre terra,
    laquale ne sustenta et governa,
    et produce diversi fructi
    con coloriti flori et herba.

Laudato si, misignore, per quelli ke perdonano
    per lo tuo amore
    et sostengo infirmitate
    et tribulatione.

Beate quelli kel sosterrano in pace,
    ka da te, Altissimo,
    sirano incoronati.

Laudato si, misignore, per sora nostra
    morte corporale,
    da laquale nullu homo
    vivente poskappare.

The Canticle of Brother Sun

A TRANSLATION

Most high, all-powerful, all good, Lord!
    All praise is yours, all glory, all honor
    And all blessing.

To you alone, Most High, do they belong.
    No mortal lips are worthy
    To pronounce your name.

All praise be yours, my Lord, through all that
      you have made,
    And first my lord Brother Sun,
    Who brings the day; and light you give to us
      through him.

How beautiful is he, how radiant in all his
      splendor!
    Of you, Most High, he bears the likeness.

All praise be yours, my Lord, through Sister Moon
      and Stars;
    In the heavens you have made them, bright
    And precious and fair.

All praise be yours, my Lord, through Brothers
      Wind and Air,
    And fair and stormy, all the weather's moods,
    By which you cherish all that you have made.

All praise be yours, my Lord, through Sister Water,
    So useful, lowly, precious, and pure.

All praise be yours, my Lord, through Brother Fire,
    Through whom you brighten up the night.
    How beautiful he is, how gay! Full of power
      and strength.

All praise be yours, my Lord, through Sister Earth,
      our mother,
    Who feeds us in her sovereignty and produces
    Various fruits and colored flowers and herbs.

All praise be yours, my Lord, through those who
      grant pardon
    For love of you; through those who endure
    Sickness and trial.

Happy those who endure in peace,
    By you, Most High, they will be crowned.

All praise be yours, my Lord, through Sister Death,
    From whose embrace no mortal can escape.

The Original Italian (*cont.*)

Gai acqueli ke morrano
   ne le peccata mortali!

Beati quelli ke trovarane
   le tue santissime voluntati,
   ka la morte secunda
   nol farra male.

Laudate et benedicite, misignore,
   et rengratiate et servaite li
   cum grande humilitate.

A Translation (*cont.*)

Woe to those who die in mortal sin!

Happy those She finds doing your will!
   The second death can do no harm to them.

Praise and bless my Lord, and give him thanks,
   And serve him with great humility.

The Canticle of Brother Sun

VERSE TRANSLATION

All creatures of our God and King,
Lift up your voice and with us sing
Alleluia, Alleluia!
Thou burning sun with golden beam,
Thou silver moon with softer gleam,
O praise him, O praise him,
Alleluia, Alleluia!

Thou rushing wind that art so strong,
Ye clouds that sail in heaven along,
O praise him, alleluia!
Thou rising morn, in praise rejoice,
Ye lights of heaven find a voice,
O praise him, O praise him,
Alleluia, Alleluia!

Thou flowing water, pure and clear,
Make music for thy Lord to hear,
Alleluia, Alleluia!
Thou fire so masterful and bright,
That givest man both warmth and light,
O praise him, O praise him,
Alleluia, Alleluia!

And all ye men of tender heart,
Forgiving others, take your part,
O sing ye, alleluia.
Ye who long pain and sorrow bear,
Praise God and on him cast your care.
O praise him, O praise him,
Alleluia, Alleluia!

The Canticle of Brother Sun

AS PARAPHRASED IN *THE CATHOLIC WORKER*

Most loving and almighty Lord,
   Yours is the power and blessing forever.

To you be honor in each of your creatures,

But first of all in radiant Brother Sun. How quietly
   he tumbles shadows into dawn, and warmth into
     our
   blood.

Be praised, my Lord, in faithful Sister Moon. By
   her
   the tides and seasons run; with her the stars
   spill across your skies.

Be praised, my Lord, in the bellows of the winds.
   In
   their channels scarlet leaves and windmills twirl
   and dance.

And be praised, my Lord, by lowly Sister Water,
   pure
   wine of your creation. She babbles and banters
   in golden streams, making us young again in
   baptism and in rain.

Be honored, my Lord, by stately Brother Fire. He it
   is who purifies our souls, and brings us homeward
   in the dark. In his friendship men recline to
   crackling warmth and mellow wine.

Be praised, my Lord, in spinning earth, in worms
and churning surf. Exalted, my Lord, in green
and red, in dark and evening's end.

Tumble down, my Lord, in colored glass, in grass
and
chimes and horns. Be praised, my Lord, in sunly
voices, scents, and sounding songs.

And yes, my Lord, be praised in chaff, in aching
lives,
on bloody trees. For it is you who make coins
thick, and cast hope on unknown seas.

O praised and blessed be you, my Lord. Let us give
you thanks and awake with the dead.

The Canticle of Brother Sun

AS PARAPHRASED IN THE OFF-BROADWAY MUSICAL, *FRANCIS*

Praise be to you, O Lord and Father
Praise be to you and you alone
We praise you, O Lord, for all of your creatures,
Especially Brother Sun

For Brother Sun, he is strong and bright
And he gives us light as we live each day

Praise also Sister Moon
And the sparkling stars
Which thy Hand made

Praise thee, O Lord, for our Brother the Wind
For weather that's cloudy and weather that's clear
Praise thee, O Lord, for sweet Sister Water
Helpful to all thy children here

Praise thee, O Lord, for our Brother Fire
Praise how he warms and lights the night

Praise thee, O Lord, for the Earth our Mother
She who sustains us that we might
Be led to a love of all creatures great and small
As they show thy grace

Lord, help us each to learn
Everywhere we turn
We can see thy Face

Praise thee, O Lord, for all those who suffer
Injuries in thy Holy Name
Blessed are they who merit to suffer
You will reward them for their pains

Praise be to you, O Lord of all seasons
Praise be to you, O Lord, for all reasons

Glory to you, O God!
Glory to you, O God!
Glory to you, O God, and you alone!

His End

Brother Ass and Saint Francis

JOHN BANISTER TABB

It came to pass
That "Brother Ass"
(As he his Body named)
Unto the Saint
Thus made complaint:
"I am unjustly blamed.

"Whate'er I do,
Like Balaam you
Requite me with a blow,
As for offense
To recompense
An ignominious foe.

"God made us one,
And I have done
No wickedness alone;
Nor can I do
Apart, as you,
An evil all my own.

"If Passion stir,
'Tis you that spur
My frenzy to the goal;
Then be the blame
Where sits the shame,
Upon the goading soul.

"Should one or both
Be blind or loath
Our brotherhood to see,
Remember this,
You needs must miss
Or enter heaven through *me*."

To this complaint
The lowly Saint
In tears replied, "Alas,
If so it be,
God punish me
And bless thee, Brother Ass."

Into Eternity Singing

JOHANNES JØRGENSEN

Francis . . . gave a last sermon of admonition to the brothers, pressed it upon them above all to be faithful to poverty, and—as a symbol thereof—to be true to poor little Portiuncula. "If they drive you out of one door, then go in the other," said he, "for here is God's house and the gate of heaven!" He blessed finally with the whole of his overflowing

heart, not only the absent brethren but also all brothers who should ever enter the Order—"I bless them," said he, "as much as I can—*and more than I can.*" Francis perhaps never said anything that better expresses the whole of his innermost nature, than this *plusquam possum* ["more than I can"]. The spirit that actuated him had never rested before it had done more than it could.

And now at the end it gave him no rest. After he had blessed his disciples, he had himself completely undressed and placed on the bare earth in the hut. Lying there he took from the guardian as a last alms the cowl, in which he was to die, and as this did not seem poor enough, he had a rag sewed to it. In the same way he received a pair of breeches, a rope, with a hat he wore to hide the scars that always showed on his temples. Thus he had held his faith with Lady Poverty to the last and could die without owning more upon this earth than he had owned when he came into it.

Exhausted, Francis fell into a sleep, but early on Friday morning he awoke with great pains. The brothers were constantly gathered about him, and Francis's love to them constantly sought some new outlet. Thinking it was still Thursday, the day on which the Lord held the Last Supper with his disciples, he had them bring a loaf of bread, he blessed it, broke it, and gave them all bits of it. "And bring me the Holy Scripture and read the Gospel of Maundy Thursday to me!" said he. "Today is not Thursday," one told him. "I thought it was still Thursday!" he answered. The book was brought, and as the day dawned the words of the Holy Scriptures were read over Francis's deathbed —the words in which were summarized all his life and learning:

Before the festival-day of the pasch, Jesus, knowing that his hour was come, that he should pass out of this world to the Father: having loved his own who were in the world,

he loved them unto the end. And when supper was done (the devil having now put into the heart of Judas Iscariot, the son of Simon, to betray him), knowing that the Father had given him all things into his hands, and that he came from God, and goeth to God: He riseth from supper, and layeth aside his garments, and having taken a towel girded himself. After that he putteth water into a basin, and began to wash the feet of the disciples, and to wipe them with the towel wherewith he was girded. He cometh, therefore, to Simon Peter, and Peter saith to him: Lord, dost thou wash my feet? Jesus answered and said to him: What I do, thou knowest not now, but thou shalt know hereafter. Peter saith to him: Thou shalt never wash my feet. Jesus answered him: If I wash thee not, thou shalt have no part with me. Simon Peter saith to him: Lord, not only my feet, but also my hands, and my head. Jesus saith to him: He that is washed, needeth not but to wash his feet, but is cleansed wholly. And you are clean, but not all. For he knew who he was that would betray him; therefore he said: You are not all clean. Then after he had washed their feet, and taken his garments, being sat down again, he said to them: Know you what I have done to you? You call me Master, and Lord; and you say well, for so I am. If then I, being your Lord and Master, have washed your feet, you also ought to wash one another's feet. For I have given you an example, that as I have done to you, so you do also (JOHN 13:1–15).

During the days Francis still lived, none of the brothers left his bedside. Again and again Angelo and Leo had to sing the "Sun Song" to him—again and again did the sick one say the last words: "Praised be thou, O Lord, for Sister Death!" Again he asked his guardian to have his clothes removed, when the last hour would come, and received permission to expire lying naked on the earth.

Friday passed and Saturday came (October 3, 1226). The physician came, and Francis greeted him with the question of when the portals to the everlasting life should be opened to him. He required of the brothers that they should strew ashes over him—"soon I will be nothing but dust and ashes."

Toward evening he began to sing with unusual strength. It was no more the "Sun Song," but Psalm 141, a Psalm of David, the one which in the Vulgate begins: *Voce mea ad Dominum clamavi* ["With my voice I have cried out to the Lord"]. As the October evening fell rapidly, and it grew dark in the little hut in the Portiuncula woods, Francis prayed in the deep stillness, among the disciples listening breathlessly:

I cried to the Lord with my voice:
   with my voice I made supplication to the Lord.
In his sight I pour out my prayer,
   and before him I declare my trouble:

When my spirit failed me, then thou knewest my paths.
In this way wherein I walked,
  they have hidden a snare for me.
I looked on my right hand, and beheld:
  and there was no one that would know me.
Flight hath failed me:
  and there is no one that hath regard to my soul.
I cried to thee, O Lord; I said:
  Thou art my hope, my portion in the land of the living.
Attend to my supplication: for I am brought very low.
Deliver me from my persecutors;
  for they are stronger than I.
Bring my soul out of prison, that I may praise thy name:
  the just wait for me, until thou reward me.

While Francis prayed, it was quite dark in the little cell. And as his voice ceased all was still as death—a stillness that this voice was never more to break. Francis of Assisi had closed his lips forever; he went into eternity singing.

  While Francis prayed it was quite dark in the little cell. And as his voice ceased all was still as death —a stillness that this voice was never more to break. Francis of Assisi had closed his lips forever; he went into eternity singing.

  But as a last greeting to the departed singer of God at this moment, over and around the house there was a loud and sudden twittering—it was Francis's good friends the larks, who said their last farewell.

Francis, Dying, Blesses Assisi

EMILE RIPERT

O Town, it was in you I knew life
  First as a kiss,
When my mother felt my lips
  Rest on her exulting face.

It was in you that later I ran
  From dawn to warm, lovely eve,
When along your walls my loud sonorous laugh
  Flowed like a bounding stream;

It was in you that, not yet knowing the Divine
    Master,
  I used to sing of that love
That is to the love I was to know
  No more than dawn is to day:

In you that bit by bit I understood
  That my soul was to know God,
That it knew him, that all base things
  Faded into the blue daylight;

In you that I heard, one evening, in the gray
    shadow
  The voice of Jesus Christ. . . .

Now, sweet Town, it is in you I am dying,
  And for eternity
You are to be, after so many days, the refuge
  Where I stopped. . . .

It is not rest that my wishes ask of you
  As before, over-weary.
In the spring you will have flowers, then almonds,
  I will not see them. . . .

You will have lilies, roses . . . I hope for
  A more radiant tomorrow;
If only, O Town, I could lead you with me by the
    hand
    Toward the Father!

I am leaving you, but I also leave you the graces
  Which pain brings.
Souls will blossom on your high terraces
  As tall as flowers.

Your beautiful bells will drive sadness
  From sad and empty hearts,
And many will find in you, O good hostess,
  Water, bread, and wine.

Be blessed, O exquisitely flowering Town,
  By the Father and the Son
And the Spirit . . . In the rose and white eve
  Your towers are roses and lilies.

The road climbing toward you, white and dotted
  Already with many lights
(For it is dark now), seems like a milky Way,
  You are so heavenward. . . .

Ah, already . . . Now I am slipping, going . . .
  Are the angels there?
Do you think that to find Paradise
  We must go still higher?

Do I not already hear, through the stone,
  Chaste and sweet singing?
That poor old man, standing by Porta San
    Pietro—
  Is it not you, Peter?

Festa di San Francesco

ERNEST RAYMOND

On October 4, which is kept as his feast, all roads lead to the Church of San Francesco.

At the beginning of our tale, we saw Francis seeking the outcasts: first, the odd man out in the Perugia prison, then the beggars, then the lepers of San Salvatore. And now at its end we shall find him, if an ancient tradition is true, still among the outcasts where he sleeps in San Francesco.

The tradition asserts that when he lay dying, he asked to be buried on the "Collis Infernus," a hill just outside the walls of Assisi, because it was there they executed the criminals and sometimes buried them. This "Lower Hill" was a rocky outwork of Assisi's hill, with steep or precipitous sides and a gully separating it from the western gate of the city. To any but Elias the difficulties of such a site might have seemed too great, but he by some masterly engineering, walling it about with lofty arches, one colonnade of arches imposed upon another, made it into a long headland and platform for the support of his proud basilica. On that platform, driving its foundations into the rocks, he raised San Francesco.

And San Francesco is acclaimed almost everywhere as the fairest, even as it was the first, among the Gothic cathedrals of Italy. No one has any-thing but praise for Elias as engineer, architect, artist, and organizer. Today, since the enlargement and embellishment of the crypt, it is really three churches piled one above another: first, the crypt containing the tomb of the saint, then the lower church, large as a cathedral, and then the soaring upper church, almost equal in size to the lower church, and very much loftier.

And the two higher churches are all color. Every inch of wall, every section of vaulted roof, every rib of the vaulting, are covered with frescoes. All the painters of the dawning Renaissance came to Assisi to spend themselves in honor of Francis—Giunta Pisano, Cimabue, Pietro Cavallini, Giotto, and their schools. San Francesco, if we compare the amount of priceless paintings with the compass of the building, is, I suppose, the richest treasure house of art in the world. It is the watershed from which fall the rivers of the Renaissance.

And on October 4, the Festa di San Francesco, the people who have come into Assisi from all parts pour into the basilica inferiore, or lower church. Last year at five o'clock in the evening, we were all summoned to the Piazza del Commune by the ringing of the lauds bell in the slender campanile that dominates the square. We climbed to the square through streets whose every house was hung with banners and flags. Pennons flew from the towers of the Rocca, just as they did in medieval times. And assembled in the square we found the heralds and halberdiers of Assisi in their parti-colored doublets and hose. The two colors in these pied garments were azure and rouge, the colors of the city's flag: azure for faith, and rouge for love. At their side, needless to say, stood the *pompieri*, shining with plumed helmets and brass epaulets, for no festival in Europe can be begun without the firemen. And because in this year the festa coincided with the closing of some Giotto celebrations, the heralds and halberdiers of Padua and Florence were also there, the lads of Padua in yellow and red, and those of Florence in white and red, with liripipe hats. Can you not see that the medieval piazza, with these quaint figures on its stones, made a picture by Benozzo Gozzoli?

The heralds stood on the steps of the Temple of Minerva, lifted their long trumpets to their mouths, and sounded the hymn of Assisi; and forthwith the procession began.

It was difficult to say who of the streaming people were in the procession and who were not; difficult to tell whether the heralds, *pompieri, podestà,* (the mayor), and chief burgesses were leading the march or being led and escorted by it; because, while some of us tramped with dignity behind the great men, others trotted like terriers at their sides or tacked like hounds in the van. Every few minutes the heralds pointed their trumpets toward heaven and addressed to it the call of Assisi; and so, with music and voices and running, we all trooped down the sunlit chasms of the streets to the Piazza Inferiore. And out of its brightness we passed with some disorder, and some dodging, into the long dim aisles and the quiet of the lower church.

I, I am ashamed to say, had joined the runners at an early stage so as to get into the north transept, from which I could command the greater part of the church, see the procession come in, and watch the picture take shape before me.

Soon every transept and chapel, every aisle, stairway, and side altar, was black and asway with people; and now above the heads of the multitude in the nave came the trumpets and the pikes and the banners. Heralds and halberdiers went to the left of the high altar, the *pompieri* to the right, and the *podestà* and chief men to important seats in front of it. Thus all color arranged itself about the altar, and the altar itself was brilliant with five rows of candles and with flowers heaped upon its steps.

In the apse, behind a woodwork screen, a hidden choir of friars was singing an office all the time, so that the picture took shape against a background of music.

And we waited. With reasonable quiet we waited. We waited listening to the steps and shuffle of crowds still packing into corners, listening to the singing of the brothers, looking up at the many-colored frescoes on roof and walls, and gazing round on the cramped multitude. The deep-toned bell of San Francesco rang above us, as the sun dimmed and the church darkened. It was sunset, and the hour that Francis passed from the world.

The bell stopped. A long procession of tonsured brothers in white cottas went to their places round the altar, the hidden choir burst into a new song, and a dazzling scarlet cardinal passed with his escort to the papal throne, sweeping the people around him to their knees, like a reaping machine ploughing through the wheat. And solemn vespers began.

After solemn vespers would come the function of the Transitus, or passing of Francis. Alas, my knowledge of Catholic ceremonial was not enough to tell me at what point, as the hours went by, we crossed from vespers to the Transitus. I cannot tell

you for which solemn office they began the vesting of the cardinal. All I know is that I watched this ceremony with a gaping interest.

The cardinal stood on the top step of the throne, a baldachin of red and gold above him, a carpet of red running across the "theater" to his feet, and dignified men in dress clothes on either side of him, to act as flunkys. Before him, in Indian file, stretched a long line of tonsured friars (white figures on the red carpet), each holding a different vestment for the clothing of the cardinal. These friars seemed to have been arranged by the master of the ceremonies, a portly and peripatetic brother, according to their heights, so that they looked like a row of white organ pipes. And to an accompaniment of music and singing they arrayed the garments around the cardinal, one over another, like the layers of an onion. I use this simile in my ignorance, not in my irreverence.

And it was just as the last vesture was being wrapped around him that I remembered we were celebrating a man who at his death had asked to have all his clothes removed that he might die faithful to poverty.

At first I considered this a witty reflection, till I remembered that Francis was as eager for the seemly glorification of Jesus in the churches as he was for the humiliation of Francis; and then I didn't know what to think. All his sons, hundreds of them, were watching the ceremony and seemed to see in it nothing out of key with their father's poverty. And it was certainly beautiful. It was beautiful as a ballet, but of a different order of beauty from that of Francis giving his cloak away.

Now certainly it was the Transitus. All the principal clergy were kneeling before the altar beneath which the little man lay; they were singing the psalm he sang as he passed from us; they were praying to him. One of them, standing by the altar, blessed the whole congregation with some holy relic in its reliquary. And then—magnificent moment!—the pikes and banners sprang to attention, the swords of the *pompieri* leapt to the salute, the trumpets turned upward to the roof and sang the call of Assisi, and the huge choir behind the screen, as the last silvery notes died away, burst into Francis's own song, the "Canticle of Brother Sun": *"Altissimu, omnipotente, bonsignore. . . ."*

The moment overwhelmed me with its splendor. I listened in a spell to the waves of triumphant sound sweeping between the dusky vaults of the roof and the black sea of people. I stared at the tableau about the altar: the rows of lights, the heaped

flowers, the heralds, the *pompieri*, the pikes, banners, and swords; behind the altar I saw through the open-work of the screen the arms of Padre Maestro Maria Domenico Stella conducting with Italian vehemence his packed, excited, and exulting choir; and just as I was standing agape and dumb with the grandeur of it, I chanced to turn my eyes to the left, and there—there from his place in huge fresco on the transept wall—was the author himself, gazing pointedly at me.

There, life-size in a painting attributed to Cimabue, he stood, in his ragged brown tunic and cowl, his face lined and haggard and kind, and his eyes fixed on mine. Fixed on mine (God pardon my presumption) as if he and I had an understanding! And I could have sworn that his right eye—but I suppose it was impossible. I stared back, and one thing was beyond question, that in Cimabue's fresco his left eye was wide open, while his right eye

might have been beginning or completing a—but enough of this. I say it was impossible. Manifestly.

After the cantico came Eucharistic Benediction, for our Holy Mother the Church does not spare her children, singing to them, praying for them, forgiving them, preaching to them, and blessing them; and when at last we came out of the basilica, it was night in Assisi. The night of the festa. From the top of the highest tower to the steps of the last building, Assisi was aflicker with little points of flame fanned by the breeze. Every inhabitant of Assisi had put out his chain of little flames; mostly they were homemade cressets, just wicks afloat in saucers of oil, but some were real "links" on their brackets of wrought iron. Every house was picked out in small flames. They stood in rows on every balustrade, in every loggia, on every sill, round all the fountains, along the cornices of the public buildings, and in the topmost windows of the tall campaniles. They burned along the streets where he rioted as a young man. The highest of all twinkled against the velvet sky. It is said that the brothers on Mount Alvernia look south on the night of the festa to see the lights of Assisi. The whole city was a constellation of scintillating stars—and all because a young man, once upon a time, dared to be real.

Lights overflowed the city walls on to the fairground outside the Porta Nuova, illuminating the swings, the roundabouts, the booths, and the big top where, with full appropriateness, the clowns and the tumblers, unshaven and ragged and lively, honored the Great Romantic by doing their turns in the sawdust with a virtuosity as brilliant as their motley was faded and their jokes were rude.

Do not tell me that Francis failed. The Spirit of Compromise captured his dream and pared it down; it captured his brothers whom he had wished to be a free and worldwide order of spiritual chivalry, and changed them—as it had tried to change him from the first—into good but commonplace monks; it captured his body and buried it in one of the greatest churches of Italy; it captured his dangerous life-story and put it into censored and adapted biographies; but it could not catch Francis.

Good-bye then, my master; and well done. I have left Don Quixote dead, and Sancho Panza can go home. The troubadour has gone singing to his tomb, and the tumbler may depart.

His spirit slipped through the stoutest of these walls. It broke through the cracks in the immuring biographies. It emerged to be the head of an invisible order, the order of those who, whether within or without his visible brotherhood, can see his vision in its fullness. As Angelo Clareno, one of the doughtiest of his champions in the next generation, said, "Francis is not in the name of an order, nor in walls, nor in anything outward whatsoever, but in his obedient sons and his lovers." Among these may we be counted. God knows that most of us are not his obedient sons, but we may claim a lowly place among his lovers.

And this, after all, means that he achieved exactly what in the first place he set out to do: he preached by his life, which is the best way, the most effective Christian sermon that has ever been preached;

a sermon that still, after all the centuries, works its gentle ferment and attains its design, because if in reading it we learn to love Francis, we must find ourselves loving also his Master and his Model. Francis succeeded; it was the others who failed. Behold the eternal paradox of the Cross: by betraying Francis and denying him and defeating him, they enabled him to rise higher, to set forth his message better, and to conquer. "No man took my life from me. I laid it down. . . ." "Daughters of Jerusalem, weep not for *me*."

Good-bye, then, my master; and well done. I have left Don Quixote dead, and Sancho Panza can go home. The troubadour has gone singing to his tomb, and the tumbler may depart. I left Assisi the next morning.

Opening the Tomb of Saint Francis

VITALE BOMMARCO, O.F.M.CONV.

On December 10, 1818, the body of Saint Francis was at long last discovered under the main altar of the middle church of the Basilica of Saint Francis in Assisi. During the next six years the crypt area of the basilica was created; during this period, the body of St. Francis remained outside the sarcophagus in the sacristy. On October 4, 1824, after all the work was completed, the body of Saint Francis was placed in a metal casket, gold lined, and then positioned inside the original sarcophagus again. The casket was closed with two special keys, and the sarcophagus was simply covered with a wooden plank. On the top of this were three metal bands with the official seal of the bishop and the Minister General. And on top of this was replaced the original grille that Friar Elias of Cortona had originally used to safeguard the body of Saint Francis when it was buried in the basilica almost seven hundred fifty years ago.

Elias had really sealed the tomb perfectly because he had the grille and the sarcophagus covered with twelve bands of metal. These were sawed in order to be able to open it in 1818, but they were not welded back together until 1824. So what happened over this period of time? With this type of situation, the tomb of Saint Francis was, as it were, in the middle of a chimney. There were air drafts from the crypt to the middle basilica. And there was an opening from above, so that every time the middle basilica was cleaned, dirt and dust kept falling through over this period of a hundred and some years. Furthermore, the brothers would occasionally try to clean the tomb and would lift the grille; more dirt in the tomb. In the meantime, two of the three seals were broken.

The time came when something had to be done about this situation. We wanted to make sure that nobody would be able to go and disturb the remains of Saint Francis because the tomb was still unsealed. At this rate, something could happen! We wanted to reweld these twelve bands the way Elias had done originally. This was the motivating cause for the action taken earlier this year. Another reason was to examine the condition of the remains. We knew from documents that the bones had been in a sort of humid condition for nearly six hundred years before they were discovered in 1818—humidity, you might say, eating away at them. For the last one hundred fifty years the bones had been elevated in such a position that they were "aerated" or dried out, since they were in this wind tunnel, a chimneylike passageway that was the driest place in the basilica. So then, we asked ourselves—and asked the Holy Father—since we had to replace the seals and weld the tomb back together, why not examine the condition of the bones to see whether any process of deterioration could be stopped?

In January of 1977 the Holy Father created a special commission—three cardinals, two bishops, and I. In our preliminary meetings we discussed what was to be done and how we were to proceed. We made on-the-spot visits to Assisi and chose a doctor to be part of the commission. And that brought us up to January 1978. Throughout this whole period the Holy Father insisted on being continually informed of the proceedings. Precisely because of the injunction of the Holy Father to maintain absolute silence, not even the friars of the basilica knew what was going on until January 23, 1978.

On the evening of January 24, the basilica was locked, the community was assembled, the Ministers General of the four branches of the Order were invited along with all the Ministers Provincial of Umbria and the guardian of the Portiuncula. The tomb of Saint Francis was opened. The casket was removed and taken in procession by the Ministers General to a special room. In that room twenty

people remained—the actual commission, the Ministers General, and the Provincials.

The casket was opened, and in it was found the document in excellent condition, as if it had been placed there a day or two previously. The bones of Saint Francis found therein were enveloped in a long piece of silk cloth. The outside of the casket looked oxidized because it was either bronze or zinc. The inside was in excellent condition; it was gilded.

Everyone, including the Ministers General, was surprised to find so many bones intact, because they all expected to find much less—more dust than bones. The bones were very varied and very coarse; one could see a type of dust, almost as if they were gradually disintegrating within the casket. This was the result of the meteorological extremes—too humid for six hundred years and then too dry for the following one hundred fifty years. The very rapid change from very humid to very dry created something like an explosion. One could see this in the tibia, as though it had burst apart like a banana being peeled.

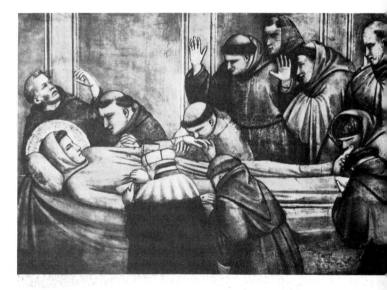

The official document had all the bones allocated and identified with their technical names. The commission decided that the bones, after being treated, would be replaced in a type of plexiglass container, hermetically sealed, and the air taken out by forcing in a neutral gas, in order to avoid the extremes of humidity and dryness and cold and heat. Prior to this, all the bones were to be immersed in a bath of alcohol mixed with a disinfecting chemical.

The bones were laid out to dry (they had to be

dry before they could be placed into the plexiglass) and eventually rearranged into the skeletal form they would naturally have.

For the last week or so the remains were on exposition to the people of Assisi in one of the chapter halls of the basilica. They did not give the impression of just a corpse or anything like that. Rather, the remains gave the impression of a very poor, small man who had a tremendously large heart. St. Francis was no more than five feet tall.

The bones gave evidence that this little poor man lived a very mortified life; a pronounced lack of calcium in the bones was evident. In opposition to some press reports, there was no evidence of malnutrition or tuberculosis. . . .

On Saturday, March 4, 1978, the remains of Saint Francis were placed back into the tomb in the crypt of the basilica. While the investigation of the bones was carried out, the crypt was cleaned and certain things repaired. They took out the grille that Friar Elias had placed over the tomb and that hadn't been touched for seven centuries; it was polished and rust-proofed.

Incidentally, it was ingenious how Friar Elias conceived the whole burial of Saint Francis. The sarcophagus, all solid rock, weighs about 200 pounds. Over it was the grill weighing about 190 pounds. Then there were the 10 arms of iron and a large circular one binding them all together; these were welded together. On top of this grille, once it was placed in the grave, he placed a big stone. On top of that was placed gravel and a stuccolike material. Then atop of this was another slab of granite. No wonder no one was able to find the body of Saint Francis for 6 centuries! Friar Elias did all this because at the time of the burial the cities used to fight over the relics of the saints. Perugia had plans to steal the body of Francis; so Elias went to all this trouble to make sure no one would find the remains and steal them.

R. Powell OFM.

His Continuing Influence

A Fourth Order?

ERNEST RAYMOND

And as I stood there thinking this, the fancy came to me that there cleaves always to Francis, whether he approves or not, a Fourth Order. It is the Order of those who do not abjure their fighting and their oaths, who cannot abandon their comfort or their fame, who still like the top table at the feasts and are not in the least eager to return their excess profits, but who, in spite of all this weakness, love Francis of Assisi and wish they were more like him. Perhaps they even, in a small way, limp after him, loose fellows though they are. They look wistfully after his disappearing figure, and wish they were not so like Brother Fly, in that they do not pray too much nor work too hard, but do eat bravely. The Limping Quaternaries, shall we call them? I have been a member of the Order for a long time, limping on as well as I may; and I suspect that most of my readers are members too, or I should have lost them long before this. God bless them all, and lead them on to better things.

The Persistence of Saint Francis's Ideals

JOHN R. MOORMAN

The fact that, in England alone, a new life of Saint Francis of Assisi appears almost every year, and that there are now in circulation at least a dozen learned periodicals devoted entirely to Franciscan history, is some indication of the unique place that the saint and his Order hold in the interest and affection of the modern world.

This is due partly to the wealth of material that has survived; but it is also due to the peculiar nature of Saint Francis's life and work. For we owe to Saint Francis a particular form of Christian dis-cipleship, an interpretation of the dominical teaching, which made a deep impression not only upon the Church of his day but also upon all succeeding centuries. What might be called the Franciscan Way was described by the saint's companion, Leo, in these terms:

> The most holy father was unwilling that his friars should be desirous of knowledge and books, but he willed and preached to them that they should desire to be founded on holy *Humility,* and to imitate pure *Simplicity,* holy *Prayer,* and our Lady *Poverty,* on which the saints and first friars did build. And this, he used to say, was the only safe way to one's own salvation and the edification of others, since Christ, to whose imitation we are called, showed and taught us this alone by word and example alike.

. . . in England alone, a new life of Saint Francis appears almost every year. . . .

Humility, Simplicity, Poverty, and Prayer are the four foundation stones on which Saint Francis built; and each was worked out on the basis of a literal obedience to the recorded sayings of Christ. It was this uncompromising challenge that drew large numbers of people to follow him into the hardships and dangers that such a way of life would inevitably contain. Scholars, explorers, poets, mystics, and evangelists all found in this adventurous way of living an inspiration that nothing else could provide. Within St. Francis's lifetime thousands had come under the spell of his holiness, some to be enrolled in the Order of Friars Minor, some to enter the convents of Poor Clares, and some to adopt a simpler Rule of life as members of the Third Order of Penitents.

But the very success of the Franciscan experiment led to difficulties. A way of life that was feasible for a small band of reckless enthusiasts under the leadership of a man of genius, became quite impossible when the leader was dead and the Order had spread far and wide. In this expansion and in the changing conditions in which men lived, some adaptation of the standards that Francis himself had set up became inevitable; and those in authority in the Church saw it as their duty to help the

Order to fit itself to meet the demands laid upon it. In so doing, it appeared to some that the ideal was in danger of being lost sight of; and the history of the Friars Minor is the story of a long struggle to find a way in which the particular "Franciscan" way of life could be fitted into the general work of the Church.

A New Form of Religious Life

P. POURRAT

It will be noticed that the Friar Minor, as understood by the poor man of Assisi, had not much resemblance to the Benedictine or Cistercian monk.

He was in the beginning a religious quite outside the traditional system, without novitiate, who did not recite the ecclesiastical office, and who went about from village to village preaching repentance and peace.

He was in the beginning a religious quite outside the traditional system, without novitiate, who did not recite the ecclesiastical office, and who went about from village to village preaching repentance and peace. Francis had not the intention of founding a new Order, and he was rather frightened by the rapidity with which the Minors multiplied. He would have been incapable of disciplining and organizing the immense religious movement that his burning soul had excited if he had not had as counselor and guide Cardinal Ugolino, the future Pope Gregory IX.

In reality, his first idea was to form traveling preachers, men practicing the Gospel literally, and going, two by two, like the disciples of Jesus (Luke 10:1), to preach peace and repentance to the world. Francis was one of these preachers. He began all his sermons by the peaceful greeting: *Dominus det vobis pacem* (The Lord give you peace). It was our Lord himself who showed him how to go about it in this way, and he obliged his disciples to do the same.

The Franciscan preachers preached in the churches; more often in public places or at the corners of streets. First of all they caused astonishment. But soon their message of peace, delivered by men who had voluntarily stripped themselves of everything, produced an extraordinary impression. There was a much-felt need of peace at that time in Italy, divided as it was, between the Guelphs and the Ghibellines, the party of the Pope and that of the Emperor. The towns were almost always at war with each other and torn asunder internally by rival factions. The preaching of Francis was remarkably effective in procuring the cessation of enmity, bringing about reconciliations, and producing startling and numerous conversions. There was also a great personal devotion to him. Men and women in crowds ran after him and considered it a happiness to touch his habit.

It is difficult for us to picture the enthusiasm that the Franciscan sermons produced. Friaries of Friars Minor sprang into being on every side. Even more, both clergy and laity came to ask of Francis rules of life, in order to follow the precepts of the Gospel in the world and work out their salvation. He gave counsel to all, and pointed out to each one the course he should follow in order to get to heaven. Such was the origin of the Third Order, or, as it was then called, the Brotherhood of Penitence.

The Brothers and Sisters of Penitence were called upon to live in great harmony with all, a harmony that at that time was greatly needed. They retained their possessions and remained in the world, in the state in which Providence had placed them. But they had to perform alms deeds as often as possible, to practice inwardly renunciation, and to pray. It was, in a measure, the religious life adapted to the secular state.

Greccio: Origin of the Drama

JAMES J. WALSH

The last place in the world, perhaps, that one would look for a great impulse to the development of the modern drama, which is entirely a new invention, an outgrowth of Christian culture, and has practically no connection with the classic drama, would be in the life of Saint Francis of Assisi. His utter simplicity, his thoroughgoing and cordial poverty, his sincere endeavor all during his life to make little of himself, might seem quite enough to forbid any thought of him as the father of a literary movement of this kind. "The poor little man of God," however, as he liked to call himself, in his supreme effort to get back to nature and out of the ways of the conventional world, succeeded in accomplishing a number of utterly unexpected results. His love for nature led to his wonderful expression of his feelings in his favorite hymn, one of the first great lyrical outbursts in modern poetry, a religious poem that . . . Renan declares can be appreciated properly only by comparing it with the old Hebrew psalms, beside which it is worthy to be placed.

It should not be such a surprise as it might otherwise be, then, to find that Saint Francis may be considered in one sense as father of the modern drama.

Those who know the life of Saint Francis best will easily appreciate how dramatic, though unconsciously so, were all the actions of his life. After all, his utter renunciation of all things, his taking of holy poverty to be his bride, his address to the birds, his sisters, his famous question of the butcher as to why he killed his brothers, the sheep, his personification of the sun and the moon and even of the death of the body as his brothers and sisters, are all eminently dramatic moments. His life is full of incidents that lent themselves, because of their dramatic quality, to the painters of succeeding centuries as the subjects of their striking pictures. Before the end of the century Giotto had picked out some of the most interesting of these for the decorative illustration of the upper church at Assisi. During the succeeding century, the author of the *Little Flowers of Saint Francis* embodied many of these beautiful scenes in his little work, where they have been the favorite reading of poets for many centuries since.

It should not be such a surprise as it might otherwise be, then, to find that Saint Francis may be considered in one sense as the father of the modern drama. The story is a very pretty one and has an additional value because it has been illustrated by no less a brush than that of Giotto. One Christmas Eve, just at the beginning of the thirteenth century, Saint Francis gathered round him some of the poor people living outside of the town of Greccio,

in order to recall vividly to them the great event that had taken place on that night so many centuries before.

A little figure of a child, dressed in swaddling clothes, was laid on some straw in a manger with the breath of the nearby animals to warm it. To this manger throne of the Child King of Bethlehem, there came in adoration, after the hymns that recalled the angels' visit, first some of the shepherds from the surrounding country and then some of the country people representing the kings from the East with their retinues and bringing with them their royal gifts. After this little scene, probably one of the first Nativity plays that had ever been given, Saint Francis, according to the old legend, took the little image in his arms and in an excess of devotion pressed it to his heart. According to the old-time story, the infant came to life in his embrace and, putting its little arms around his neck, embraced him in return.

Of course our modern generation is entirely too devoted to "common sense" to accept any such pretty, pious story as this as more than a beautiful poetic legend. The legend has provided a subject for poet and painter many a time in subsequent centuries. Perhaps never has it been used with better effect than by Giotto, whose representation is one of the favorite pictures on the wall in the upper church of Assisi. Whether the little baby figure of the play actually came to life in his arms or not we do not know, but one thing is certain, that infant modern dramatic literature did come to life at the moment and that before the end of the thirteenth century it was to have a vigor and an influence that made it one of the great factors in the social life of the period. The Franciscans were soon spread over the world. With filial reverence they took with them all the customs of their loved Father of Assisi, and especially such as appealed to the masses and brought home to them in a vivid way the great truths of religion. By the middle of the century many of the towns had cycles of mystery plays given at various times during the year, associated with the different feasts and illustrating and enforcing the lessons of the liturgy for the people in a manner so effective that it has probably never been equaled before or since.

While the most potent factor in the dissemination of the early religious drama can be traced to Francis and the Franciscans, they were but promoters of a movement already well begun. Mystery plays were attempted before the thirteenth century in England and in North France. . . .

Saint Francis in Art

REINHOLD SCHNEIDER

Francis woos every age, as Christ does, Christ the "great king" whose "poor herald" Francis was—and woos like him as a man scorned, mishandled, beaten, and offered up. A sign pointing to Christ, the saint of Assisi, with his high endowment of divine grace and his power to transform the world, was nevertheless in himself nothing but this sign, pointing to Christ. Who dares say where his path leads? No one has followed it to the end; all give up sooner or later. But by choosing it a man comes to understand and love all creatures. He will be marked by his love for creation, by sympathy for the semisaved and patiently waiting part of it.

Where this path leads, a man becomes incapable of harming any living thing because of Christ through whom it was created. It is the path to a life that appears impossible and yet may be the nearest thing we have to the Gospel itself, or at least an ineffable attempt to realize it in practice, regardless of cost in suffering and endurance, letting come what may, be it grace or truth, be it truth against truth! Only those actually on this path can have any real idea of it. It is the grain of corn seed that never loses its germinating power even when capsuled in worldly wisdom. The saints are pioneers; they break new ground, and none of them ever intended that we should gather round where they left off. It was not their concern to serve as models for other men but to be a reflection and imitation of their own supreme model. Our part—incredible as it may seem—is to go ahead where they left off.

The road the saint of Assisi took remains open. No power can close it. We are equipped for it and cannot be stopped if the true picture of Francis lives in us: Francis, for whom it was the greatest honor to be greeted by the Lady Poverty, who found his mission in limitless self-sacrifice, and who has something about him of those unknown witnesses through whom Christ is to be manifest during the horrors attendant on the end of the world. This trait, the prophetic one, is what brings him nearest to us today, hourly and daily our wise and helpful brother in need. Among our ruins we catch a glimpse of his shadowy upright figure; he is our companion on all our ways, present in prayer in the night of our death. However briefly we encounter him, we know how true the legend is of the cup he left behind in a solitary cell, how bees settled in it and filled it with honey.

From all the many pictures that exist of Francis and his world, we learn a good deal of the way forms of piety change with the times. His main characteristic was his nearness to Christ, and the painters of his portraits will attempt to convey this. There arises the difficult question of how far art can be effective here and how its function is to be understood.

The oldest portrait we know—the fresco in Sacro Speco, Subiaco—was made shortly after the saint's death (in 1228 according to Thode's conjecture) in commemoration of Francis's visit to St. Benedict's hermitage to honor the founder of Western monasticism. From the historical point of view a good likeness is less interesting than the picture in men's minds. It may well be that art is attempting the impossible when it tries to depict the saint of Assisi: he unites so many contraries!—humility and power, innocence and experience, joy and bitter sorrow, audacity and scrupulousness, nobility and poverty ("his garment was dirty, his person contemptible, his countenance unlovely," runs a report from Bologna in 1220). Add to this his capacity for love and his incidental harshness, his liking for popular devotions and for the strictest form of early Christian monasticism. How can art cope with all this?

It was art that conveyed to posterity the idea of the saint as a star in the east, heralding the rise of a new age.

But something that applies in Christian living applies also in art: an ideal arises that is to all appearances humanly irreducible, and yet by grace it finds its niche in the year's round, bears fruit, transforms the world. So in art: in the endeavor to find a satisfactory form for St. Francis and for what we term Franciscan, art attained to such luminosity and spirituality, such knowledge of men's souls and such power of expression, such illumination of minds, such love of creatures and landscape, that we can see no end to its potentialities. It was art that conveyed to posterity the idea of the saint as a star in the east, heralding the rise of a new age. It is true he would never have countenanced nor understood such enhancing of his person—one can imagine his blaze of fury, consigning all such

works to utter destruction as he did the house at Portiuncula.

In our selection of pictures we wanted to keep as close to the saint as possible, leaving out any that tend to show him too weak or too worldly or too insipid for the truth, even when painted by famous artists. A few pictures belonging to the last phase of the Middle Ages will show how he lived on in the conception of the peoples of Europe. The German fifteenth-century master has caught a true aspect of him, with our Lord's Passion exposed in all its human tragedy as the very core of Franciscan piety: Francis kneeling before the pillar of the mocking and scourging, rather than before the throne of the king of the world. El Greco's study is highly spiritualized, showing him noble in his poverty and inner serenity, his wisdom and renunciation. We include necessarily that master painter of poverty, Rembrandt. Francis is one of his very few nonbiblical saints; he has made him Flemish, transferring him from Umbrian light to pregnant shadow, the sole light coming from the book exalted by Rembrandt's preachers—illuminating those Dutch interiors. The saint is on his knees and does not appear to be reading; his gaze is turned inward, as he contemplates the cross with the body of his Lord. Book and crucifix, tokens of a divided Christianity, unite in Francis.

The earlier pictures describe his life devoted to preaching and missionary activity. Art followed the records and reproduced them faithfully, depicting man and God's grace at one in the work. The scenes are self-explanatory, almost biblical, and they are of such force that there is little to add. Only this: in these dramatic clashes with the world, what is at stake is the reversing of worldly values for the restoration of their original intention. The saint appears on the scene at the moment when the kingdom of God is about to erupt into the visible order of things—with the reenacting of the Passion.

Saint Francis and Art

WILLIAM FLEMING

While opposing, systems of logic were being argued in the universities, the Friars of Saint Francis were bringing his message to town and country folk. With them, religious devotion became a voluntary, spontaneous relationship between man and God rather than an imposed obligation, an act based on love rather than on fear. The Franciscans also sought to establish a common bond between a man, whatever his station in life, and his fellow men—an important shift from the vertical feudal organization of society in which men were related to those above and below them by a hierarchical authority, to a horizontally oriented ethical relationship that bound man to his fellow men.

Saint Francis everywhere saw evidence of God's love in everything, from the fruits and flowers of the earth to the winds and the clouds in the sky—a concept that was to have great consequences for the course of art. The birds to which Saint Francis preached, for instance, were the birds that were heard chirping and singing every day, not the symbolic dove of the Holy Ghost or the apocalyptical eagle of Saint John. While this tendency toward naturalism was already noticeable in the thirteenth-century sculpture of Chartres and elsewhere, it became widespread in the fourteenth century. As this view of the natural world gained ascendance over the supernatural, based as it was on concrete observation rather than on metaphysical speculation, it released the visual arts from the perplexing problems of how to represent the unseen. The love of Saint Francis for his fellow-men and for such simple things as grass and trees, which could be represented as seen in nature, opened up new vistas for artists to explore.

Saint Francis's message was taught in parables and simple images of life that all could understand, and Giotto succeeded in translating these into pictorial form. In this favorable naturalistic climate, he found his balance between the abstract and the concrete, between divine essence and human reality. By refraining from placing his accent on symbolism, Giotto moved away from medieval mysticism and in his pictures portrayed understandable human situations. To him, the saints were not remote transcendental spirits but human beings, who felt all the usual emotions from joy to despair, just as did the people in the Italian towns he knew so well. Now that he no longer had to be concerned mainly with allegories but could reproduce the world of objects and actions as he saw it, a new pathway was opened. Even his contemporaries could see that Giotto was blazing new trails. Yet when they extolled him for his faithfulness to nature, their praise must be measured by the art that had preceded his time rather than by fifteenth-century or later standards. While Giotto undoubtedly showed a love of nature as such, he never accented it to the point where it might weaken his primary human emphasis. His interest was less in nature for its own sake than in its meaning in the lives of his subjects.

In viewing a Giotto picture, one does well to begin with his people and be concerned only secondarily with their natural surroundings, because his pictures are in psychological rather than in linear perspective. His subjects seem to create their own environment by their expressive attitudes and dramatic deployment. While his work shows an increasing preoccupation with problems of natural space, this space remains subordinate to his expressive intentions, and his use of color and shading gives his human figures the sense of depth and volume that brings them to life. In this way, both human nature and nature as such attain an intimate and distinctive identity in Giotto's pictorial conceptions.

Long before, Cluny * had changed the character of monasticism by uniting cloistered life with feudalism. Now the new orientation of the Franciscan order was no less revolutionary. St. Francis did not confine his friars in cloisters but sent them forth as fishers of men. The idea of evangelical poverty, humility, and love for mankind expressed through living and working with simple people resulted in a union with, rather than a withdrawal from, society. The Franciscans did not shun the world so much as they shunned worldly pursuits, and, as G. K. Chesterton has remarked, what Saint Benedict had stored, Saint Francis scattered. The Cluniacs were, in the proper sense of the word, an order—that is, a strict hierarchical organization. The Franciscans, by contrast, were, in every sense of the word, a movement.

The icy intellectualism of the medieval universities was bound to thaw in the warmth of Franciscan emotionalism.

The icy intellectualism of the medieval universities was bound to thaw in the warmth of Franciscan emotionalism. Asceticism and self-denial held little appeal for an increasingly prosperous urban middle class. The mathematical elegance of Gothic structurality began to yield to more informal types of buildings. The logical linear patterns of the surviving Byzantine pictorial style gave way to the expressive warmth of Giotto's figures, and the vac-

* Referring to a Catholic monastic order founded by William I of Aquitaine and the monk Berno in 910 at the Benedictine abbey of Cluny, France.

uous stylized faces of Byzantine saints pale in the light of the human tenderness found in a smiling mouth or tearful eye in a Giotto picture. The formal architectural sculpture and abstract patterns of Gothic stained glass were replaced by the colorful informality of mural paintings in fresco. St. Francis in his music, as in his religious work, drew the sacred and popular traditions closer together, and in the lauds he encouraged people to sing; he gave them a music that they could feel in their hearts without having to understand with their brains.

The Roots of Saint Francis's Poetry

FREDERICK OZANAM

A country must not only be beautiful and fertile; it must also be rich in historical associations to produce great men. This preparation was not wanting in Italy at the very end of the twelfth century.

The second conflict between the papacy and the empire had just ended gloriously, under the leadership of Alexander III. It had resulted in liberty, power, and glory—all that most nearly concerns the people, that inspires them, and gives them the right and the desire to immortalize themselves in its monuments. All the arts awoke. The religious and political ideals that had led the Italians to the fields of battle for a hundred years were to be pursued by word as they had been pursued by arms. If they were to move the heart of the people it was necessary for them to be expressed, not in the idioms of scholars, but in homely language, and after having formed a nation to found a literature. An example was ready at hand. The poetry of France had already crossed the Alps; her songs were sung in the castle halls and in the public squares. If these models were not entirely without blemish, if the fabliaux of the trouvères and the irreverent sirventes of many of the troubadours were addressed to the dissolute, there were also pious lays like those of Rambaud of Vaqueiras, heroic legends such as the battles of Charlemagne and the death of Roland, quite capable of kindling the imaginations of Christians. Undoubtedly political activity and literary intercourse were more rife in the Lombard towns, which had

129

borne the chief brunt of the war and had gathered the first fruits of peace.

Nevertheless the cities of Umbria had not been the last to rally under the banner of papacy and liberty. They hastened to confirm their victory by showing their sovereignty, by fortifying themselves, and by raising troops. Assisi had her nobles, her soldiers whom she sent to make war on Perugia. She had also merchants who carried their trade be-

yond the Alps, and who brought back great profits and some useful information. In this way a cloth-seller called Pietro Bernardone, having visited France in 1182, and finding on his return that his wife had presented him with a son, named him Francis in memory of the beautiful country where he had just made large profits. The humble merchant little thought that this name of his own invention would be invoked by the Church and borne by kings.

"Whatever merit there is in these writings belongs neither to paganism nor to humanity but to God alone, who is the author of all good."

The young Francis, entrusted at an early age to the priests of the Church of Saint Giorgio, had received from them the elements of the humane sciences. He is too often represented, as he depicted himself, as a man without culture and without knowledge. He retained from his short studies enough Latin to understand readily the holy books, and a genuine respect for letters. This was not one of the joys he abandoned after his conversion. He cherished it to such a degree that if he found on the road a scrap of writing, he picked it up carefully for fear of trampling on the name of the Savior, or on some passage that treated of divine matters. And, when one of his followers asked him why he picked up pagan writings with equal care, he replied, "My son, it is because I find in them letters that compose the glorious name of God." And he completed his thought by adding: "Whatever merit there is in these writings belongs neither to paganism nor to humanity but to God alone, who is the author of all good." And, indeed, what are all the sacred and profane literatures but the characters with which God imprints his name on the human mind, as he imprints it on the heavens with the stars?

However, the literary education of Saint Francis was accomplished less by classical studies, to which he devoted little time, than by the French language, which was already esteemed in Italy as the most melodious of all, and as the preserver of the traditions of chivalry that softened the uncouthness of the Middle Ages. He had a secret attraction for that country of France to which he owed his name; he loved her language; though he expressed himself in it haltingly, he spoke it with his brothers. He made the neighboring woods resound with French canticles. He was to be seen, in the early days of his penitence, begging in French on the steps of Saint Peter's at Rome, or while he was hard at work rebuilding the Church of San Damiano, addressing the inhabitants and passers-by in French, invoking them to raise up the house of God.

If he borrowed the French idiom, if he gained inspiration from French poetry, he found in it sentiments of courtesy and generosity that took root in his heart and were revealed in his actions. He was the life of the joyous bands that were formed there under the name of *corti* in the town of Assisi as throughout Italy, and which popularized the frivolity, the romantic customs, the sensuous pleasures of the Provençals. Often his companions, captivated by his chivalrous manners, chose him for their leader and, as they expressed it, for the lord of their banquets. When they saw him pass by in rich apparel, with staff of office in his hand, surrounded by his friends who roamed the streets each evening with torches and singing songs, the crowd would admire him and proclaim him as "the flower of the nobility."

He himself took literally the noisy flatteries murmured on his path. This merchant's son who impoverished his father by his bounty did not give up hope of becoming a great prince, and books of chivalry told him of no adventures he had not dreamed of.

At first he conceived the idea of conquering his principality with lance in hand, of attaching himself to the suite of Walter de Brienne, who was about to reclaim from Frederick III the beautiful kingdom of Sicily.

Then it was that he had a mysterious vision. He saw himself in the middle of a superb palace, filled with arms and rich accoutrements; glistening shields were hanging on the walls, and when he asked who was the owner of this castle and armor, he was told that all would belong to him and his knights. We need not suppose that later the servant of God forgot this dream, or that he did not see anything more in it than a delusion of an evil mind; he recognized in it a warning from heaven and thought to interpret it by instituting that religious life of the Brothers Minor, which was in his eyes like a knight-errantry, established, as the other had been, to redress wrongs and to defend the weak.

This comparison pleased him, and when he wished to praise those of his followers whom he fa-vored on account of their zeal and sanctity, he said, "These are my paladins of the Round Table." Like a true knight, he had to respond to the call of the Crusades. In 1220 he crossed over the sea and joined the army of the Christians at Damietta. Bolder than all those knights encased in armor, he forced his way right up to the Sultan of Egypt, preached the faith publicly, and challenged the priests of Muhammad in the ordeal by fire. At last he departed, having won the respect of the infidels, and left in the holy places a colony of his followers, who established themselves there under the name of Fathers of the Holy Land, and who are there still as guardians of the Holy Sepulcher and of the sword of Godfrey. After that, it is not surprising that the biographies of Saint Francis ascribe to him all the merits of military glory, and that St. Bonaventure, when he had nearly finished the account of the life and combats of his master, cried:

And now, valorous soldier of Christ, bear the arms of that unconquerable chief who will put your enemies to flight. Hoist the banner of the King Most High; at sight of it the courage of all the fighters in the heavenly host will be revived. That prophetic vision is now accomplished, according to which, O Captain of Christ's soldiers, you were destined to don the heavenly armor.

But, as all true knights were devoted to the service of some lady, Francis had to choose his. Indeed, a few days before his conversion, his friends, finding him rapt in thought, asked him if he were thinking of taking a wife, and he replied: "It is true. I am contemplating taking the noblest, richest, and most beautiful lady that ever lived." This was the description he gave of his ideal of all perfection, the type of all moral beauty, namely Poverty. He loved to personify this virtue according to the symbolic genius of his time; he imagined her as a heavenly damsel whom he called in turn the lady of his thoughts, his betrothed, his spouse. He bestowed on her all the power that the troubadours attributed to the noble ladies celebrated in their poems— the power of wresting from the souls captivated by her all worldly thoughts and inclinations, of elevating such souls to the society of the angels. But while with the troubadours these Platonic loves were merely witticisms, the invisible beauty that had ravished Saint Francis wrung from him the most impassioned cries. Open any of the medieval poets, and you will find no song bolder, no words more impassioned, than this prayer of the penitent of Assisi:

O my most sweet Lord Jesus Christ, have pity on me and on my Lady Poverty, for I burn with love of her, and without her I cannot rest. O my Lord, who didst cause me to be enamored of her, thou knowest that she is sitting in sadness, rejected by all; "the mistress of nations is become as a widow," vile and contemptible; the queen of all virtues, seated on a dunghill, complains that all her friends have despised her, and are become her enemies—they have proved themselves deceivers, and not spouses. Behold, O Lord Jesus! how truly Poverty is the queen of all the virtues; for, leaving the abode of angels, thou didst come down to earth that thou mightest espouse her to thyself with constant love, and produce from her, in her, and by her, the children of all perfection. . . . At thy birth she received thee in a manger and a stable; and during thy life she so stripped thee of all things that she would not even allow thee a stone whereon to rest thy head. As a most faithful consort she accompanied thee when thou didst go forth to fight for our Redemption; and in the conflict of thy Passion she alone stood by as thy armor-bearer; when thy disciples fled, and denied thy Name, she did not leave thee, but with the whole band of her princes, she fearlessly adhered to thee. On account of the height of thy Cross, even thy Mother (who devotedly loved thee, and shared so deeply in the bitterness of thy Passion could not reach thee; but thy Lady Poverty, with companion Want, embraced thee more closely than ever, and was more firmly united to thee in thy sufferings. Therefore she would not allow thy Cross to be smoothed or in any way polished; the very nails were (as it is believed) too few in number, not sharpened nor ground; but she provided only three—blunt, thick, and rough—in order to increase thy torments. And when thou wast consumed with thirst, she, thy faithful spouse, was there, and did not allow thee to have even a drop of water; but by means of the impious executioners she prepared for thee a draught so bitter that thou couldst only taste, not drink it. In the strong embrace of this thy spouse, thou didst breathe forth thy Soul. Nor did she forsake thee at thy burial, but she took care that thou shouldst have neither sepulcher, nor ointments, nor winding-clothes, except what were lent thee by others.

This thy holy spouse was not absent from thy Resurrection, for rising gloriously in her embrace thou didst leave in the sepulcher all these borrowed things. Thou didst bear her with thee to heaven, leaving all that is in the world. And now thou hast given to thy Lady Poverty the seal of thy kingdom, that she may sign the elect who walk in the way of perfection. Oh! who would not love the Lady Poverty above all! I beseech thee to grant me this privilege: I beg to be enriched with this much-desired treasure. O most poor Jesus, I ask this favor for myself and my children forever, that for love of thee they may never possess anything of their own, that they may use the goods of others sparingly, and that they may suffer Poverty as long as they live in this miserable world. Amen.

132

The Father of the Renaissance

JAMES J. WALSH

The Renaissance is often thought of as a movement that originated about the middle of the fifteenth century. Careful students sometimes trace its origin back somewhat farther. In recent years it has come to be realized, however, that the great intellectual development that came in Italy during the century after the fall of Constantinople, and gradually spread to all the civilized countries of Europe, had been preparing for at least two and a half centuries. Although the period from the middle of the fifteenth to the end of the sixteenth centuries well deserves the name of Renaissance, because one of the most important fructifying principles of the movement was the rebirth of Greek ideas into the modern world after the dispersion of Greek scholars by the Turkish advance into the Byzantine Empire, the term must not be allowed to carry with it the mistaken notion, which only too often has been plausibly accepted, that there was a new birth of poetic, literary, and esthetic ideas at this time, just as if there had been nothing worth considering in these lines before.

Undoubtedly the leader in that great return to nature, which constitutes the true basis of modern poetic and artistic ideas of all kinds, was Saint Francis of Assisi.

Any such notion as this would be the height of absurdity in the light of the history of the previous centuries in Italy. It was a cherished notion of the people of the Renaissance themselves that they were the first to do artistic and literary work; hence they invented the term *Gothic,* meaning thereby barbarous, for the art of the preceding time, but in this they were only exercising that amusing self-complacency that each generation deems its right. Succeeding generations adopting their depreciative term have turned it into one of glory so that Gothic art is now in highest honor.

Fortunately in recent years there has come, as we have said, a growing recognition of the fact that the real beginning of modern art lies much farther back in history, and that the real father of the Italian Renaissance is a man whom very few people in the last three centuries have appreciated at his true worth. Undoubtedly the leader in that great return to nature, which constitutes the true basis of modern poetic and artistic ideas of all kinds, was Saint Francis of Assisi.

"The poor little man of God," as in his humility he loved to call himself, would surely be the last one to suspect that he should ever come to be thought of as the initiator of a great movement in literature and art. Such he was, however, in the highest sense of the term, and, because of the modern appreciation of him in this regard, publications concerning him have been more frequent during the last ten years than with regard to almost any other single individual. We have under our hand at the present moment what by no means claims to be a complete bibliography of Saint Francis's life and work; yet we can count no less than thirty different works in various languages (not reckoning translations separate from the originals) that have issued from the press during the last ten years alone. This gives some idea of present-day interest in St. Francis.

It must not be thought, however, that it is only in our time that these significant tributes have been paid him. Much of his influence in literature and art, as well as in life, was recognized by the southern nations all during the centuries since his death. That it is only during the last century that other nations have come to appreciate him better, and especially have realized his literary significance, has been their loss and that of their literatures. At the beginning of the nineteenth century, Görres, the German historian who was so sympathetic toward the Middle Ages, wrote of Saint Francis as one of the troubadours, and even did not hesitate to add that without Saint Francis at the beginning of the thirteenth century there would have been no Dante at the end. Renan, the well-known French rationalist historian and literateur, did not hesitate to proclaim Saint Francis one of the great religious poets of all time and his famous "Canticle of Brother Sun" as the greatest religious poem since the Hebrew psalms were written. It was from Renan that Matthew Arnold received his introduction to Saint Francis as a literary man, and his own studies led him to write the famous passages in the *Essays in*

Criticism, which are usually so much a source of surprise to those who think of Mr. Arnold as the rationalizing critic, rather than the sympathetic admirer of a medieval saint. . . .

It was the great body of legends that grew up about Saint Francis particularly, all of them bound up with supreme charity for one's neighbor, with love for all living creatures, even the lowliest, with the tenderest feelings for every aspect of external nature, that appealed to the painters as a veritable light in the darkness of the times. It was especially in the churches founded by the disciples of "the poor little man of Assisi" that the world saw burst forth before the end of the century the first grand flowers of that renewal of art that was to prove the beginning of modern art history. It is hard to understand what would have happened to the painters of the time without the spirit that was brought into the world by Saint Francis's beautifully simple love for all and every phase of nature around him. This it was, above all, that encouraged the return to nature that soon supplanted Oriental formalism. It was but due compensation that the greatest works of the early modern painters should have been done in Saint Francis's honor.

On Saint Francis

MATTHEW ARNOLD

In the beginning of the thirteenth century, when the clouds and storms had come, when the gay, sensuous pagan life was gone, when men were not living by the senses and understanding, when they were looking for the speedy coming of Antichrist, there appeared in Italy, to the north of Rome, in the beautiful Umbrian country at the foot of the Apennines, a figure of the most magical power and charm, Saint Francis. His century is, I think, the most interesting in the history of Christianity after its primitive age, more interesting than even the century of the Reformation; and one of the chief figures, perhaps the very chief, to which this interest attaches itself, is Saint Francis. And why? Because of the profound popular instinct that enabled him, more than any man since the primitive age, to fit religion for popular use. He brought religion to the people. He founded the most popular body of ministers of religion that has ever existed in the Church. He transformed monachism by uprooting the stationary monk, delivering him from the bondage of property, and sending him, as a mendicant friar, to be a stranger and sojourner, not in the wilderness, but in the most crowded haunts of men, to console them and to do them good. This popular instinct of his is at the bottom of his famous marriage with poverty. Poverty and suffering are the condition of the people, the multitude, the immense majority of mankind; and it was toward this *people* that his soul yearned. "He listens," it was said of him, "to those to whom God himself will not listen."

He brought religion to the people. He founded the most popular body of ministers of religion that has ever existed in the Church.

So in return, as no other man, he was listened to. When an Umbrian town or village heard of his approach, the whole population went out in joyful procession to meet him, with green boughs, flags, music, and songs of gladness. The master, who began with two disciples, could in his own lifetime (and he died at forty-four) collect to keep Whitsuntide with him, in presence of an immense multitude, five thousand of his Minorites. And thus he found fulfillment to his prophetic cry: "I hear in my ears the sound of the tongues of all the nations who shall come unto us: Frenchmen, Spaniards, Germans, Englishmen. The Lord will make of us a great people, even unto the ends of the earth."

Prose could not satisfy this ardent soul, and he made poetry. Latin was too learned for this simple, popular nature, and he composed in his mother tongue, in Italian. The beginnings of the mundane poetry of the Italians are in Sicily, at the court of kings; the beginnings of their religious poetry are in Umbria, with Saint Francis. His are the humble upper waters of a mighty stream; at the beginning of the thirteenth century it is Saint Francis; at the end, Dante. Now it happens that Saint Francis, too, like the Alexandrian songstress, has his hymn for the sun, for Adonis. "Canticle of Brother Sun," "Canticle of the Creatures"—the poem goes by both names. Like the Alexandrian hymn, it is designed for popular use, but not for use by King Ptolemy's people; artless in language, irregular in rhythm, it matches with the childlike genius that produced it, and the simple natures that loved and repeated it. . . .

It is natural that man should take pleasure in his senses. But it is natural, also, that he should take refuge in his heart and imagination from his misery. And when one thinks what human life is for the vast majority of mankind, how little of a feast for their senses it can possibly be, one understands the charm for them of a refuge offered in the heart and imagination. Above all, when one thinks what human life was like in the Middle Ages, one understands the charm of such a refuge.

Now, the poetry of Theocritus's hymn is poetry treating the world according to the demand of the senses; the poetry of Saint Francis's hymn is poetry treating the world according to the demand of the heart and imagination. The first takes the world by its outward, sensible side; the second by its inward, symbolical side. The first admits as much of the world as is pleasure-giving; the second admits the whole world, rough and smooth, painful and pleasure-giving, all alike, but all transfigured by the power of a spiritual emotion, all brought under a law of supersensual love, having its seat in the soul. It can thus even say: "Praised be my Lord for *our Sister, the Death of the Body*."

But these very words are, perhaps, an indication that we are touching upon an extreme. When we see Pompeii, we can put our finger upon the pagan sentiment in its extreme. And when we read of Mount Alvernia and the stigmata; when we read of the repulsive, because self-caused, sufferings of the end of Saint Francis's life; when we find him even saying, "I have sinned against my Brother the Ass," meaning by these words that he had been too hard upon his own body; when we find him assailed, even himself, by the doubt "whether he who had destroyed himself by the severity of his penances could find mercy in eternity," we can put our finger on the medieval Christian sentiment in its extreme. Human nature is neither all senses and understanding, nor all heart and imagination. Pompeii was a sign that for humanity at large the measure of sensualism had been overpassed; Saint Francis's doubt was a sign that for humanity at large the measure of spiritualism had been overpassed. Humanity, in its violent rebound from one extreme, had swung from Pompeii to Mount Alvernia; but it was sure not to stay there.

The Only Perfect Christian

ERNEST RENAN

Francis of Assisi possesses an extraordinary interest for religious criticism. He is, after Christ, the man who had the most limpid conscience, the most absolute naïveté, the most vivid sentiment of himself as a son of the heavenly Father. God was in a very real sense his beginning and his end. His life is a poetic madness, a perpetual intoxication with divine love. For a whole week he delighted in the song of a cicada. His eyes, clear and deep like those of a child, penetrated to the inmost secrets, those things that God conceals from the wise and reveals to the humble.

The thing that distinguishes him in his age and in every age is his complete originality. . . . His kind of piety comes solely from himself. . . . He despises nothing; he is indifferent to nothing; he loves everything. For everything he has a smile and a tear. A flower throws him into an ecstasy—in nature he sees only brothers and sisters. . . . All things for him possess meaning and beauty. We know that admirable hymn that he himself calls the "Canticle of the Creatures," the most beautiful piece of religious poetry since the Gospels and the most complete expression of modern religious feeling. . . . In it there is nothing strained as in the mode of Port Royal and the mystics of the French school of the seventeenth century, nothing exaggerated or frenzied as in the Spanish mystics.

One might say that Francis of Assisi was the only perfect Christian since Christ. . . . After Christianity itself, the Franciscan movement is the greatest popular achievement known to history.

One might say that Francis of Assisi was the only perfect Christian since Christ. His great originality lies in his having undertaken—with boundless faith and love—to carry out the program of Galilee. . . . The thesis of the *Book of the Conformities* is true. Francis really *was* a second Christ, or, rather, he was a faithful mirror of Christ. The fundamental theme of the Gospel is the vanity of earthly things, which turn man aside from the kingdom of God. This is likewise the main theme of Francis of Assisi. The bird appears to him, as to Jesus, to lead a perfect life. For a bird has no barn; it sings without ceasing; it lives by God's grace, and it wants for nothing.

After Christianity itself, the Franciscan movement is the greatest popular achievement known to history. One feels in it the simplicity of men who know only nature and what they have seen or heard in church, and who combine the whole in the freest fashion. We are a thousand miles away from Scholasticism. Francis of Assisi is virtually the only man in the Middle Ages . . . whose mind was never infected by the subtleties of the Schools.

On Francis and Franciscans

ALBERT CAMUS

THURSDAY, SEPTEMBER 9

Pisa and its men lying in front of Duomo. The Campo Santo, with its straight lines and cypress trees at all four corners. One comes to understand the quarrels of the fifteenth and sixteenth centuries —here each town is important, with its own features and profound truth. . . .

He justifies those who have a taste for happiness.

The Giotto in the Santa Croce. The inner smile of Saint Francis, lover of nature and of life. He justifies those who have a taste for happiness. A soft and delicate light on Florence. The rain is waiting and swelling up the sky. Christ in the tomb by Giottino: Mary clenching her teeth with grief. . . .

SEPTEMBER 15

In the cloister of San Francesco in Fiesole there is a little courtyard with an arcade along each side, full of red flowers, sun, and yellow and black bees.

In one corner, there is a green water sprinkler, and everywhere the humming of bees. A gentle steam seems to rise from the garden as it bakes in the heat. Sitting on the ground, I think about the Franciscans whose cells I have just visited and whose sources of inspiration I can now see. I feel clearly that if they are right then it is in the same way that I am. I know that behind the wall on which I am leaning there is a hill sloping down toward the town, and the offering of the whole of Florence with all its cypress trees.

But this splendor of the world seems to justify these men. I put all my pride in a belief that it also justifies me, and all the men of my race, who know that there is an extreme point at which poverty always rejoins the luxury and richness of the world. If they cast everything off, it is for a greater and not for another life. This is the only meaning that I can accept of a term like "stripping oneself bare." "Being naked" always has associations of physical liberty, of harmony between the hand and the flowers it touches, of a loving understanding between the earth and men who have been freed from human things. Ah, I should become a convert to this if it were not already my religion.

Fascism Takes Francis as Patron Saint

ANNE O'HARE McCORMICK

Not by chance in new Italy does the beginning of the Franciscan year coincide with the promulgation of another decalogue of "Thou shalt nots" for the Italian people. Not by chance was the Fascist government—in the person of the minister of public instruction, Signor Fedele, escorted by a convoy of official delegates—a part of the candlelit midnight procession that made Assisi the seven-hundred-year-old "capella ardente" of a new national faith.

At the same hour, the gaunt and ravaged face of the old Church of the Aracoeli was illuminated with the Franciscan emblem, so that the crossed hands of Saint Francis blazed side by side with the lighted bundle of fasces on the Roman Capitol itself. Even the king was drafted into the pageant. He dedicated the wide road that opens to all Italy the rocky cell at Alvernia, where the cheerful ascet-

icism of the most seductive of saints received its heavenly imprimatur.

Italy has become Franciscan. The virtues of the Little Poor Man of Assisi are proclaimed as a formula of national salvation. The Lady Poverty to whose austere worship were consecrated these blue-walled, vine-carpeted valleys is the mistress glorified in one after another of the encyclicals issued from the Viminal.* Asceticism is preached as the patriot's rule of life. Black bread and no cake, the nine-hour-day, silence, obedience, order, the hard gospel of giving up and doing without—by such monastic laws and counsels does the present government invoke again the spirit that once before took fire from a flame kindled on this hill and swept Italy into the glory of the Renaissance. When Mussolini makes his pilgrimage to Assisi, he will hail St. Francis as the patron saint of Fascist Italy.

In Rome—listening to these proclamations and prescriptions, seeing all the past, from Caesar to Cavour, so deftly used to feed the new "Italianità" fusing this people into a power that already marches no one yet knows where—one begins, indeed, to regard Saint Francis as a national symbol. Hearing him constantly exalted as "the most Italian of saints" has the effect of stressing his nationality at the expense of his saintliness.

One sits with Gibbon on the steps of the old Franciscan church crouching more formidably than the Roman wolf beside the Campidoglio and wonders whether the Fascists are right in assuming that it was built as a bulwark instead of as a challenge to the secular empire here typified and centralized since the Alban and the Sabine hills were sheepfolds.

Watching from that top gallery seat the hardening once more of "the will to power," one thinks the inevitable thoughts of the rise and fall of empires, and descends to go to the inauguration of the Franciscan year, considering it another episode in the oldest of human dramas.

The Roman Campagna, in the midafternoon sun, broods too, a little cynically. No will to power and progress, however it fights battles of the grain in other fields or strews suburbs and factories around other cities, is able to impress itself on the empty plain that surrounds the Seven Hills. The Campagna seems tired of buildings and of battles. It is a dry moat of weariness, as eternally sepulchral as Rome is eternally alive.

Even beyond, where Socrates, the Horatian mount, stands like the prow of some submerged

---

* One of the seven hills on which ancient Rome was built and the seat of Italian fascism.

136

Eichenberg 1979

leviathan; where a herd of cows grazes within the still strong walls of a Roman town; where Etruria persists in the tombs and temple of Falerii, Rome is still enveloped in a kind of hot haze formed of the dust of empires. And then suddenly the sun lowers and the road enters green valleys between hills crested with towns the color of old umber, the color of the faded brown habits worn by poor old friars trudging along.

This is Umbria. You would know it from the backgrounds so carefully painted behind the madonnas and saints in every picture of the Umbrian school—from the first gropings at perspective in Gentile da Fabriano to the mellow fluency of Raphael. It has not changed seemingly since then by so much as a single straight campanile or one little pointed tree. You would know it by something else, simpler and more archaic; by a serenity and otherworldliness as tangible as is the tension of Rome becoming great or as is the exhaustion of the Campagna from the strain of too much greatness.

"Silenzio!" murmurs the Fascist militia officer who had pushed open all doors for us, even the gates at railway crossings. He was discovering for the first time, I fancy, what is meant by the precept that must be the hardest of all the new commandments for Italians to keep.

We were on the Flaminian Way, the route of so many marches on Rome before Garibaldi's and Mussolini's. In silence we sped through Terni, four years ago a Red barricade and now as busy and blackshirted as the best. There was no sound in Narni except the purl of the chalky little Nera at its feet. Spoleto was hushed in the dusk. The hills I had once heard echoing with "Evivas!" for Lenin were now dark and quiet. Only the sunset blared like a cannonade in the sky. It was a strangely stationary sunset, and as we issued from the gorge behind Spoleto we saw that it hung behind a distant dome, a golden ball floating on the billowing valleys, like one of those impossible clouds of glory seen on baroque altars of the most flamboyant period.

It was the dome of Saint Mary of the Angels, reared on the plain below Assisi to cover the poor little chapel of the Portiuncula, built by pilgrims from Jerusalem in the fourth century and rebuilt by the young Francis with his own hands on the day when he flung away his ermine cloak of the silk merchant's son, so fond of cutting a dash in his home town, and resolved to be free of houses and possessions forever. In that same place, only twenty years later—twenty years during which he accom-

plished a spiritual revolution—Francis of Assisi sang his "Canticle of Brother Sun" and died. It was as if the sun remembered.

One had a sense that all the little tucked-in towns leaned breathless, afraid to light a candle, waiting to see some apparition in the sky. Perhaps they did. Who is to know what is beyond the vision of political pilgrims in a motorcar, raising dust upon the hill between the Portiuncula and the gate of Assisi? What wonders may those pilgrims have seen who climbed up and down that road all night long on foot, making prayers our shamefaced progress could not interrupt?

In Umbria, Francesco Bernardone is as little a Fascist saint, pattern of Italy's new asceticism, as he is a Protestant saint, precursor of the Reformation.

From that point, indeed, the seven-hundred-year-old saint got the better of the five-year-old symbol. In Umbria Francesco Bernardone is as little a Fascist saint, pattern of Italy's new asceticism, as he is a Protestant saint, precursor of the Reformation.

Brother Dog

LUIS ANIBAL SANCHEZ

In the enormous tragic silence of the night,
 Francis, the monk of Assisi, with sunken eyes
 of immense tenderness, caressed the white
 body, the snow-white body, of a poor dog that
 died in the war.

To that body, which had no soul, but which felt
 much, loved much, suffered much, Francis has
 given a tear and infinite pity.

Francis has wept, while afar nations made war.

It is the apocalyptic hour. Humanity is condensed
 into one long shriek. Hate asserts its supremacy.
 The great red cataclysm sows earth with tears
 and blood; tears of the child and of the beloved,
 and ancient crystallized tears of the venerable
 mothers who weep in dark alcoves where the
 cat whines sybaritically without knowing why.

Before the white body of the poor dog slain by
 chance bullets, the divine Francis wept.

Europe's Greatest Religious Genius

SIR KENNETH CLARK

In the years when the north portal of Chartres
was being built, a rich young dandy named Francesco Bernardone suffered a change of heart. He
was, and always remained, the most courteous of
men, deeply influenced by French ideals of chivalry.
And one day when he had fitted himself up in his
best clothes in preparation for some chivalrous campaign, he met a poor gentleman whose need seemed
to be greater than his own, and gave him his cloak.
That night he dreamed that he should rebuild the
Celestial City. Later he gave away his father's possessions so liberally that his father, who was a rich
businessman in the Italian town of Assisi, was
moved to disown him; whereupon Francesco took

off his remaining clothes and said that he would
possess nothing, absolutely nothing. The Bishop of
Assisi hid his nakedness, and afterward gave him a
cloak; and Francesco went off into the woods, singing a French song.

The next three years he spent in abject poverty,
looking after lepers, who were very much in evidence in the Middle Ages, and rebuilding with his
own hands (for he had taken his dream literally)
abandoned churches. One day at mass he heard the
words "Carry neither gold nor silver, nor money in
your girdle, nor bag, nor two coats, nor sandals,
nor staff." I suppose he had often heard them before, but this time they spoke directly to his heart.
He threw away his staff and his sandals and went
out barefooted onto the hills. In all his actions he
took the words of the Gospels literally, and he
translated them into the language of chivalric poetry and of those *jongleur* songs that were always
on his lips. He said that he had taken Poverty for
his Lady, and when he achieved some still more
drastic act of self-denial, he said that it was to do
her a courtesy. It was partly because he saw that
wealth corrupts; partly because he felt that it was
discourteous to be in the company of anyone poorer
than oneself.

From the first everyone recognized that Saint
Francis (as we may now call him) was a religious
genius—the greatest, I believe, that Europe has ever
produced; and when, with his first twelve disciples,
he managed to gain access to Innocent III, the
toughest politician in Europe (who was also a great
Christian), the Pope gave him permission to found
an order. It was an extraordinary piece of insight,
not only because Saint Francis was a layman with
no theological training, but also because he and his
poor, ragged companions were so excited when
they went to see the Pope that they began to dance.
What a picture! Unfortunately the early painters of
the Franciscan legend do not reproduce it.

The most convincing illustrations of the story of
Saint Francis are the work of the Sienese painter
Sasetta, although he painted so much later, because
the chivalric, Gothic tradition lingered on in Siena
as nowhere else in Italy, and gave to Sasetta's
sprightly images a lyric, even a visionary quality
more Franciscan than the ponderous images of Giotto. But they have more authority, not only because Giotto was working almost a hundred and
fifty years nearer to the time of St. Francis, but also
because he, and his circle, were chosen to decorate
the great church dedicated to Saint Francis in
Assisi. And when it comes to the later and—how

shall I say it—less lyrical episodes in the saint's life, Giotto's frescoes have a fullness of humanity that was beyond Sasetta. Where they seem to me to fail is in their image of the saint himself. They make him too grave and commanding. They don't show a spark of the joy that he valued almost as highly as courtesy. . . . The earliest representation that must date from just after his death is (appropriately enough) on a French enamel box. The best-known early painting is attributed to the first famous Italian painter, Cimabue. It looks quite convincing, but I'm afraid that it is entirely repainted, and shows us only what the nineteenth century thought Saint Francis ought to have been like.

Saint Francis died in 1226 at the age of forty-three, worn out by his austerities. On his deathbed he asked forgiveness of "poor Brother Donkey, my body" for the hardships he had made it suffer. He had seen his group of humble companions grow into a great institution, and in 1220 he had, with perfect simplicity, relinquished control of the Order. He recognized that he was no administrator. Two years after his death he was canonized, and almost immediately his followers began to build a great basilica in his memory. With its upper and lower church, jammed onto the side of a steep hill, it is both an extraordinary feat of engineering and a masterpiece of Gothic architecture. It was decorated by all the chief Italian painters of the thirteenth and fourteenth centuries, from Cimabue onward, so that it became the richest and most evocative church in Italy. A strange memorial to the little poor man, whose favorite saying was, "Foxes have holes, and the birds of the air have nests; but the Son of Man hath not where to lay his head."

. . . his belief that in order to free the spirit we must shed all our earthly goods . . . is an ideal to which, however impossible it may be in practice, the finest spirits will always return.

But of course, Saint Francis's cult of poverty could not survive him—it did not even last his lifetime. It was officially rejected by the Church; for the Church had already become part of the international banking system that originated in thirteenth-century Italy. Those of Francis's disciples, called Fraticelli, who clung to his doctrine of poverty were denounced as heretics and burned at the stake. And for seven hundred years capitalism had continued to grow to its present monstrous proportions. It may seem that St. Francis has had no influence at all because even those humane reformers of the nineteenth century who sometimes invoked him did not wish to exalt or sanctify poverty but to abolish it.

And yet his belief that in order to free the spirit we must shed all our earthly goods is the belief that all great religious teachers have had in common—Eastern and Western, without exception. It is an ideal to which, however impossible it may be in practice, the finest spirits will always return. By enacting that truth with such simplicity and grace, Saint Francis made it part of the European consciousness. And by freeing himself from the pull of possessions, he achieved a state of mind that gained a new meaning in the late eighteenth century through the philosophy of Rousseau and Wordsworth. It was only because he possessed nothing that Saint Francis could feel sincerely a brotherhood with all created things, not only living creatures, but Brother Fire and Sister Wind.

This philosophy inspired his hymn to the unity creation, the "Canticle of Brother Sun," and it is expressed with irresistible naivety in a collection of legends known as the *Fioretti*, the *Little Flowers*. Not many people can make their way through the arguments of Abelard or the *Summa* of St. Thomas Aquinas, but everyone can enjoy these holy folktales, which, after all, may not be completely untrue. They are, in contemporary jargon, among the first examples of popular communication—at any rate since the Gospels. They tell us, for instance, how St. Francis persuades a fierce wolf that terrified the people of Gubbio to make a pact by which, in return for regular meals, he will leave the citizens alone. "Give me your paw," said Saint Francis, and the wolf gave his paw. Most famous of all is the sermon to the birds—those creatures that seemed to the Gothic mind singularly privileged. Seven centuries have not impaired the naive beauty of that episode, either in the text of the *Fioretti* or in Giotto's fresco.

Saint Francis is a figure of the pure Gothic time —the time of Crusades and castles and the great cathedrals. Although he interpreted it in a curious way, he belonged to the age of chivalry. Well, however much one loves that world, it must, I think, remain for us today infinitely strange and remote. It is as enchanting, as luminous, as transcendental as the stained glass that is its glory—and, in the ordinary meaning of the word, as unreal. But already during the lifetime of Saint Francis another world was growing up, which, for better or worse, is the ancestor of our own, the world of trade and banking, of cities full of hard-hearted men whose aim in life was to grow rich without ceasing to appear respectable.

The First of the First Californians

LEONARD JOHN FRANKISH

When miles are the consideration, it is a far cry from California to Italy, where just now in the little hill-town of Assisi is being staged a great, yet dignified, celebration, to mark the seven hundredth anniversary of the passing of St. Francis. But if one stops to reflect how the early history of the Golden West is woven with the activities of that other great Franciscan, Fra Junipero Serra, the matter of material distance fades into insignificance.

Italy is celebrating the seven hundredth anniversary of the passing of the founder of the order that played such an important part in early California history.

Even an indifferent study of the aims of the Order, as established by Francis of Assisi, must give the student of California history a better understanding of the quality of that indomitable courage and surpassing fortitude with which the Franciscan friars, coming here from Mexico in 1769, met and surmounted hardships and privations innumerable in carrying out their purpose of bringing Christianity to the Indians. Had it not been for Giovanni Bernardone—fondly called Francesco by those who loved him—born in the far hill-town of Assisi in 1182, it is doubtful if the old Spanish missions, which are one of California's chief attractions, would now be in existence, and all the romance attached to them would not be our heritage.

His Name Is on America

FRANCIS AND HELEN LINE

In 1609, nearly a dozen years in advance of, and two thousand miles westward from the Pilgrims' landing on Plymouth Rock, an obscure follower of Saint Francis gave the name to Santa Fe, now New Mexico's capital city. *La Villa de Santa Fé de San Francisco,* he called it—The Town of the Holy Faith of Saint Francis. That is still its full name.

A lifetime earlier—1539—a Franciscan who was scouting the land for the eventual exploration by Coronado raised a flag near what is now the boundary between New Mexico and Arizona, naming that vast area of the southwest the Kingdom of Saint Francis. Today, Arizona's highest mountains—the San Francisco Peaks—rise over that land, commemorating the name of the Assisi saint.

The name of Saint Francis is on the land in English, Spanish, and French. Mid-America is dotted with places named in his honor. A portion of the Missouri Ozarks is called the Saint Francis Mountains. The Saint Francis River rises here, flowing through Saint François County, Missouri, and past Saint Francis, Arkansas.

In 1776, the de Anza expedition journeyed from Mexico to the central California coast for the express purpose of establishing a city to honor the Franciscan founder—San Francisco. The Mission Dolores, which still serves the city, is officially Mission San Francisco de Asis.

A few miles southward is Mission Santa Clara de Asis and the city and county of Santa Clara, commemorating the lovely girl of Assisi whom Francis loved, and with whom he helped found the Second Order of Franciscans—the Poor Clares.

In 1769, the Spanish explorer Ortega—advance scout for the Portola Expedition—pitched camp near a small Pacific Coast river. The date was August 2, sacred day of the tiny Portiuncula chapel, which had been Francis's headquarters in Assisi. So the spot was named *Nuestra Señora la Reina de*

142

los Angeles de Portiuncula, or Our Lady the Queen of the Angels of Portiuncula. Twelve years later, when de Nave founded a city here, it was given this name—later shortened to Los Angeles.

To the north, the Sacramento River was named by the Spaniards for the sacraments, which were so precious to Francis, and later California's capital city was given the name Sacramento.

The degree of Franciscan influence on California place names is shown by the fact that more than fifty of her communities, a quarter of her counties, and more than three hundred rivers, peaks, islands, and other geographic features are named after saints or religious objects.

The name of Saint Francis is on the land in English, Spanish, and French. Mid-America is dotted with places named in his honor. A portion of the Missouri Ozarks is called the Saint François Mountains. The Saint Francis River rises here, flowing through Saint François County, Missouri, and on past Saint Francis, Arkansas.

The name of Francis of Assisi is also on the land in Texas. In the 1680s a cluster of missions was established by the Franciscans near what is now El Paso. In 1690, in what is now East Texas, Franciscans built the first mission in this part of the country. The mission, moved to San Antonio, was originally called *San Francisco de la Tejas,* after Saint Francis and the Tejas, or Texas Indians.

In San Antonio the Franciscans also founded the Mission San Antonio de Valero. Nearby grew some cottonwood trees, which in Spanish are known as alamos. This became the popular name for this part of the old mission when, in 1836, it became the Cradle of Texas Independence.

Francis of Assisi died more than half a thousand years before America became a nation, but across the entire continent, from Florida to the Golden Gate, his name is on the land.

Saint Francis in Modern Times

CATHERINE DE HUECK DOHERTY

If Pope John's *aggiornamento* or Vatican Council II needed a patron saint, Saint Francis of Assisi would be the one chosen for both. Saint Francis is also one of the few saints who would feel completely at home in our modern world.

He was a lover of poverty. He spoke about it as a poet and a mystic speaks. But he practiced it as Cardinal Lercaro, Father Gauthier of Bethlehem, and so many theologians, bishops, priests, and lay people desire to practice it in our day. Saint Francis knew the essence of poverty, its soul, and sang of it and lived it.

He might smile indulgently at our efforts to abolish poverty in our own affluent society. He might weep at the abyss still separating the haves and have-nots in the world, but he certainly would be at home among us moderns in this field too. He would not allow us to rationalize away the Gospel. He would cut through all red tape, all hypocrisy, all verbiage, whatever its name, and lead us directly to the heart of the matter, asking, begging, compelling by the very force of his love of God and his shining personality, the rich to give of their abundance to the poor.

He would do it with his simple eloquence, as Martin Luther King, Jr., does it, only better. His bare feet and his brown habit would be seen marching across the world, and he would be more effective than Gandhi.

He would do the same again with our atomic energy. He would divert it from being used in weapons for annihilating man and his earth, and put it at the service of mankind, turning "swords into ploughshares."

If anyone could solve the question of war and peace that tears Christian souls apart, Saint Francis would be the saint to do it. For even in the cold appraisal of a historical monogram on the subject, the breaking up of the feudal system of medieval times is attributed to him. Somewhere in Europe there is a hill that men dig in today to find the arms, the shields, etc., which medieval knights heaped one on top of the other, after hearing Saint Francis speak on peace and love.

He would do the same again with our atomic energy. He would divert it from being used in weapons for annihilating man and his earth, and put it at the service of mankind, turning "swords into ploughshares."

Because he himself was a flame of love, he would bring us love . . . for he would bring us God, who

is Love! He would make clear the knotty question of "authority versus obedience"! He was a lover, and only lovers can make obedience clear to modern man, who so desires to learn to love.

Saint Francis would be relevant to the modern Church in the modern world because he would bring perfect love and perfect joy to it, showing us all by the grace of God that indeed Perfect Love casteth out fears and brings joy into the world.

Francis would be completely in accord and at home among the "New Breed," be it of bishops, clerics, religious, or lay people, because he would understand and clarify their search for truth, their desire to return to the pristine purity of the Gospel, their desire to incarnate it in its fullness into the modern Church—the people of God.

Yes, if Pope John's *aggiornamento* or Vatican Council II needed a saint, Saint Francis of Assisi would be the one chosen for both.

Miracle of 32nd Street

FRANCIS AND HELEN LINE

Mid-town Manhattan, off Broadway,
Is not the most inspiring place in our land.
Clerks and shop people, spewed from the subways,
Hurry to offices and stores.
Commuters, jolted into Penn Station from Long
    Island,
Scurry to sanctuary skyscrapers.
Tourists, streetwalkers, panhandlers,
Motley habitants of a brick-encased jungle,
Stream back and forth along 32nd Street's
    crowded sidewalks
Intent on the tasks of the day,
Or the pleasures of the evening.

But in a tiny court
Not a dozen feet from this traffic,
Nestled behind a church of St. Francis,
Is a kneeling statue of the Assisi saint.
Some people step into the church,
Others pause a second
And whisper a prayer.
Some touch Francis's hand or knee with their
    fingers,
Some just hesitate—to look,
And then continue on.

There has been a moment of uplift.
Inspiration has found its way to these sidewalks.
The spirit of a saint has blessed the multitudes,
And the bronze statue is shiny with gentle touches
   of love.

A never-ceasing miracle
Is unfolding in the canyons of mid-Manhattan
Because Francis of Assisi is there.

My Southwest Canticle

DECLAN MADDEN, O.F.M.

Tomorrow when I leave our southwest desert country there will be one sharp regret—how deeply Saint Francis would have enjoyed these past weeks. His would have been a father's pride as he walked the mission trails etched by his Padre followers; his a poet's pride as he saw God's beauty splashed in harsh, brilliant colors and shapes. Had he been here, perhaps in some small way I could have shown him new facets in his *Canticle of the Sun*.

---

*Do not such extremes describe Francis in
his later life? A man vibrant with love
of God yet his body twisted in pain; a man
sharply aware of naure's beauty, yet
his eyes dimming in blindness. This, the
Francis of the Sun's Canticle.*

New facets? Yes, for no other writing of the saint blends so well with this land of contrast. Here in one small area nature is extreme. Searing daytime heat, numbing nighttime cold; dryness which forces even the cactus to lift suppliant arms, then rain, hammering, ripping new gashes in the earth. A stark land defying vegetation, a soft land lavish with flowers. Do not such extremes describe Francis in his later life? A man vibrant with love of God yet his body twisted in pain; a man sharply aware of nature's beauty, yet with his eyes dimming in blindness. This, the Francis of the Sun's Canticle.

Our tortured canyons and sere mesas would be merely the reverse of his gentle Umbrian hills and fertile plains; our cactus blooms and desert flowers wayward sisters of his roses and mountain violets. Yes, I wish he were here today. I wish I could show him our "Canticle of Brother Sun."

Praise for Brother Wind would be the first thing we would discuss. It would have to be. The desert wind is something you can't overlook, it is with you always. Still, I know even now the reaction of Francis—complete enchantment with this capricious architecture of the Lord.

For a fine example of the wind's work, I would like Francis to see Monument Valley in southern Utah. We would approach it from the town of Kayenta so its stunning grandeur would burst full upon him. A land of gigantic spires and mesas, of arches and buttes; a tortured, twisted land red with nature's suffering. Only the wind could have chiseled these giants of stone. Even as we stood, awed and humble, I would point wordlessly to a dust column whirling across the valley floor and perhaps hear the saint's remark, "And He shall go before them by day . . ."

Leaving the Valley we would travel southward to the Sonoran desert of Arizona where, most casually of course, I would show Francis our own Sister Moon. As we neared my surprise there would be no need to mention Brother Sun. He is with you each day—a molten orb doing his work as the Creator commanded. A diligent worker this one, brooking no nonsense, demanding your instant respect. He has a job to do and do it he will. Respect him and he makes the desert live; ignore him and you have none but yourself to blame for his wrath.

Francis and I would cross the Chiricahua Mountains, and late one day I would show him our Sister Moon. Those dark eyes would flash and a tentative smile play about his lips. "This cactus plant in the afternoon, with Brother Sun scorching us—this is Sister Moon?" Ever mysterious, still enjoying his puzzled look I would say only, "Let's sit here in the car and eat our sandwiches, then when night comes I'm sure the moon will appear."

"I see now why you stopped here. How dark your Arizona nights, how countless the stars in God's heaven. Why, they look as if you could reach out and gather an armful." And for once, I would remain quiet. Any reply would irreverently shatter the awesome display of God's beauty.

With a dramatic gesture I would turn on the headlights and say to Francis, "There is Sister Moon." And his reaction? Tell me, what would be yours if the cactus of the afternoon were now a sea of delicate white flowers? For a few nights, and only at night, does this cactus bloom—star-shaped flowers, soft and shimmering. The desert queen of the night we have named it. Truly, our earthbound moon.

The man who quieted the wolf of Gubbio and talked to the larks of Umbria would smile in appreciation as their less civilized relatives performed before him. That same evening we would listen to a coyote serenade—not a mournful, frightening cry but always to me a happy expression from this wary animal. Our headlights would pick out the glowing eyes of a deer, perhaps the solemn look on the tiny, old-man face of a cactus owl. Yes, I'm sure I would search the saguaros until I could point out this elf to Francis. And how he would laugh to see this little face peering solemnly from a hole in the huge cactus.

Dawn would find us near Tucson in the Saguaro National Monument, just in time to show Francis our open-air cathedral filled with early morning worshipers. I know what Francis would say: "How very much these saguaros look like gigantic people, their twisted arms reaching out in prayer or bent groundward in supplication." And then with a smile, "These are all men aren't they? See those waxy flowers in the very top of each arm? Why, they look like the fringe of white hair on an elderly man."

"And our candles, Father Francis! The tall shapely ones are ocotillo, each slender arm aglow with tiny scarlet flowers. And look, over there, see the yucca in bloom? That long green shaft with the huge cluster of white flowers? Is it any wonder the early explorers called them Candles of the Lord?"

"And who are the choir members I hear? Such a variety of song from our Sisters."

"Wait only a minute," I would smile, "and you will see our choir. There in that palo verde tree. See her? Yes, one member only—a mockingbird gaily offering the Lord her extensive, slightly off-key repertoire of song."

Since it is only natural to save the best till last, Brother Water would be the final verse in our modern canticle. First we would stop along the stream which cuts through Sabino Canyon only a short distance from our open-air cathedral. A happy stream, sparkling silver in the sun or mysteriously dappled with shadow of willow and cottonwood. A singing stream lending a green touch to the canyon floor, refreshing anyone who pauses beside it. Perhaps we would walk along this narrow creek, stilling

for a moment the cicada hum, pleased to catch the sudden flash of a startled trout.

"This is Brother Water in a gentle mood, Father Francis. Such streams are so very rare in this country that they soon become favorite playgrounds. Even our rivers are different, most of them nothing but sandy beds months on end. Only when it rains heavily do they have any water. And then you would think Brother Rain is trying to make up for his long neglect. The Rillito—you remember we laughed together at the large bridge across a dry river bed—now there is a wild one when the desert has rain. I only wish we could stand on that same bridge and watch the sudden, almost terrifying change. From far upstream you hear a deep roar as a wall of water flings itself from the hills. A maddened stream, five to six feet deep, stained by dirt and sand, choked with trees and rocks, rips and tears in a journey to complete oblivion in the desert."

"You make Brother Water sound awesome. I think I prefer him in this more gentle mood."

"As I do, Father Francis. Only once have I been in a flash flood such as I described; and believe me, once is enough. But before we leave the desert let me show you a patient, helpful Brother Water."

A long drive would take us deep into the Rincon Mountains. Leaving the car we would walk along an ancient trail traced by a race long dead. Sand and rock shimmering in an oven's heat would give sharp testimony: this is a waterless land. Finally, we would stop near a jumble of rocks, the result of a slide ages ago. House-sized boulders surrounded and crowned with smaller rocks resemble a ruined castle.

"Now Father Francis, if you are in a climbing mood, I'll show you a secret which decades ago saved many a life. There isn't a drop of water visible for miles around. A man traveling through this country could soon exhaust his supply of water. Some died of thirst in this very area, yet only twelve feet above us there is water. Let's climb to the top of the large boulder and you'll see what I mean."

Huffing and puffing like an arthritic mountain goat I would lead Francis to a tinaja. On the flat top of the rock lies a small depression perhaps two feet by two feet, a few inches deep. Protected by the overhang of the nearby rock this tiny pool stores the water of a storm or the runoff from the canyon rim above. It stays surprisingly cool and clean, a water hole for small animals and birds, a true life-saver for man.

Such is our Southwest Canticle.

Il Poverello and Technology

LUKE R. POWER

. . . Although a theology of technology has not yet been completely elaborated, a portion of our Franciscan heritage—Saint Francis's attitude toward creatures—strongly suggests itself as a basic framework orienting theology for this problem of our age.

Is it naive to propose the simple thought of medieval Francis as insight for the complex issues of our age? Yet, it took the genius of a Bonaventure and a Duns Scotus to *begin* to elucidate the profound implications in the spirit of Saint Francis. We here propose a further consideration of these implications that are relevant for the problems of today.

The attitude of Francis was radically *Christian*, essentially religious, and therefore fundamentally optimistic. He had the gift of unifying in one dynamic view God, men, and all creation. God was the center of all to Francis, the Supreme Being, the Lord of Creation and Goodness himself. To him, in whom all things live and move and have their being, Francis abandoned himself with genuine dependence upon his Providence. Having so sought and embraced God, having abandoned all else for his sake, Francis merited to discover all things anew.

Because he was given a special insight into material things, Francis could see that God's self-diffusive Goodness communicated itself in all ways, even into the finite order. The divine Goodness was for him the explanation of all creation. God willed all that was created, and in willing it, oriented the entire order of creation to return glory to himself.

Francis was not a lover of nature in a sentimental, pantheistic sense. Rather, it was his reverence for God that was communicated to creatures, for he saw in each of them the vestige of their Creator. In themselves they were good: perfect in their nature and in the laws that governed their development. Each thing, giving glory to God not only by being but also by becoming what it was intended to be, drew from Francis a response proportionate to its inherent dignity.

Francis, however, was also aware that man works out his salvation by using material things, and he understood that part of the value of a creature was its capacity for use by men. This is apparent in the constant acknowledgment he gave to creatures for their help in his climb to God. To Francis himself is attributed the following statement of his motivation in composing the "Canticle of Brother Sun":

> For his praise, therefore, and for our consolation and the edification of our neighbor, I want to compose a new hymn about the Lord's creatures, of which we make daily use, without which we cannot live, and with which the human race greatly offends its Creator.

Realizing that men have the dual capacity to misuse and debase created things as instruments of evil, or to consecrate and develop them, he could never make these material things ends in themselves, for that would have been irreverent abuse of their goodness. Thus it was that Francis felt a fellowship with each creature, for every tree and every rock was the progeny of the same Creator who had created him.

In the spirit of Saint Francis, with his appreciation of creation and man's dominion over it, we can view technology as a gift of God.

In the spirit of Francis, with his appreciation of creation and man's dominion over it, we can view technology as a *gift of God*. This is not really a new thought, for the idea that the state of man could be improved materially and spiritually has deep roots in the Judeo-Christian tradition. It is expressed in Isaiah: "Behold, I have created the smith that blows in the fire the coals and brings forth an instrument for his work" (54:16). Saint Thomas acknowledges it when he states in the *Summa Theologiae:* "In the state of corrupt nature man can indeed achieve some particular good by the power of his own nature, as for example, the building of houses, the planting of vineyards, and things of this kind" (I:109:2).

Now, armed with that pervading reverence that Francis had for material things and their potentialities, man can understandingly exercise his prerogative to perfect creation. Since man was created with an ability to develop those potentialities, it is proper that he do so, for it is an *aspect of reverence* to see seminal possibilities mature in the creation of God. Such a spirit, drawing out the hidden forces of nature with the tools of technology, can be instrumental in drawing men closer to God and at the same time can give glory to God by the positive transformation of matter. Francis could see that to make the earth bear fruit was to share in the act of creation and to render formal glory to God. In the "Canticle of Brother Sun" he sang:

> Be praised, O Lord, through our Sister
> Mother Earth,
> For she sustains and guides our life,
> And yields us diverse fruits, with tinted
> flowers and grass.

It is certain, then, that if he could praise God because the earth yielded its fruit, he would also say that to take the ore from the earth and to process steel from it was also a godly act.

Rather than being fearful for his fate in a technological society, the man of faith can share a true Christian optimism, since the development of God's creation can be a means to recapitulate all things in Christ. This optimism is underscored by Bishop (later Cardinal) John J. Wright, who, taking note of man's new vantage point at the frontier of space, anticipates that the departure of man and his machine from the very earth itself is bound to have a profound influence on human thought. Acknowledging the past tendency of modern science to be man-centered and materialistic, he contrasts this with the confidence that

> the new age of science, gazing out into God's clear space instead of back into our own murky psychological depths, may let fresh air into modern thought . . . this mood is more likely to prove theocentric, rather than narrowly "humanistic" in any man-centered, materialistic sense. It is the mood in which a new Saint Bonaventure or Scotus could talk to us of a Christocentric universe.

How would this technological movement appear to the Scotist as he elaborates on the Franciscan vision? To him, Christ is preeminent, the Beginning, the Final Cause, the Primate and King of the Universe. "He is the image of the invisible God, the firstborn of all creation. For in him were created all things. . . . All things have been created through him, and he is before all creatures, and in him all things hold together" (Col. 1:15–18).

Christ, therefore, is center, the principle of unity of a creation that is incomprehensible without him. Everything in creation was made through him as its meritorious efficient cause. Since creation is the work of a single plan of Wisdom, all things are pointed toward Christ for termination and meaning. This orientation toward Christ is the dynamic tendency in matter urging it to become what it was intended to be from all eternity.

Whether one speaks of a universe in evolution or a creation made capable of expansion through its potentiality, our technology can be understood as an instrument in that development. In a creation that is unfinished, man as a technician has a role to play in its development, and as a Christian he has the task of extending to the universe the effects of the Incarnation. As a collaborator in creation, he perfects; as a protractor of the Incarnation, he divinizes and restores—drawing all things to recapitulation in Christ. Man's tools and his power, his nature and his grace, are brought to bear on created things, and thereby created things come to share in the promised fulfillment of a new creation.

But man's salvation is not necessarily effected by the perfection of creation. True human development is in the "supranature" of man, and its fulfillment can be accomplished only through grace. A transformed world can only be the environment in which God's gift of grace might abound the more. Man's earthly labor will constitute a means of sanctification only insofar as it makes him more truly human—when Christ is the measure of what is human. Man must use his talents and his creative power to make the forces of the physical world the instruments of his freedom. This freedom will in turn serve to bring out the relation between the individual and Christ, and man will then transcend an existence centered upon himself and physical things to one centered upon God.

This freedom can be achieved by the total Christian dedication to transform the world while paradoxically maintaining a certain diffidence toward it. To be committed to the development of the seminal possibilities latent in matter can reduce man to a place of subservience to material demands. On the other hand, to divorce himself completely from the work of creation and development of God's universe is unrealistic for a modern man. Saint Francis again exemplifies for us a Christian life in this world. Francis practiced a positive asceticism to prevent his own fallen nature from seducing him to an inordinate love of the creatures in which he rejoiced. Prayer, proper humility, the spirit of poverty, plus an all-embracing Christocentric vision—all these must be exercised if the individual is to be free to attain to God and to draw all things with him. He will have true power over creation and will possess a restraint in exploiting his technological achievements only when his spiritual vision is articulated in mature moral control. Thus the advances of our age have dramatized in bold relief the need for moral excellence. This was the means used by Francis to attain his concord with nature; it is the technique of modern man's attainment of God through the world. This is the modern adaptation of that same balanced discipline that enabled Saint Paul to say:

I know how to live humbly and I know how to live in abundance (I have been schooled in every condition), to be filled and to be hungry, to have an abundance and to suffer want. I can do all things in him who strengthens me [PHIL. 4:12–13].

Thus, to interpret material progress in terms of Christ-centered cosmic development is not only valid but even essential. Only when God preempts in the minds of men the place he deserves, will technology be understood as a means of sharing in the act of creation. The significance of technology in this light would not be in terms of material development alone, but in terms of man's personal orientation to Christ—a conformity that would say to man, "All things are yours, and you are Christ's, and Christ is God's" (1 COR. 3:23).

Saint Francis of San Francisco

VACHEL LINDSAY

But the surf is white, down the long strange coast
With breasts that shake with sighs,
And the ocean of all oceans
Holds salt from weary eyes.

Saint Francis comes to his city at night
And stands in the brilliant electric light
And his swans that prophesy night and day
Would soothe his heart that wastes away:
The giant swans of California
That nest on the Golden Gate
And beat through the clouds serenely
And on Saint Francis wait.

But Saint Francis shades his face in his cowl
And stands in the street like a lost gray owl,
He thinks of *gold . . . gold.*

Francis weeping over the assassination of San Francisco mayor George Moscone in 1978

He sees on far redwoods
Dewfall and dawning:
Deep in Yosemite
Shadows and shrines:
He hears from far valleys
Prayers by young Christians,
He sees their due penance
So cruel, so cold;
He sees them made holy,
White-souled like young aspens
With whimsies and fancies untold:—
The opposite of gold.
And the mighty mountain swans of California
Whose eggs are like mosque domes of Ind,
Cry with curious notes
that their eggs are good for boats
To toss upon the foam and the wind.
He beholds on far rivers
The venturesome lovers
Sailing for the sea
All night
In swanshells white.
He sees them far on the ocean prevailing
In a year and a month and a day of sailing
Leaving the whales and their whoop unfailing
On through the lightning, ice, and confusion
North of the North Pole,
South of the South Pole,
And west of the west of the west,
To the shore of Heartache's Cure,
The opposite of gold,
On and on like Columbus
With faith and eggshell sure.

What a Fine Place This World Would Be

PETER MAURIN

What a fine place
this world would be
if Dualist Humanists
tried to be human
to men.
What a fine place
this world would be
if Personalist Theists
tried to be
their brother's keeper
as God
wants them to be.
What a fine place
this world would be
if Fundamentalist Protestants
tried to exemplify
the Sermon on the Mount.
What a fine place
this world would be
if Roman Catholics
tried to keep up
with Saint Francis of Assisi.

Troubadours of Christ

DOROTHY DAY

More than ever am I convinced that the solution lies only in the Gospel and in such a leader as Saint Francis. Peter Maurin has been talking these past two years of recruiting troubadours of Christ. More and more am I convinced that together with our purely material efforts of building up hospices and farming communes we need these fellow travelers with the poor and the dispossessed to share with them their poverty and insecurity and to bring them the reminder of the love of God.

May 1940

Saint Francis and the Church of Tomorrow

MARIO VON GALLI, S.J.

Not long ago a woman journalist who had worked as a reporter at the Second Vatican Council asked me what I was doing at the moment. I told her that I was completely absorbed in writing a book about Francis of Assisi. "Oh, nothing interesting there," was her disappointed reply. She is a Catholic of the "progressive" sort. A book about Francis: that could only be a pious work, one that smacked of the "edification" that people do not welcome today. At best it would be a historical study, but even that would be oriented toward the past, not at all topical.

So how did the idea of writing a book about Francis of Assisi come to me? It grew—as is so often true—out of a series of accidental circumstances. First of all, Dennis Stock's photographs of the Umbrian landscape were there before me, such peerless reproductions they almost make you believe you can hear the clear voice of the Poverello of Assisi. He was the Provençal minstrel of these woods and fields and streams; of these gnarled, tapering olive trees and cypresses and thistles; of these oxen, sheep, and doves. Their voices are heard through the mouth of this man who was so intertwined with his native home that he became one with it—even though he began a world-wide movement that, as he wished, was to encompass all the countries of Europe and even the Orient. This was the place he chose to be the midpoint, the pulsing heart as it were. From it blood would be pumped through the arteries. To it blood would return for revitalization after its wearisome journey.

So the pictures were the occasion and also the starting point of this book. I saw them and they appealed to me. But I had not thought then of writing a book. Others urged me to do it. I protested that I did not know any more about the saint than any average Catholic. I pointed out that there were scores of learned Franciscans (friars, nuns, priests, etc.) who by their vocation were better acquainted with their founding father than I, a Jesuit. I referred to the vast literature that exists on Francis. Just to survey it takes time. But no one listened to

my objections. They didn't want a scholarly book. They wanted a book of spontaneous impressions such as a man of today might be able to offer.

Was I supposed to have a soul somehow akin to that of Francis? Those who plied me openly hinted in that direction. Whether they were right about that, I cannot decide. But in any case, I can't deny that although I began the study of Francis of Assisi half-heartedly, I proceeded to fall under his spell.

I must admit that I carried out my reading as unsystematically as you can imagine. First I read Gilbert Chesterton's little book about the saint. I love Chesterton. His mind and spirit bore an original stamp. He holds to his own judgment, and he is not at all inclined to give the customary edifying portrait that I dread so much in literature on the saints. So I read Chesterton, and I was richly rewarded. His Francis is certainly not a stereotype! But what in his presentation is really Francis, and what is the poetic creation of Chesterton? And what about the fascinating but controversial idea posed in the second chapter? There he describes the awakening of the world in the twelfth and thirteenth centuries as the end of the penitential period that necessarily followed paganism: "The purge of paganism is complete at last" (p. 36). At that moment

a figure appeared silently and suddenly on a little hill above the city, dark against the fading darkness. For it was the end of a long and stern night, a night of vigil, not unvisited by stars. He stood with his hands lifted, as in so many statues and pictures, and about him was a burst of birds singing; and behind him was the break of day [pp. 36–37].

Even if that holds true for the High Middle Ages, what significance does this figure still have for us today? At the end of his fine monograph on Francis of Assisi (1958), Ivan Gobry gave a surprising view of the impact of the saint in today's non-Catholic world. There he says that the "heretic" Renan called Francis "the only perfect Christian since Jesus," and that Gandhi praised him as one of the greatest wise men of the world. There are also testimonials from Rainer Maria Rilke and Max Picard. And Gobry maintains that there are clear "points of contact" between the spirit of Saint Francis and the following: the theandry of a Solovyev and Berdyaev, the personalism of Gabriel Marcel and Emmanuel Mounier, and Teilhard de Chardin's idea of the progressive upward transformation of creation. Here in his view it is evident that Francis reaches beyond the Middle Ages. He

even goes so far as to attribute to the Franciscan spirit the fact that already in the thirteenth century, "in opposition to the accepted methods," the Franciscan Roger Bacon became a forerunner of experimental science.

I could go no further. I had to go back to the sources. First I found the anthology edited by Otto Karrer, *Franz von Assisi: Legenden und Laudes* (1951). There I actually had all the essentials together. On the one hand it contained the old sources: the so-called *Legend of the Three Companions* (Ceprano), the oldest biography by Thomas of Celano, the legend of young Clare, the saintly portrait of Saint Francis by the great Bonaventure, the *Fioretti*, the songs of praise by the saint, and his *Testament*. And on the other hand it had critical introductions and notes for all these pieces. I was delighted as I read it because I was now seeing a saint from the inside. I don't believe there is another saint whose thoughts and feelings, loving and suffering, one is permitted to enter into in this way. Critical distance from the standpoint of history was provided by the introduction and commentary of the editor, for Karrer is a recognized historian. But while the keen analyst is almost always in control of his material in his other writings, here the soul of a great man, a saint, takes over and carries him beyond himself.

Was I on the right track? The remarks of a young Capuchin convinced me that I was. I asked him what actually fed his spiritual life as a Franciscan, as a follower of Francis. Was it biographies, modern critical studies, books about Franciscan spirituality?

He replied, "Certainly, there are many studies of all sorts that are very valuable: the biography of Father Cuthbert (Wildlöcher), the studies of Laurentius Casutt and Hilarin Felder."

"A member of the Third Order named Jørgensen's biography to me as the best book," I said. "And a Protestant referred me to the life of the Calvinist minister and Franciscan scholar, Paul Sabatier—you can't very well pass that up even today. Another showed me the voluminous work of Henry Thode, which describes the spreading influence of Francis at the start of Renaissance art. Or maybe I should go more deeply into the source material edited by the German Franciscans?"

My young Capuchin was silent for a while. Then he said, "Personally, I live by Karrer's anthology. Further research—and it is not at an end by a long shot—will shed light on the scholarly study of many important questions and details, such as the four distinct rules. Maybe you know how much is unclear there: whose influence plays a part, why the one rule was "lost" or permanently "misplaced" by Brother Elias, and so forth. But for laying hold of the Franciscan spirit, all that is of secondary importance after all."

I believe the young Capuchin was right. To be sure, I have read Casutt, Felder, Jørgensen, Cuthbert (Wildlöcher), Thode. In each I discovered new details that rounded out my picture. But Karrer's anthology remained for me the center around which everything clustered. I also looked into the modern presentations and analyses, such as those of Romano Guardini and Walter Nigg, and even the novel *Saint Francis* by Nikos Kazantzakis. They all attest that Francis has not vanished along with the world picture of the Middle Ages. Indeed he has not even faded. And that is truly amazing. That is the thing that attracts me.

How account for the fact that although we live in an age in which everything is planned (and whether we like it or not must be planned), we are not seeking the "man of the future" in orders that look back to founders whose chief traits are planning and organizing, but on the contrary, in the Franciscan mentality and spirit?

How is it that in our day, long before ecumenism became the rage among the Christian confessions, and long before a deep desire for ecumenical encounter found expression in the Protestant Ecumenical Council at Geneva and confirmation on the Catholic side in Vatican II, the figure of Francis of Assisi has exerted a fascination of its own upon everyone? How is it that in our era of science —the "scientific age" we like to call it—this wholly unscientific man, who by many is even called an enemy of science, nevertheless appears as an ideal? How can it be that today when we only too gladly pride ourselves on an empty and false maturity, a man addicted to childlike play, to actions that seem even downright *childish*, appeals to us? How account for the fact that although we live in an age in which everything is planned (and whether we like it or not, must be planned), we are not seeking the "man of the future" in orders that look back to founders whose chief traits are planning and or-

ganizing, but on the contrary, in the Franciscan mentality and spirit?

I will cite here a witness who is completely beyond suspicion, the Jesuit Peter Lippert:

The organization principle that leads from Benedict through Dominic and Ignatius to the newer communities seems to have practically exhausted its inner possibilities. That, of course, does not mean that it could ever become superfluous or replaceable. But the fundamental newness, which is precisely the thing being sought today by countless souls and in countless attempts at innovation, is to be found only along a completely different line: along the line of the original ideal of Francis. In other words: in the direction of a freely chosen lifestyle and freely chosen bonds of love; in the direction of a life that operates through spontaneous initiative of the self rather than through great constructs of the will; in the direction of a truly living and individual personality shaped by its own inner laws and standards. If God should someday deign to reveal the order of the future to his Church, the order so longingly sought by many of our best people, it will surely bear the stamp of Francis's soul and spirit.

Lippert wrote that in *Stimmen der Zeit* in 1927. In the meantime much has happened, even in the spiritual realm; yet his words are still to the point today.

I admit that much seems to contradict this, but we cannot let appearances deceive us. Maybe the Little Brothers of Charles de Foucauld are closer to the "original ideal of Francis" than the present-day organizations of the Franciscan family. To the modern temperament the very name "Little Brothers" accords much better with what Francis meant than the now incomprehensible term Friars Minor. And what is more, the manner of living, the activities, and even the clothing of the Little Brothers are more strongly suggestive of Francis than those of the Franciscans. That is also true of their distinctive way of linking the eremitical life with active apostolic work, and of the high value they place upon the simple witness of their lives in preference to preaching.

But I prefer not to pursue this line further. I do not care to offend my beloved Franciscans, who could scarcely become other than they have been constrained to become within their own stream in history. Nor do I want to rob the Little Brothers of their Charles de Foucauld, who certainly understood the Muslims better than Francis of Assisi. But still the strange parallels exist—and perhaps the Little Brothers of Charles de Foucauld had to be in order that the branches of the Franciscan family would not have to be painfully sundered once again.

I mention the example of the Little Brothers only so people cannot say it is abstract speculation or backwards-looking romanticism to say that Francis still lives today. . . .

It is something else that concerns us here. Namely, our future, which we would like to measure against Francis as he really was. Certainly he was a man of his time, and much in him was conditioned by that time. It could not be otherwise. Still a timeless element came to light in his time-bound figure, became clear and tangible as never before. That can be said of every saint, of course. But it cannot be said of them all that their peculiar timelessness is relevant precisely for our own age. But with Francis this seems to be true. So more than the others he is a guide to the future for us. Since the days of John XXIII, Pope and Council have been urging us to interpret the signs of the time. The unexpected and surprising thing to me was that the longer I studied Francis of Assisi, the more that study helped me to read the signs of the time. Although our critical juncture in history is not the same as that faced seven hundred years ago, the same figure stands "on a little hill above the city, dark against the fading darkness." He stands with raised hands, and around him the songs of birds echo, and behind him is the dawn. That is why I have tried to write this book.

A Franciscan Prayer

ENID DINNIS

When I am old and tutored by
   The grim experience of days;
   When I have proved men in their ways,
Oh, do not let the dreamer die.

When I have learned aside to toss
   The foolish things that wise men hate,
   Lest Littleness should hold me great,
Be mine the folly of the Cross.

When comes detachment's strength to me,
   Let mine the weakness be that wept
   O'er Lazarus' grave and kept
Three comrades in Gethsemane.

When head bids heart herself forget,
   When Reason's lure would love deceive,
   May my poor foolish heart achieve
A few life-giving blunders yet.

When I have grown too sane, too sad,
   To join the angels' faerie ring
   And serve the playtime of the King,
Then, Sweet Saint Francis, make me mad.

Franco Zeffirelli on Saint Francis

ENZO NATTA

I found Franco Zeffirelli at Assisi not filming a scene on set, but amongst a group of brown-robed Franciscan clerical students and novices. They were bombarding him with questions. One young student friar asked him: "Do you think it can fairly be said that one finds a resemblance between the state of society in Francis's time and that of the Western world in our time? I mean, was there something in his surroundings that provoked in the heart of the saint a disgust for his external world and made it seem necessary for him to throw everything overboard and to dedicate himself totally to the life of the spirit? Is it the same nowadays?"

"Yes, in our day too," answered Zeffirelli, "there is a towering build-up and confusion of problems. And that is what has provoked a very definite return to the spiritual, just as in Francis's day. For that reason, the parallel between Francis's life and ours seems to me quite relevant. However, I'd like to make it clear that what I intend is not a religious film, but a film that rethinks human values that lead up to religious values. I do not intend to touch the inside sphere of his sanctity, for Francis's sanctity was too great for anyone to master it at will. Instead, my film will be a story of young people, of Francis and his set of friends who live in an affluent society where each one has his own neurosis bending him in a characteristic direction, and that direction is clearly indicated by Francis. You see, this film deals with a set of friends—five of them—and this extraordinary being, Francis, emerges to lead the others onward. His companions think him a bit crazy. The life to which he points is hard, almost impossible, but in spite of that they cannot ignore it. They discern an ultimate rightness about this new folly proposed by Francis. It comes to exert a pull from which they cannot escape.

I do not intend to touch the inside sphere of his sanctity, for Francis's sanctity was too great for anyone to master it at will.

"Now, as regards the parallel of which we just spoke: I think it interesting to seek another affinity. Has our society produced any figure like Francis? Do we expect to find anything like the phenomenon of Francis among the people who count in our society? I'd say that the reply would surely be: 'I wish we had one of his type around today!' A figure like Francis is what we badly need. But I'm convinced that we actually have many figures like him. That far-off medieval world was one of isolated personalities. Their sentiments and spiritual forces were precisely centered, whereas today the seed of good is scattered, and it is difficult to find one single person who concentrates in himself all the virtues or defects. Still, I get the impression that the seed of good sprouts in our times, too. After a whole generation of horror and wickedness, after years of violence during which men became conditioned to resolving all problems, even personal ones, by the use of maltreatment, today there arises a new generation. Unfortunately, it, too, is a torn generation: it is misguided and disorderly; it does not know how to use its immense inheritance; it does not know what it wants. Yet, in spite of all its excesses, when

we see its sense of fairness and justice together with its anguished thirst for goodness, we cannot but look forward to a better tomorrow."

Another question put to Zeffirelli: "Do you think that it would be possible for Francis to 'do his thing' in our society? After all, in that past society he was surrounded by a simple feudalistic world that was passing through the Crusades and developing a new merchant class. But our society is a pluralistic one. It is differently structured, differently organized."

Zeffirelli answered: "When all is said and done, the society in which we live is rather simple. Young people nowadays think of it in just the same way as Francis and his young companions thought of theirs. In our day, Che Guevara becomes an idol of many young people by playing on a few fundamental themes. Imagine what a saint could achieve in these circumstances! I'm convinced that Francis's power to command the attention of the masses would be here, too. He would not fail to capture the ear and eye of the crowds. When a man lacks clear ideas, he feels the need of a light that should shine. Of course, we live in sad confusion nowadays. I talked about Saint Francis with some hippies who claim to have the authentic Franciscan outlook. They asserted that they were the true inheritors of Saint Francis's wisdom. I told them: 'Let's have some plain truths about this: you try to base your lives and order your horizons on a return to paganism; you seek an earthly paradise where everything turns up easily, simply, and automatically, where achievements will not demand effort or sacrifice. Meanwhile, you have the gall to claim identity with a man who made self-sacrifice the badge of his very survival. I see in Francis the typical so-called 'martyr mechanism' that prompts a man to seek inner perfection through renunciation.

"Hippies have the opposite attitude. They want to find perfection in a lazy way of life, to pluck apples from trees they have not tended, to drink pure water from unguarded streams, to fornicate and go their careless way. And they call that Franciscanism? The worst of it is that many of them think it is really so, and for that reason I have tried to play a trick on these false mystics in my *Brother Sun, Sister Moon*. Up to a certain point in the film I let them believe that they are right, that they are like Saint Francis. Later they are shown the difference, the profound difference, that separates them from the Poor Man of Assisi. The difference arises from the obstinate fact that in real life nothing comes as a gift without strings, and that sacrifice is

the coin in which we must pay for things worth having."

Another young Franciscan asked: "Would Francis find followers in this day and age? I wonder, where? Sacrifice strikes fear into modern hearts. As Francis grew in self-purification he also grew in self-sacrifice. One of the keenest reproofs to modern society pillories its common neglect of training in self-sacrifice, but in Francis's day it was acknowledged as the basis of civilized society."

Zeffirelli answered: "I think he would still find sincere followers. Let me repeat: the seed of good is still here; it needs only to sprout and to be encouraged to grow. Today's society is indeed materialistic, and it tends to turn each of us into soulless brutes. But the young are still open to a frank and earnest proposal, an authentic message, so long as it is a precise spiritual message. Modern confusion of ideas and popular confusion of language cause many young minds to miss the point in Francis's message, and they suffer from that lack of precision. Let's refer to Guevara again. Che leaves immature and superficial minds thunderstruck because they interpret him as a kind of Robin Hood. They see only his heroic, adventurous side."

Another question: "Will your film highlight only the humanism of Francis, or also his sanctity? Youth's sacrifice today is tied to humanism rather than to Christianity. They strive for human solidarity more than for Christian charity."

Zeffirelli replied: "Well, when I said that I don't intend to touch the sanctity of Francis, I meant that I do not deal with the aspect or 'moment' of his sanctity. It ought to be evident that I cannot prescind from his sanctity; I can't ignore it. If I dealt only with his humanism I would be replaying a common, hackneyed tune: rich man chooses rags. That would be a cliché, a miserably banal stereotype, because it is normal for a rich man to pose as a man of the people. Sensitive children of rich parents can and do have 'guilt-feelings' about their condition. Rich men commonly feel a need to give themselves to the poor; this need is a sincere desire, even though it has an equivocal, ambiguous tendency in many cases.

"However, that guilt-feeling of a rich boy is certainly not what I'm handling in this film, nor did I ever discern it in St. Francis. In him, poverty is not a rejection of societal property or wealth as such. He loves poverty and praises it for all mankind to hear and is convinced that it offers us the key to truth and happiness. Love of poverty becomes a basic Christian theme in the mouth of Francis. It

is a developing conversation concerning all of humanity and the Christian liberation of mankind. For this reason, the story of Francis's life is a Christian parable. I confess that at one stage I was about to drop the film. I went through a big crisis over it. I said to myself: 'I am not fit to confront such a stupendous personality as Saint Francis of Assisi. I have not got that kind of ability. I'm simply not competent in that field.' Then, later, I came to understand that his message is, at its core, a simple one. It is so simple that anyone who truly wants to tell it to others can tell it."

Brother Sun, Sister Moon

A REVIEW BY
JOHN FELICE, O.F.M., AND
ROY M. GASNICK, O.F.M.

There have been three major films about Saint Francis of Assisi, none of which was really successful in getting to the dramatic essence of this most extraordinary man. There was a Spanish version some twenty-five years ago that was strong on sentiment but weak in everything else; it presented a sapless Francis: nice, nondemanding, and saccharine. Rossellini's Italian *The Little Flowers of St. Francis* gave us something of the exuberance of the first Little Brothers but missed completely the passion, the vision, and the strength of the little poor man; this Francis was not only sapless but also sappy. Hollywood's *Saint Francis of Assisi,* released thirteen years ago, wound up being patronized mostly by Catholic school groups who probably felt an obligation to support a movie about a saint; this was a Francis so watered down that his life seemed a rivulet instead of the torrent it really was.

Now there is a fourth film, Paramount Picture Corporation's *Brother Sun, Sister Moon,* an Italian-English production directed by Franco Zeffirelli, whose last picture, *Romeo and Juliet,* was a triumph not only artistically and at the box office, but also in making Shakespeare contemporary to the young people of a few years ago.

Let it be said immediately that *Brother Sun, Sister Moon* is something of a Franciscan masterpiece and that Zeffirelli's achievement on the screen calls

to mind Giotto's frescoes in Assisi. The film is visually stunning. Zeffirelli said that he wanted to show nature, color, light, animals, people in a way that only someone with the innocent eyes of a Francis could see them. English folk singer Donovan's music score and lyrics are as fresh and charming as the original "Canticle of Brother Sun."

Let it be said immediately that Brother Sun, Sister Moon *is something of a Franciscan masterpiece and that Zeffirelli's achievement on screen calls to mind Giotto's famous frescoes in Assisi.*

More importantly, here is a flesh-and-blood Francis: real, powerful, passionate in his values, tender in his relationships, uncompromising in his principles. Zeffirelli has gotten Saint Francis out of the birdbath, hopefully, once and for all.

Though the film covers only the first part of Francis's life (it ends with Pope Innocent III approving the Order), all of his basic values are vividly, honestly, and movingly revealed: his uneasiness with a wealthy and powerful Church; his disdain for civil rulers who are more concerned about their power than the needs of the people; his concern for the poor, the oppressed, the little ones; his rejection of wealth and status in favor of a life of poverty and minority; his human and popular approach that brought religion back to the people; his abhorrence of war and violence; his fidelity and reverence for the Church in spite of abuses; and, of course, his vision of the brotherhood of creatures.

Francis's poverty and simplicity are never sermonized, but lived. Lady Poverty is never mentioned, but is assumed as an essential fact in Francis's vision. Simplicity is embraced as a sort of odd characteristic of the first brothers as if they had discovered a logic beyond the logic of man.

You do not see Francis the mystic, the ascetic, the

158

sufferer, the man of prayer—but you do not doubt for one moment that he is all these and more. What you do see is a man truly fascinated with God and men, and hence fascinating: a dreamer, a visionary, a gentle rebel, a seeker of freedom, a man challenging the status quo. You watch, and you begin to silently cheer him on, hoping that he will make it.

There is no deep-voiced God telling Francis what to do, no talking crucifix of San Damiano, no dreaming Pope Innocent III seeing Francis holding up a falling Church, though all these are subtly suggested by Zeffirelli's directional techniques.

There is just a young man caught up with the futility of human toil and aspiration, caught up with the Gospel vision of something better. "If the purpose of life is this loveless toil we fill our days with," says Francis to Bishop Guido of Assisi after his father had denounced him, "then it's not for me. There must be something better. There has to be. Man is a spirit. He has a soul. And *that* is what I want to recapture. My soul."

Francis is never seen hating what he is trying to overthrow, never seen judging the world he has taken on. When he discovers that one of his brothers has been killed at San Damiano during a raid instigated by one of his former friends and reluctantly permitted by Bishop Guido, Francis says, "Why? Why? Who could have such hatred? For such a creature? What did I do wrong? I must know. I must—understand."

(The incident itself is historically inaccurate—Bishop Guido was actually close to Francis and was his adviser from the beginning, and there was no such raid or killing—but it is dramatically acceptable.)

Francis goes to Rome with his first followers to find out what, if anything, he has done wrong. The encounter with Pope Innocent III is the most powerful and moving part of the film. After the papal court has Francis violently ejected from the Lateran, the Pope calls him back. Francis says, "Simple people understand us. But the others—perhaps we have

159

made mistakes. This is what we want to know. Is it not possible, Holy Father, to live according to the teachings of our Lord, or have we sinned through presumption?"

The Pope replies, "My dearest son, in our obsession with Original Sin, we too often forget—original innocence. Go in the name of our Lord Jesus Christ. Preach the truth to all men. May your disciples increase a thousandfold, and flourish."

We suspect that not everyone will react favorably to *Brother Sun, Sister Moon* for a number of reasons: the slight but nonessential tampering with history will offend the historical purists; Zeffirelli's romantic approach will probably turn off those whose outlook is more intellectual; the allusions to the contemporary hippie movement will disturb some adults; the antiestablishment nature of some of the scenes will provoke rumbles among those committed absolutely to law and order; and an activist Francis is bound to disturb those who be-

lieve that Francis's place is in the birdbath.

Some will be hostile to the film because it presents the medieval Church in unfavorable light. But how else to dramatize "Francis, repair my Church, which you see is falling into ruins"? Actually, the film ends with a strong statement of fidelity to the Church. Zeffirelli's intent is clear from the way he movingly handles the meeting between Francis and Pope Innocent: Francis is a reformer, not a revolutionary, whose work is for the Church and *within* the Church and decidedly not against the Church; Innocent III is a great and gentle Pope who recognizes the need for a Francis and opens the doors for him. A message, certainly, for the "alienated" young Catholics of today who mistakenly feel that all doors are closed to them.

But the essential message about Francis is there for the rest of us. For a world grown cold, it prompts us once again to reconsider and to wonder one more time.

160

The Franciscan Style of Communications

ANTHONY SCANNELL,
O.F.M.CAP.

Last summer I visited Assisi for the first time. It was a tremendously moving experience for me, as I knelt before the tomb of Saint Francis in wonder and prayer, and as I walked the streets of his city, visited the churches, the hills, and the caves where he prayed. What amazed me most was that this little man, from this remote, walled city, still fascinated followers and attracted visitors seven hundred and fifty years after his death and is still the most popular Catholic saint.

How did he do it? He had no publicity agent; he didn't have his own radio or television program; he lived even before the printing press was invented. What made his style of communication so effective and so enduring that it lives on dynamically even seven hundred and fifty years later?

Francis was an evangelizer. He lived and preached the Gospel of Jesus.

Francis was not just interested in communicating; he had a very definite message to communicate. That message was Jesus Christ. Jesus had become his total life; he was eager to talk about him, to witness to him, to minister to others in Jesus' name. So if we simply call Francis a communicator, we are not saying enough about the message, the content of his communication. Francis was by his own admission a "herald of the Great King."

Francis's incarnational sense not only saw the Living Water in every brook, the Light of the World in the sun, the Lamb of God among the flocks, the Grain of Wheat in the fields, but also he wanted others to see them, too. That's why he constantly taxed his imagination, his creativity, his poetic sense and love of music, his flair for the dramatic, and his genius for parable and symbol. He had a style in everything he did, but it was born of love and a real desire to evangelize. If it were just for effect, the effect was to make Jesus better known and loved. The effect was to evangelize without overpowering, without manipulating. The effect was to make the revelation of God go on, continue in the events of every day.

If we call Francis an evangelizer, we more pre-

cisely focus on the heart of Francis's whole life and activity, on the purpose for which he communicated. And by talking about the Franciscan style of evangelization, we not only italicize that Francis's communicating and ours are Christ-centered, but also we remind ourselves that communication is a service of evangelization, and that makes communicating a ministry, and not just a job, a hobby, or a technique.

The Franciscan style of communication is, and always has been, *close to the people.*

Francis didn't live in, nor evangelize from, a high office on Madison Avenue. Whenever he went up high, such as on Mount Subasio or Mount Alvernia, it was always to come down, as Jesus did, to live and work among the people. His experiences were those of real life; he put on real armor to fight in a real war; he was thrown into a real prison. When he wanted to know what it was like to be a beggar, he changed clothes and tried to live the life of a real outcast. He went out to serve among real lepers; he even tried to rebuild a real church. He wanted to do real work. He went on a real Crusade, and went to see the real Sultan. He really wanted to suffer the same wounds as Jesus. And from all these real experiences, he learned.

From real life he drew the stories that he told, the songs that he sang, the parables that he fashioned, the language and imagery he used. This, he knew, of course, was what Jesus did. It has been Christ's style of communicating and evangelizing.

That's why there was such a human touch in all that Francis wrote or spoke or said. This is why he was understood so well by the people and loved by them. And this is why, wherever there has been effective communication, evangelization, by Franciscans all over the world, to the cities or in the missions, it's because that contact with life, that human touch, that understanding and sympathy were there.

What was unique about Francis's style of communicating was that he was actor, poet, musician, artist, author, preacher—a multimedia man.

Francis was an effective communicator, an effective evangelizer, because everything he said and did came from the heart. It was a heart he opened fully to God, to receive his love, and a heart he opened fully to people, to share their pain and their promise. Out of the abundance of that heart came wondrous creative ways to communicate and evangelize.

What was unique about Francis's style of communicating was that he was actor, poet, musician, artist, author, preacher—a multimedia man.

He always had a flair for the dramatic. For instance, his response to his father before the Bishop of Assisi was the X-rated dramatic gesture to throw off all the clothes his father had given him and declare that he had only one Father in heaven. He acted out other messages, such as displaying his displeasure by dismantling the roof of a friary he thought too sumptouus, going out to beg before dining with a bishop, and eating morsels on the floor when he couldn't stomach his feasting friars.

Symbols and images were another important part of Francis's communication style. After his nude scene in Assisi, he was given the garb of a peasant, and on it he marked the sign of the cross. That symbol represented a special image for Francis—that of the knight. It was an image that had fascinated him from childhood, and one that he sought to ful-

fill by going out to war and battle. But through symbols and images in his dreams, he had been drawn to a new understanding of what knighthood meant, had been knighted by Christ from the cross at San Damiano, and now as knight and herald of the great King, he went out to claim his lady, Lady Poverty, the only bride he would ever take. That symbol of the cross dominated his whole life. It was the only symbol he used on his letters and writings, in the then customary form of the tau, or T-shaped cross.

Francis also had a great respect for verbal and written communications. He knew how to preach well and effectively, and those he could not reach by his spoken words he attempted to evangelize by his writings, such as his *Letter to All the Friars*, and even a *Letter to All Christians*.

But words about Christ were never enough for Francis. He wanted to show and tell, and that's why he made the story of Christmas come alive in the first crib at Greccio. He wanted to sing out his love, and that is why he is said to be the founder of the Christmas carol. He harmonized audio and visual in his splendid "Canticle of Brother Sun."

He himself, in fact, had become a symbol and an image, so much so that all he had to do was walk through a village and say nothing, but he knew that he had preached a powerful sermon.

When Francis was able to do that, he had become the most effective communicator. He had become an integrated image, at once the medium and the message. He was a "single image projection": a person simple, thorough, and integral. What he *was* communicated more effectively than anything he said or did.

The Father recognized this, too, and one day, before Francis's death, the Lord made him a living audiovisual of himself on Mount Alvernia. But those external stigmata really exposed wounds that had been cut deeply in Francis's heart ever since the encounter with the crucifix of San Damiano. Out of the abundance of that heart the wounds bled.

I think it is the same with us today. We will never become effective communicators, effective evangelizers, by learning all the techniques of mass media—radio, television, public relations, advertising, photography, script writing, editing, composing. We need expert skill in them, but I think the basic Franciscan truth is that the message is the medium, not vice versa, and if the message has truly changed our hearts, and we live it as totally and as close to real life as we can, the media will take form from it.

When we do that, the Franciscan message will go on.

A Personal Friend of Jesus Named Francis

ARLO GUTHRIE

I was perfectly happy, as a nothing could be perfectly happy. I also was perfectly sad as well. It occurred to me one day that a personal friend of Jesus named Francis has made it possible for a fraternity to exist among people that theretofore had not been recognized by the official Church and therefore by anyone else. The faithful, in terms of having not just a position but an obligation, were increased and encompassed. By this encompassing they changed their nature. The people took seriously their baptism and what it implies. Maybe it has taken eight hundred years for that to be actualized. In some ways it is going to take longer. It hasn't occurred yet. It is not enough to sing "Priestly People" every two months. Francis made it possible for us in a way that is within the limits and structures of the Church to be a community.

Saint Francis of Assisi ... Superhero

GENE PELC

In the beginning there was the comic.

And the comic was without form, and was void; and darkness was upon the face of the artists. And the spirit of Francis moved upon the face of Marvel.

And Marvel said, "Let there be a Saint Francis comic magazine."

And there was a Saint Francis book.

And the Church saw the book. And it was good.

How do you start talking about a wild and wonderful project such as a comic magazine about the life of Saint Francis of Assisi? Wild . . . the Church and comic books? Wonderful . . . why not the Church and comics!

Well, there I was, in the midst of plotting the further expansion of the Marvel Universe: *The Incredible Hulk, Spider-Man,* ad infinitum, and how to endear ourselves further into the hearts and minds of Japandom, and the phone rang. It was Father Campion Lally, O.F.M., of the Rappongi Chapel Center in Tokyo, and after the opening amenities, Father first introduced me to the idea. "You know, 1982 will be the eight hundredth anniversary of the birth of Saint Francis of Assisi," said Father Campion, "and it'll be one of the greatest worldwide celebrations of all time. Saint Francis is such a popular figure, especially with the children. What would you think about doing a comic book about the life of Saint Francis?"

"Church . . . comics . . . Saint Francis . . . Superheroes?" I thought, "Well, why not? If we can call Superman and Captain America superheroes in our magazines, then how much more so is Saint Francis! He has shaped events and influenced millions of people's minds, particularly the young, for centuries. In my book that's a real Superhero!" "Of course," I said, "it's probably something we'd have to make up for the Church. I don't know if it would have any commercial value in the places where comics are usually sold. But then again . . . let's talk about it."

Sitting at the chapel center with Fathers Campion, Flavian Walsh, O.F.M., and William De Biase, O.F.M., I became more excited. I began to

163

FRANCIS' PRAYERS HAVE BEEN ANSWERED IN A WAY HE NEVER DREAMED OF!

IN HIS OWN MOMENT OF TORMENT, HE HAS BEEN SHOWN A VISION OF THE GREATER TORMENT SUFFERED BY *CHRIST*, WHOSE MEMORY FRANCIS HAS TRIED TO LIVE BY.

THE VISION IS ACCOMPANIED BY THE FLIGHT OF A *SERAPHIM*.

FRANCIS IS THE ONLY ONE WHO IS HERE ON *MOUNT VERNA* TO WITNESS THESE HEAVENLY SIGHTS...

realize that this could be much more than a simple Sunday-morning church item. "We have been planning many projects to celebrate this occasion of Saint Francis's anniversary," said Father Campion, "and I have always been intrigued by and interested in comics, especially as an expression of the culture. I've seen Buddhist comics about Shinran, Buddha, etc. I'm also fascinated by the Japanese *emaki* or pictured scroll, which is a type of comic, and began to think it would be wonderful to have a really good comic, or illustrated story, to put it better, about the life of St. Francis in English. And that's when we thought of you."

Father Flavian introduced me to Father Conrad Harkins, O.F.M., head of the U.S. Franciscan Institute at St. Bonaventure University in New York. Father Conrad was most enthusiastic and wanted the Church, specifically the Franciscans, to write the story. "What particularly interests me," said Father William, "is that many people who otherwise have been unreached by the Church will read this work. We're reaching out to a new audience."

The next step was a late-night call to Marvel Comics headquarters in New York and publisher Stan Lee. "Sounds great," Stan said, "but I also want a new audience to realize that our work is more than kid stuff . . . funny books. I want them to realize that cartooning and illustration are a legitimate art form and means of expression, just as valid, rich, and meaningful as any other!"

So comics and the Church have joined hands. An unlikely couple? Maybe, but made possible by a few people who believe— and a man whose spirit continues to touch all of mankind 800 years after his birth. A man who truly can be called, as in the title of the forthcoming Marvel Comic Magazine: Francis—Brother of the Universe!

And so it came to pass. The Franciscan Order would write the book; Marvel would illustrate, publish, and distribute it through its channels. The Church would also distribute it through its channels. But—who could write it? Fathers Flavian and Conrad had the answer and introduced me to Father Roy Gasnick, O.F.M., Director of the New York Franciscan Communications Office, who had already worked with Paramount Pictures on Zeffirelli's *Brother Sun, Sister Moon,* with NBC for the development of *Francis, a Search for the Man and*

BUT THEY LEAVE BEHIND THEM EVIDENCE FOR ALL THE WORLD TO SEE.

≥UUHHN≤

ALL HIS LIFE, FRANCIS HAS CARRIED THE LORD'S PAIN IN HIS HEART.

NOW, HE SHARES IT WITH HIS BODY.

His Meaning, and on the off-Broadway musical, *Francis.*

I met with Father Roy in New York, and he went right to work. He wrote the text and plot. That went to Marvel's studios and comic artist supreme, John Buscema, who is now creating the artwork at his home in California.

Publication is expected sometime next year. If the enthusiasm and spirit for the work continue, further vistas will unfold: a syndicated newspaper strip, perhaps; translations into foreign languages; and maybe a TV animation special that has all the earmarks of a classic.

So comics and the Church have joined hands. An unlikely couple? Maybe, but made possible by a few people who believe . . . and a man whose spirit continues to touch all of mankind 800 years after his birth. A man who truly can be called, as in the title of the forthcoming Marvel Comic magazine: *Francis—Brother of the Universe!*

In Detail: Bellini's Saint Francis

COLIN EISLER

Wandering through the baronial splendors of New York's Frick Museum, the visitor suddenly comes upon an extraordinary view—not of neighboring Central Park or the museum's garden court, but of Saint Francis in a north Italian landscape. The painting is done with such phenomenal clarity and intensity as to seem beyond art and style. Never before had a religious picture shown so much nature and so little man.

This great work was painted in the late 1470s (the precise date is unknown) by Giovanni Bellini, a member of one of the most renowned families in Renaissance Italy and the acknowledged leader of the contemporary Venetian school. The scene represented in the picture is Mount Alvernia, where Saint Francis is said to have received the stigmata—the imprint of Christ's Crucifixion wounds, here barely visible on his hands and foot. . . .

At first sight, Bellini's *Saint Francis* suggests the fertility of a late medieval millefleurs tapestry or manuscript margin, teeming with life's infinite variety. But as we look closer, the painting reveals a

new sense of order. Trees and rocks, the birds, and foreshortened donkey, are all carefully arranged to move the eye backward and forward. This is no mirror of medieval piety—but a vista shrewdly assembled by a Renaissance artist.

What we see is a mystical event placed in an extraordinarily realistic setting, a unity of Christian symbolism and Renaissance rationalism. Bellini's treatment clearly reflects the intellectual climate of the time, in which humanists and scholars at the University of Padua (Venice's university town) often worked and prayed side by side with the Franciscans at the great local shrine of Saint Anthony, himself a follower of Saint Francis.

Curiously, when modern scholars began to study Bellini's painting in the nineteenth and early twentieth centuries, they showed far more interest in the wonderfully luminous landscape than in the enigmatic subject. Such a secular view was, for instance, taken by the noted art historian Bernard Berenson. Writing in 1916, Berenson argued that the inclusion of Saint Francis was nothing more than a religious justification for painting an extraordinary natural setting. But once one analyzes the details, the work abounds with religious symbols and references. Francis's rustic retreat evokes Adam and Eve's first house; the bell and vine symbolize the Church. Christ's presence and Passion are alluded to by the cross with its crown of thorns and by the saint's clogs, removed in the presence of divinity. A skull, the standard reminder of man's fate, refers to Adam's death. The closed text on the rustic desk is perhaps a book of hours, with prayers for the different times of day. Facing the sunset, his chest raised, arms outstretched, mouth open in song, Francis may be reciting vespers for the twilight hour, with the sun's last rays streaming from a gloriously turbulent blue and white sky.

A hollyhock rises at the saint's side, planted in a little herb-and-flower garden. Long known for its healing properties, the hollyhock was believed to cure snakebite. Saving man from the serpent that caused his Fall, the flower became a symbol of salvation. Growing immediately behind the hollyhock is a small juniper, whose thorny leaves were often compared with the crown of thorns, and its wood to the Cross. The shrub was a symbol of Christ's humility and thus a most appropriate name for Juniper, Francis's favorite and humblest brother.

But the most eloquent messengers of the divine presence flooding this painting are the laurel in the sky and the stone below the saint's bare feet. The bowing tree is a *Laurus nobilis,* long believed to

be fireproof and so compared with the wood of the Cross, which kept mankind from the fires of damnation. Just as the laurel bends and dips, animated by the ray of golden light through its leaves, so does the extraordinary bluish stone outcropping where Francis stands seem to be rendered suddenly molten, as if sharing the entranced singer's ecstasy. Often tied to the imagery of divinity, the stone and the stream of water at its side may be linked to the rock and the waters of salvation. Just as Francis repeated Christ's Passion, he also appeared as a new Moses, striking water from the rock.

Bellini's painting is so freshly felt and clearly perceived that one could easily see it as simply the work of a highly trained eye. Indeed, the panel reflects an intense study of ancient theories on perspective and Renaissance inquiries into perception and optics. But the underpinning, the dominant spirit, remains religious.

For the first time color and shadow permeate a landscape with a sense of sound—Francis's song of praise to the Creator.

In the end the secret of Bellini's art lies in his ability to unite in a single work sight and sound, light and movement, scientific detail and glowing generalization. For the first time color and shadow permeate a landscape with a sense of sound—Francis's song of praise to the Creator. As Francis's prayer rises, the setting sun directs heavenly light to the earth, glorifying his miraculous sharing of the Passion.

The warm light suffusing the painting might be seen as the first radiance of the coming High Renaissance. The shepherd taking his flocks to the fortified city is like a messenger of the future and, indeed, the same figure reappears in the Arcadian paintings of younger Venetian artists, among them Giorgione and Gellini's pupil Titian. With seamless skill and grace Bellini has incorporated an extraordinary multiplicity of experience into a single work. What we see is nearly as wondrous as the saint's own vision.

His Universal Appeal

Fools for God in the Franciscan, Jewish, and Russian Traditions

JOHN GARVEY

There is probably no saint as appealing to so many people as Francis of Assisi. He has been called the saint who is most like Christ. Even in the wild company of the saints his literal acceptance of the Gospel stands out. But much of the appreciation of Francis has been sentimental, and it ignores aspects of his life that are difficult to understand and not very sympathetic. The popular picture of Francis is one of unrelieved pleasantness: he was an advocate of simple living who gathered like-minded Christians around him; he was good to animals, could talk to them and tame them; everyone liked him.

It is true that early accounts of Francis's life stress his attractiveness to many people, people who might have found another person insane if he were to act the way Francis did. And the taming of the wolf of Gubbio and Francis's sermon to the birds are stories that circulated within a couple of generations of the first Franciscans. There must be some truth to the pleasant picture of Francis that has come down to us.

Here, however, we are confronted with the same problem Jesus poses. Our tendency is to look only at the Jesus who was kind to children and sinners, and not the severe Jesus, the one who was quick to expose hypocrisy, drive moneylenders from the temple, whose behavior to his mother and his followers seems at times abrupt, if not rude. However likable Francis was, however tender, there is another and more paradoxical facet of his life that may be more important to an understanding of Francis. It may be more important because if it is true that Francis was like Christ, the vital point is not to emphasize those virtues that everyone understands, but those strange things that almost nobody understands, and hardly anyone likes. We love the

Francis who was kind, and the Francis who composed hymns to the sun is marvelous; but it is hard to feel near to the Francis who stripped himself naked to show his independence from his family, or who threw himself into thorn bushes. Francis was, in worldly terms, uncompromising and unrealistic. When his followers asked for some of the security every other religious order knew, he was furious. Although by the time he died he was loved by thousands, during the time immediately following his conversion he was considered mad and was beaten by people who were offended by his rags and his eccentric behavior.

It is this Francis we must try to understand—the fool for Christ, who said that the Passion and humiliation of Jesus were all the instruction he needed.

The notion of becoming a fool for Christ's sake goes back to the passage in the Gospel where Jesus rejoiced that God had revealed his truth to the temple and had hidden it from those the world calls wise; and the theme is taken up by Paul, who calls the Cross a scandal because it contradicts the wisdom of the world . . . it is folly. John Saward writes (in *The Fool for Christ's Sake in Monasticism*— 1975), "The most important characteristic of the fools, the basis and inspiration of all that they do and are, is identity with Christ crucified, their participation in the poverty, nakedness, humiliation, and abandonment of the Lord; and here the spirit of folly for Christ's sake comes close to the spirit of martyrdom." Saward quotes Kologrivov, who writes that the basis of the fool's vocation "is the awareness of the soul's terrible responsibility toward God," a responsibility that consists of "taking voluntarily on oneself humiliations and insults, in order to increase humility, meekness, and kindness of heart, and so to develop love, even for one's enemies and persecutors."

The fool for Christ's sake has appeared again and again in Christian history. In Russia it became a kind of charismatic institution. Saward mentions the fact that Russian fools for Christ usually appeared as pilgrims, who frequently offended the pious. Saint Basil the Blessed stole the merchandise of dishonest tradesmen, stoned the houses of the respectable, wept with sinners, and denounced the injustice of the Czar. He once offered Ivan the

169

Terrible a piece of raw meat; Ivan refused, and Basil then showed him in the sky the souls of innocent people Ivan had murdered. In the West the same phenomenon occurred. Saint Philip Neri shaved half his beard off, wore his coat inside out, walked past the tabernacle without genuflecting; and like Basil he combined this with a sense of social justice, working to prevent Gypsies from being used as galley slaves by the papal fleet. Following his conversion, Saint John of God was considered a lunatic, and there are numerous other examples of this strange way of responding to the Gospel.

Of course we have to consider the possibility that such people really were mad. But as easy as this judgment might be in the case of some saints whose havior strikes us as outrageous (Christina the Astonishing, for example, whose weird behavior is frankly described as schizophrenic by her most recent Catholic biographers), it doesn't hold up for others. Saint Basil's mad behavior before the Czar told a truth that the more restrained sanity of the "respectable" did not dare to tell. The Gospel reveals things hidden from the beginning of time, and the uncovering of those things can lead to strange behavior—Bartimaeus calls out to Jesus for mercy, while his embarrassed companions try to silence him; Zacchaeus climbs a tree to get a glimpse of Jesus, leaving respectability behind. What the world considers crazy makes sense in this context.

It is not possible to retain both our sense of having an easy place in this world and the notion that we are following Christ. Kierkegaard calls the desire to maintain respectability and worldly honor while calling oneself a Christian "wanting to have a mouthful of flour, and to blow." Jesus said that his followers were to leave all they had behind, not looking back; he said that following him meant taking up the cross daily, and dying to self. What this means will vary, life to life. But what it does *not* mean is peace, as the world gives it. It does not mean an easy life, or a life that is at home in any society. To the extent that we are willing to serve both God and Mammon, we are not followers of Christ; and we are not, in fact, following God at all. Jesus did not say that it is undesirable to follow God and Mammon. He said you *cannot* do it. What you serve is not God, but an idol of the same name, as long as your allegiance is half-hearted.

In writing this way I have to be careful; I can't claim to have made the move Jesus asks of us. I may have met one or two people who have. At best I'm a fellow traveler, sympathetic, not yet completely committed. Perhaps this is why we are more comfortable calling ourselves "Catholic," "Anglican," "Protestant" than we are calling ourselves "Christian." And this may be why we are uncomfortable around those who "get saved," who are easy about calling themselves Christians, or who claim that their commitment is total. Our embarrassment is not, as the saved sometimes seem to think, that we have not made their noble decision. It is rather a feeling of embarrassment for them, because what they say is obviously not the truth.

Faced with this common discomfort, a discomfort around those who say that they are saved, and a discomfort at our own lives, since we do not live what we profess to believe—we can respond in a number of ways. It seems to me that the least healthy is to seek a means of making ourselves feel committed without having to change our lives in any but an emotional way, through involvement with enthusiastic group movements that reinforce our belief that we really *are* committed to the following of Jesus; the more sophisticated version of this move is to seek help from the *Zeitgeist*, reading the Gospels in the light of the last issue of *Psychology Today,* proving to ourselves that we really are O.K. and that our discomfort is merely a matter of conditioning. In either case we are looking toward the preservation of the self we are asked to leave behind. We can't believe that "sell all you have, give it to the poor, and follow me" really means "sell all you have, give it to the poor, and follow me." Here we fall back on Kant's ethical imperative and ask (knowing that there is no real danger of this happening), "What would happen if everyone did that?" But the statement is not addressed to everyone, only to you. That fact is one we fall all over ourselves to avoid.

The response we should make to this impasse is to take some encouragement from the answer of Jesus to his Apostles when they asked, in response

to his hard sayings, "Who then can be saved?" He answered that what was impossible for man was possible because of God's mercy. Some of our dilemma was described by Paul, when he said, "The good I would do, I do not." We believe that we are baptized into Christ's death as well as his Resurrection. Our consciousness of failure may be part of the death we are asked to acknowledge. It becomes fatal only when we stop acknowledging it, or try to justify it.

This is one aspect of the confession of sin that often escapes us, because we have made of sin a legal thing, a matter of "committing sins" rather than a matter of the condition in which we ordinarily find ourselves: half-hearted, distracted from what we are, and what we are called to. When Christians stop confessing that they are sinners, unprofitable servants, and to that extent that they are not Christians, then Christian faith ends. Consciousness of sin is in this sense the result of baptism: we are baptized into the death of Christ, who was "made sin for us," as well as his Resurrection. Sin is death, and to acknowledge this is the beginning of freedom from death. This means a ruthless honesty, however. You cannot confess sin in the abstract. When John says that the person who denies that he is a sinner is a liar, he does not mean that our response should be an abstract confession of sin but rather an acknowlegment of the sin that is *really* there; and he associates this with the divine Light, which reveals darkness. Kierkegaard defined the best Christian confession as a confession of the fact that we are not Christians.

The problem with the confession of sins, the acknowledgment of the death into which we are baptized, is that it is meant to lead to life. "Wherever we go we carry with us in our body the death that Jesus died, that in this body also life may reveal itself, the life that Jesus lives. For continually, while still alive, we are being surrendered into the hands of death, for Jesus' sake, so that the life of Jesus also may be revealed in this mortal body of ours" (2 Cor. 4:10–11). The form of this life is something revealed to us not only in the person of Jesus, but also in the lives of those who, like Francis, made deliberate, mad-seeming efforts to break with the world of death. Their foolishness is a measure of how radical the break may have to be; our instinctive reaction against the behavior of the fool for Christ is not necessarily a measure of our sanity, but may be the death-world's way of fighting back.

Before his conversion, Francis was a pleasant young man who was known for his cheerfulness and

"He's playing back his sermon."

for his generosity to beggars. When he was about twenty he was imprisoned with a number of others who had been caught up in the battle between the cities of Perugia and Assisi. His imprisonment lasted about a year, and upon his release Francis became dangerously ill. The illness was lengthy, and it may have been the beginning of his conversion. He set out to join the Pope's armies, having bought expensive equipment and clothing, but along the way he met a poor man and felt such compassion for him that he exchanged his own clothes for the other man's rags. Shortly afterward Francis became ill once more. Instead of proceeding to battle, he returned to Assisi, realizing that a change was demanded of him. One day he encountered a leper and at first was horrified. But then his horror at the leper turned around to become a horror at his own revulsion. He embraced the leper, and from that time onward his life turned toward the radical following of the Gospel message.

This incident is one that seemed pivotal to Francis himself. In his *Testament* he wrote, "The Lord God gave me, Francis, this way of doing penance: I was a sinner and found it hard to look at lepers, and the Lord God led me among them, and I was merciful to them. As I left them, what had previously seemed bitter turned into sweetness of body and soul. And then, soon after, I left the world."

Francis began to spend time caring for the ill, giving what he could to the poor; and then came the incident that marked him as a fool for Christ. One day as he prayed in the Church of San Damiano he heard a voice tell him: "Repair my house, which is falling down." With his usual literalness Francis assumed that this meant the church in which he was praying; so he set about repairing it. Unfortunately, he used some of his father's goods in the process, selling them and offering the proceeds to the poor priest who lived at the church. The priest refused the money, which Francis left lying on a window sill.

Francis's father was understandably angry. When he finally caught Francis (who had retreated for prayer and fasting, and possibly to avoid his father), he took him home forcefully, and kept him locked up there. Francis escaped, returning to Saint Damian's, where his father angrily confronted him with a choice: return home or renounce his inheritance, and return the stolen goods. Francis told his father than he was willing to lose his inheritance, but he insisted that the money received from the sale of his father's goods belonged to the poor. Francis's father tried to take him to court; Francis refused the authority of a civil tribunal. The Bishop of Assisi therefore became the judge. He told Francis that he should return what he had taken from his father. Francis agreed, and saying, "These clothes also belong to him," he stripped himself naked. He repudiated his father, telling him, "Until now I have called you my father on earth; now I say, 'Our Father, who art in heaven.'" His father went home, angry and extremely distressed, and Francis was given the tunic of a laborer who worked for the bishop. From that day he was in every way "the poor man of Assisi," who depended only on God and the charity of others.

Legend should not blind us to what happened here. Francis's treatment of his father was not fair, in any sense of the word. He had in fact stolen his father's property, he tried to refuse restitution, and his repudiation of his father seems self-dramatizing and insensitive. Forgetting that it is Saint Francis who did these things, we would be inclined to say of a person who behaved this way that he was mad, ungrateful, disrespectful, and unkind.

Singing the praises of God, Francis left the bishop and accepted a life that included abject poverty, beatings, and the ridicule of those who could see only foolishness in his repudiation of his family and his odd habit of repairing churches. He lived by begging. He also began to try to live a literal interpretation of the words of the Gospel, so that when he heard "Provide no gold, silver, or copper to fill your purse, no pack for the road, no second coat, no shoes, no stick," he gave away the few clothes he had begged from others and kept only one shabby coat, which he tied with a rope.

Gradually, the abuse of the townspeople turned to admiration. Francis's charity to the sick and the deformed proved that there was more than eccentricity at work in his life. There were rumors of cures performed by Francis, and a community began to form around him. Men from the region were led by his example to undertake the same life. They joined him, leaving their former comfortable lives for a life of poverty and manual labor; where work could not be found, they were told to "have recourse to the table of the Lord"—which is to say, they were to beg. In his *Testament*, Francis insists upon poverty: "Let the brothers see to it that they do not receive, on any account, churches and houses made for them, if these are not in keeping with holy poverty . . . let them always adhere to these injunctions and live in the world like strangers and pilgrims."

Francis's view of poverty was absolute, and so was his view of self-discipline. He threw himself into a thorn bush when troubled by temptation; he fasted frequently; he insisted upon obedience but at the same time was willing to be rebuked by his followers—in fact he frequently demanded it. When the Order had become established and somewhat respectable, Francis fought unsuccessfully to keep it from becoming attached to property. Many of the friars had come to feel that the absolute poverty and the unproscribed asceticism advocated by Francis should be placed within a more secure framework, one which could include ownership of land and a regulated form of self-denial. Francis was enraged. "My brothers," he said, "the Lord has called me to the way of simplicity and humbleness, and this is the way he has pointed out to me for myself and for those who will believe and follow me. The Lord told me that he would have me poor and foolish in this world, and that he willed not to lead us by any other way than by that. May God confound you by your own wisdom and learning and, for all your faultfinding, send you back to your vocation whether you will or not." When some members of the Order wanted to receive official Church recognition for their preaching, in the form of a license from the Pope to preach in every diocese, Francis said that they should live lives that by their holiness would lead bishops to ask the friars for their help. "Let it be your unique privilege to have no privilege," he said.

He did nothing by halves. The *Fioretti* says that when Brother Ruffino did not obey him instantly, Francis, to chastise him, ordered him to preach naked to the people in Assisi. Then, when Ruffino had left, Francis was angry with himself for the harshness of his order and so he too went naked to Assisi, to join Ruffino. The people who saw them assumed that they were mad, until they listened to the words of Francis, who "spoke so marvelously of the contempt of the world, of holy penance, of voluntary poverty, of the desire of the heavenly Kingdom, and of the nakedness and humiliation of the Passion of our Lord Jesus Christ, that all those present, a great number of men and women, began to weep aloud with great devotion."

What can we make of this extreme behavior, of a man who takes such abrupt leave of his family and refuses to compromise at any point? His father had reason to be angry with him; his friars later found his way of life too demanding, and their desire for some security was certainly reasonable. His behavior was always a bit wild.

First of all, it should be said that the age was in need of a shock. The Church was decadent in the extreme. During the late twelfth and early thirteenth centuries, the time of Francis's life, the Cathari church was making converts—largely because of the corruption of the established Church. The Cathari were dualists, who believed that the world was the creation of a fallen spirit; to be freed from the demonic spirit that ruled the world, to free the divine Light imprisoned in the flesh, severe asceticism was necessary. The Cathari *perfecti*—the closest thing to a Cathari clergy—received a sacrament called the *Consolamentum*, following which they were not allowed to marry or eat meat. Their fasts were extreme. Their poverty was exemplary—so much that the poverty of the Dominican friars, whose Order was founded to combat the Cathari, had more to do with countering the powerful Cathari influence than with evangelical poverty. The Cathari combined their ascetic living and voluntary poverty with a compassion for all life, and their kindness to animals was considered unusual. Their teachings were widely accepted in the south of France and the north of Italy, though few Cathari believers felt able to accept the rigors of the life demanded of the *perfecti*. Cathari doctrine was frequently spread by two odd groups of travelers: troubadour poets and weavers.

Although his Catholicism isn't in question—he insisted on his absolute acceptance of Church teaching—Francis's way of life was, in the opinion of many scholars, influenced by Cathari thought. His radical poverty, his extreme asceticism, his feeling for animals, his poetry, his pacifism (he forbade the lay people who joined his Third Order to carry arms for any purpose)—all of these were closer to Cathari thinking than to the conventional Catholic thought of Francis's day. How direct the influence was is impossible to determine, and it is probably best to say that Francis and the Cathari responded to the same set of problems, though Francis's response was a kind of unorthodox orthodoxy, whereas the Cathari (more rulebound than Francis ever was) were orthodox heretics. In any case, it took a radical effort to understand the Gospel clearly in a time when the Church was both established and decadent. Francis's movement served as a reforming influence, and some have gone so far as to say that if it had been more successful there would never have been a Reformation (though the rise of nationalism and consequent anti-Roman feelings make this doubtful).

But his major purpose was not reform. Francis simply tried to live what he heard in the Gospel, and the simplicity and wholeheartedness of the attempt made him appear foolish.

It is hard, in any terms that we can understand, to see all of his actions sympathetically. It is better to see in them the literal application of such Gospel counsels as "If anyone comes to me and does not hate his father and mother, wife and children, brothers and sisters, even his own life, he cannot be a disciple of mine. No one who does not carry his cross and come with me can be a disciple of mine." This demand for single-mindedness and total surrender to God led to Francis's repudiation of his father, his obsession with Jesus' Passion, and his definition of obedience: it meant, he said, that you should be like a dead body. Before words like those of Jesus, and lives like those of Francis, we are uncomfortable. Rather than offer a defense of the words it is important to see the fruits of trying to live them, something the Gospel shows us in the Resurrection and the joy of Pentecost, and the lives of saints show us by revealing a little of the kingdom of God. In Francis's case we find tales of the kingdom in the *Fioretti*, a collection of Franciscan stories that was compiled within a couple of generations of Francis's death. The spirit that informs the *Fioretti* is the spirit of poverty—what it means to leave absolutely everything for the sake of the kingdom of God. The impression is one of sustained ecstasy, and it is sometimes frightening:

St. Francis went behind the altar and began to pray. In that prayer he received a divine visitation that inflamed his soul with such love of holy poverty that from the color of his face and the frequent opening of his mouth it seemed as if flames of fire came from him. Coming toward his companion as if aflame he cried out, "Ah, ah, ah! Brother Masseo, come to me'" He repeated this three times, and the third time lifted Brother Masseo into the air with his very breath, and propelled him the distance one could hurl a spear. Brother Masseo . . . later told his

companions that when he had been raised by the saint's breath and so softly thrown, he had felt such sweetness of soul and consolation of the Holy Spirit as he had never felt before or since.

Stories like this one remind us of something so simple we tend to forget it: God is much stronger than we think. I am reminded of a story repeated by Elie Wiesel in *Souls on Fire* (Random House, 1972) about the son of the Baal Shem who asked his dead father in a dream,

"How can I serve God?" The Baal Shem climbed a high mountain and threw himself into the abyss. "Like this," he answered. Another time the Baal Shem appeared to him as a mountain on fire, erupting into a thousand flaming fragments: "And like this as well."

Wiesel relates another story, one close to the story of Brother Masseo:

"One day," Rebbe Wolfe of Zhitomir tells us, "we were all sitting around the table in the House of Study. It was a Friday afternoon. We could hear the Maggid, in his study next door, reading the Sidra, the weekly portion of Scripture customarily read on Shabbat. Suddenly he stopped, the door opened, and there he was, standing motionless in the doorway, staring at us, or perhaps at someone beyond us. His whole being was on fire, but most of all, his face, most of all, his eyes. Seized with panic, Rebbe Pinhas, Rebbe Shmelke, Rebbe Elimelekh, and Rebbe Zusia ran into the street. Rebbe Levi-Yitzhak hid under the table. As for me, gripped by a strange exultation, I began to applaud with all my strength—and to this day I regret it."

These stories come from the Hasidic tradition, a Jewish movement that has much in common with Franciscanism, including tales of conversion, enthusiasm, asceticism, and ecstasy. They remind us that God is not an idea, a static being toward whom we aspire, but instead is a fire. From the burning bush, God gave his name to Moses: I am. And that Being was not a metaphysical notion but a fire that burns without consuming. That fire led to the ecstasy known by one of Francis's first followers, Brother Giovanni, who was so given over to God that

at times when he would hear his master speak of God, his heart would melt like wax near a fire; and the love of God so inflamed him that he was not able to stand still and endure it. He would get up and, as if drunk in spirit, would go about now through the garden, now through the woods, now through the church, talking as the flame and the impetus of the spirit moved him.

Brother Masseo, after a period of torment, was given such a joyful humility that

frequently when in prayer he would make a steady jubilant sound, like a soft dove. . . . When asked by Brother Jacopo de Fallerone why he never changed the tone of his rejoicing, he answered with great joy that when something goes well there is no need to change it.

The ecstatic element of Franciscan spirituality is balanced by a deep sense of compassion and mercy. One young friar, on seeing that a criminal had been sentenced by a harsh mayor to have his eyes put out, "asked that one eye be taken from him and the other from the evildoer, so that the criminal would not be completely deprived of his sight. The mayor and the council, seeing the fervent charity of the friar, pardoned both him and the criminal."

These stories come from the Hasidic tradition, a Jewish movement that has much in common with Franciscanism, includes tales of conversion, enthusiasm, asceticism, and ecstasy.

The Franciscan approach to life takes us to what we would normally regard as extremes: extremes of charity, of asceticism, of ecstasy, and certainly extremes of behavior. The madness involved in being a fool for Christ could have to do with the words of Scripture: that no one can look upon the face of God and live. There is a story told by the Hasidim about four men who made their way into the presence of God. One upon seeing God went mad, another died, another lost his faith, and only one survived intact. A clear sense of God could so unmoor a person from ordinary allegiances, ordinary behavior, that he might seem genuinely insane to us. But the insanity of a Francis is more sane than our caution, and his concentration on the death of Christ is more life-giving than our pursuit of self-fulfillment. The medieval fascination with Jesus' suffering has been criticized by a number of commentators, who point out that where Eastern Christianity emphasizes the Transfiguration, Western Christians emphasize the stigmata and the Passion.

Finally it is all one. The Russian Church, with its transfigured saints, saw a great mystery in the humiliated Christ. Our culture is puritanical about suffering and forgets that it is not a Christian obsession but a permanent reality. It is the beginning of Buddha's revelation, and Plato said that the love of wisdom meant learning how to die. Francis received the stigmata, but the Resurrection and the Transfiguration are there. The *Fioretti* speaks of Francis transfigured, so that "his five stigmata were as five beautiful stars and so radiant that they lit the entire palace with their rays." Reading the *Fioretti*—especially at points like this one—we feel a certain embarrassment, as if we had outgrown that kind of story. But learning to read that kind of story "with eyes that can see" might be the most important task for modern Christians, who should not be embarrassed by this any more than they are by the miracle of loaves and fishes multiplied, or water changed to wine. We can be refreshed in all of this attempt at coming to renewed understandings by the life of Francis. But it is also a challenge to the lukewarmness, which without his life, and the lives of others who have tried to understand the Gospel radically and wholeheartedly, would be reinforced without a challenge on any side.

"The humble pie is delicious here."

Francis, the Whirling Dervish?

IDRIES SHAH

Most people know that Saint Francis of Assisi was a light-hearted troubadour of Italy who experienced a religious conversion and became a saint with an uncanny influence over animals and birds. It is on record that the troubadours were a relic of Saracenic musicians and poets. It is often agreed that the rise and development of the monkish orders in the Middle Ages were greatly influenced by the penetration of Muslim dervish organization in the West. Studying Saint Francis from this point of view makes possible certain interesting discoveries.

Francis was born in 1182, the son of Pietro Bernardone, a merchant of fine stuffs, and his wife, Madonna Pica. He was originally named Giovanni, but his father was so attached to France (where he spent much of his commercial life) that "for love of the land he had just quitted" he renamed the child Francesco.

Although considered an Italian, Francis spoke Provençal, the language used by the troubadours. There is little doubt that he felt in the spirit of the troubadours a glimpse of something deeper than appeared on the surface. His own poetry so strongly resembles in places that of the love poet Rumi that one is tempted to look for any report that might connect Francis with the Sufi Order of the Whirling Dervishes. At this point we come across the first of a number of tales considered inexplicable by Western biographers.

The whirling dervishes can attain intuitive knowledge partly by a peculiar form of spinning, presided over by an instructor. Rumi's school of whirling dervishes was in full operation in Asia Minor, and its founder was still alive, during the lifetime of Saint Francis. Here is the puzzling "spinning" tale:

Francis was walking through Tuscany with a disciple, Brother Masseo. They arrived at a fork in the road. One path led to Florence, another to Arezzo, and a third to Siena.

Masseo asked which branch they should take.

"The road that God wills."

"And which is that?"

"We will know by a sign. I command you, by your path of obedience, turn round and round as children do, until I tell you to stop."

So poor Masseo twirled and twirled, till he fell down from giddiness. Then he got up and looked beseechingly at the saint; but the saint said nothing, and Masseo, remembering his vow of obedience, began again to twirl his best. He continued to twirl and to fall for some time, till he seemed to have spent all his life in twirling, when, at last, he heard the welcome words: "Stop, and tell me whither your face is turned."

"To Siena," gasped Masseo, who felt the earth rock round him.

"Then to Siena we must go," said Francis, and to Siena they went.

That Francis felt the source of his troubadour inspiration to lie in the East, and that he was connected with the Sufis seems clear.

That Francis felt the source of his troubadour inspiration to lie in the East, and that he was connected with the Sufis, seem clear from much evidence. When he went to the Pope, trying to have his order accepted, he used a parable that shows that he must have been thinking in terms of the orphaning of a tradition and the need to reestablish its reality. The phrases he uses in the parable are of Arabia; and the terminology, of a king and his court, of a woman and her sons in the desert, is not Christian but Saracen.

Francis [says Bonaventure, recording an audience with Pope Innocent] came armed with a parable. "There was," he said, "a rich and mighty king who took to wife a poor but very beautiful woman, who lived in a desert, in whom he greatly delighted and by whom he had children who bore his image. When her sons were grown their mother said to them, "My sons, be not ashamed; ye are the children of a king." And she sent them to the court, having supplied them with all necessaries. When they came to the king, he admired their beauty; and seeing in them some resemblance to himself, he asked them, "Whose sons are ye?" When they replied that they were the sons of a poor woman dwelling in the desert, the king, filled with much joy, said, "Fear not, ye are my sons, and if I nourish strangers at my table, how much more you, who are my legitimate children."

The tradition that the Sufis are the esoteric Christians out of the desert, and that they are the children of a poor woman (Hagar, wife of Abraham, because of their Arab descent) fits completely with the probability that Francis had tried to explain to the Pope that the Sufi stream represented Christianity in a continuing form.

At his first meeting with the Pope, we are told, Francis did not make much impression, and he was sent away. Immediately afterward, however, the Pope had a strange dream. He saw "a palm tree gradually grow up at his feet until it grew a goodly stature, and as he gazed upon it wondering what the vision might mean, a divine illumination impressed on the mind of the Vicar of Christ that this palm tree signified the poor man whom he had that day driven from his presence."

The palm tree is the symbol used by the Sufis, and this dream is probably the consequence of Francis's using it as an analogy during his audience.

In the early part of the thirteenth century, Pope Innocent III, convinced of the validity of the saint's mission, granted permission for the foundation of the Minor Brothers, or Franciscans. The "Lesser Brethren," considered to be a title assumed from pious humility, might lead one to ask whether there was any Order known as the "Greater Brethren." If so, what might the connection be?

The only people known in this way who were contemporary with Saint Francis were the Greater Brothers, an appellation of the Sufi Order founded by Najmuddin Kubra, "the Greater." The connection is interesting. One of the major characteristics about this great Sufi teacher was that he had an uncanny influence over animals. Pictures of him show him surrounded by birds. He tamed a fierce dog merely by looking at it—just as Saint Francis is said to have cowed the wolf in a well-known tale. Najmuddin's miracles were well known throughout the East sixty years before Saint Francis was born.

When Saint Francis was praised by anyone, it is reported, he replied with this phrase: "What everyone is in the eyes of God, that is, no more."

It is related that the dictum of Najmuddin the Greater was: *El Haqq Fahim ahsan el-Haqiqa*—"The Truth it is which knows what is True."

In or about 1224, the most important and characteristic of all of Saint Francis's songs was composed: the "Cantico del Sole"—"Canticle of Brother Sun." Jalaluddin Rumi, the whirling dervish chief and greatest poet of Persia, wrote numerous poems dedicated to the Sun, the Sun of Tabriz. He even called a collection of his poems the *Collection of the Sun of Tabriz*. In this poetry the word *sun* is used again and again.

If it were true that Saint Francis was trying to establish contact with the sources of his troubadour poetry, we would expect him to visit, or try to visit, the East. We would also expect him to be well received by the Saracens if he reached them. Further, he would be expected to produce Sufic poetry as a result of his Eastern travels. Now we can see whether these facts accord with history, and whether they were understood by his contemporaries.

When he was thirty, Francis decided to try to reach the East, and specifically Syria, which abutted upon the area of Asia Minor where the whirling dervishes were established. Prevented by financial troubles, he returned to Italy. Then he started out again, this time toward Morocco. He set off with a companion and traversed the whole kingdom of Aragon in Spain, though nobody can say why he did this, and some biographers are actually puzzled. Spain was very much penetrated with Sufi ideas and schools.

He did not actually reach Morocco, being driven back by illness. In the spring of 1214 he returned home.

Now he set out for the Crusades, where the siege of Damietta was in progress. Sultan Melek el-Kamil was encamped across the Nile—and Francis went to see him. He was well received, and the theory is that he went there to try to convert the Sultan to Christianity.

The Sultan [says a chronicler] not only dismissed Francis in peace, with wonder and admiration for the man's unusual qualities, but also received him fully into his favor, gave him a self-conduct by which he might go and come, with full permission to preach to his subjects, and an entreaty that he would frequently return to visit him.

This visit to the Saracens is assumed by biographers to be prompted by a desire to convert the Sultan. And yet it is said of him that "these two aimless journeys break in somewhat strangely upon the current of his life." They would be strange if they were not those of a troubadour looking for his roots. His desire to get to Morocco is dismissed in terms such as these: "It is impossible to tell what incident in his unrelated story may have suggested this new idea to the mind of Francis."

The Saracenic armies and the courts of their princes were at that time foci of Sufi activity. There can be hardly any doubt that it was here that Francis found what he was looking for. Far from having converted anyone in the Muslim camp, his first action upon recrossing the Nile was to try to dissuade the Christians from attacking the enemy. By the usual process of hindsight, this is explained by historians as being due to the saint's having had a vision of the forthcoming calamity to Christian arms. "His warning was received with contempt, as he had foreseen, but in the month of November following was fully verified when the Crusaders were driven back with great loss from the walls of Damietta. The sympathies of Francis under such circumstances must have been divided, for it is impossible that he could have been without some personal feeling toward the tolerant and friendly prince who had received him with such kindness."

The "Canticle of Brother Sun," hailed as the first-ever Italian poem, was composed after the saint's journey to the East, although because of his troubadour background it is impossible for his usual biographers to believe that he was not composing similar poetry before this:

It is impossible to suppose that during all these years [before 1224, when he wrote the "Song"] Francis, who was the leader of the young troubadours of Assisi in his early days, and who went through the woods and fields, after his conversion, singing to himself, still in French, songs that could not surely be the same songs he had sung through the streets among his joyous companions—the lays of war and love—it is impossible, we say, to suppose that it was for the first time at this late date that he had woven together canticles to the glory of God; but we are assured that these quaint and unskilled rhymes were the first beginning of vernacular poetry in Italy.

The atmosphere and setting of the Franciscan Order are closer to a dervish organization than anything else. Apart from the tales about Saint Francis that are held in common with sufi teachers, all kinds of points coincide. The special methodology of what Francis calls "holy prayer" indicates an affinity with the dervish "remembering," quite apart from the whirling. The dress of the Order, with its hooded cloak and wide sleeves, is that of the dervishes of Morocco and Spain. Like the Sufi teacher Attar, Francis exchanged his garb with a mendicant. He saw a seraph with six wings, an allegory used by Sufis to convey the formula of the *bismillah*. He threw away spiked crosses that were worn for purposes of self-mortification by many of his monks. This action may or may not have been exactly as it is reported. It may resemble the dervish practice of ceremonially rejecting a cross with the words, "You may have the cross, but we have the meaning of the cross," which is still in use. This, incidentally, could be the origin of the Templar habit, alleged by witnesses, that the Knights "trod on the cross."

Francis refused to become a priest. Like the Sufis, he enrolled laymen into his teaching, and again like the Sufis, but unlike the Church, he sought to spread the movement among all the people, in some form of affiliation. This was "the first reappearance in the Church, since its full hierarchical establishment, of the democratic element—the Christian people, as distinguished from the simple sheep to be fed, and souls to be ruled."

The striking thing about the rules laid down by Francis was that, like the Sufis and unlike the ordinary Christians, his followers were not to think first of their own salvation. This principle is stressed again and again among the Sufis, who consider regard for personal salvation to be an expression of vanity.

He "began his preaching everywhere with the salutation that God, he said, had revealed to him— 'The peace of God be with you!' " This is, of course, an Arab salutation.

In addition to having Sufi ideas, legends, and practices, Saint Francis retained many Christian aspects in the Order.

The consequence of this amalgam was to produce an organization that did not fully mature. A nineteenth-century commentator sums up the inevitable development:

We who, with all the enlightenment of six additional centuries, can look back and see the Inquisition grimly shadowing from under the robes of the Spanish priest, and see hordes of mendicant friars, privileged and impudent beggars, appearing behind the genial countenance of Francis, may perceive how much of evil mixed with the good, and how the enemy of all truth had cunningly mixed the seed of the tares with that of the wheat.

Saint Francis and Russian Monasticism

G.P. FEDOTOV

[Saint] Theodosius [d. 1074], from childhood, liked uncouth garb and bequeathed this predilection to the whole of Russian monasticism. But with him it was only a part of a total life orientation.

After his father's death, he used "to go to the fields with the slaves and work humbly." In this social humiliation or degradation, and only in this, the ascetic inventiveness of the Russian saint manifested itself. In the peasant labor of her son, as later in his profession of baker of wafers, the mother of Theodosius was right to see a social degradation, a stain on the family honor. The saint, however, liked to be "as one of the poor" and persuaded his mother: "Listen, O mother, I implore, listen: our Lord and God, Jesus Christ, became poor and humiliated himself, giving us the example that we also should humiliate ourselves for his sake."

This self-impoverishment of Theodosius is nourished by the vivid contemplation of Christ's *kenosis,** of His "slave's form," and of His suffering body. One recalls in this connection Theodosius's attempt to escape to the Holy Land, "where our Lord was walking in the flesh." Having chosen for himself the humble vocation of a wafer-baker, he justifies himself before his mother not on the ground of his love for the liturgy, but in regard to the body of Christ. With extraordinary force he expresses his religious attitude: "I ought to rejoice that the Lord has vouchsafed me to become maker of his flesh." These features, which have no Greek parallels, are evidence of Theodosius's strong religious intuition. . . .

Theodosius belonged to a newly converted nation, hardly to the second Christian generation in Russia. Boris and Gleb belonged to the very first. This spiritual youth of Russian Christianity turned out to be a great advantage rather than a handicap. The old and ossified Byzantine tradition had still little sway over Russian religious consciousness. The shock of the Gospel was more immediate and overwhelming: it determined for all time the main Russian approach to Christianity.

The kenotic idea has its practical expression with Theodosius in three Christian virtues: poverty, humility, and love, in their complete unity as one inseparable whole. Poverty and humility or obedience are virtues inherent in monasticism from its very beginning. Here, however, their meaning is changed. With Theodosius they are not ascetic means for shaping Christian personality. They are rather an end in themselves, expressing different

* The acceptance by Christ of the limitations of human nature in becoming man, but without the impairment of his divinity.

sides of the same personality: the Incarnate Christ and his ideal disciple. Obedience is not an exercise for eradicating self-will and shaping another higher self. It is a direct way to Christ. With Theodosius it is better not to speak of obedience, but of humility. He was supremely and perfectly disobedient through all his life. But he remained humble even in his disobedience. Love is not the last and the most difficult degree of perfection, as it is with most of the Greek ascetic writers. It is a simple, immediate, and self-evident implication of Christ's love for man. Love of one's fellow-men does not need to justify itself as if it were robbing something from the love of God.

Indeed, Theodosius seems to ignore *Eros* in the sense of passionate and mystical love of God as celestial Beauty. *Agape* remained for him the only type of Christian love. That is why there is nothing mystical about him. Contemplation was not his business. When Nestor speaks of his secret prayers, they are not silent states of contemplation, but loud ejaculations with tears and violent gestures. In terms of Latin theology, it is *oratio jaculatoria,* the expression of contrition, and not of beautifying vision. In this respect also Theodosius is the spokesman of ancient Russia. Mysticism is a rare flower on the Russian soil. Perhaps he even gives the key to his limitations. The terms in which he speaks, in his childhood, of his love for Christ, are quite remarkable: the Eucharistic bread and the land of Palestine speak to him not only of Christ, but especially of Christ's flesh. Theodosius's religion is not a kind of spiritualism; neither is Russian religion in general. The distance between the two worlds is not the gulf between flesh and spirit—as in Platonic mysticism—but between the fallen and the transfigured and deified flesh.

This lack of *Eros,* in the mystical as well as esthetic sense, constitutes the main difference between Theodosius and Francis of Assisi. Otherwise, the Russian apostle of poverty and kenotic love has his nearest Western counterpart in the Umbrian Poverello. Theodosius, besides, is more moderate and reserved. He shrinks from all external gestures revealing his inner life. In this he is also typically Russian. He did not seek new forms for the evangelical ideal revealed to his intuition. Humbly, he tried to realize it in the traditional forms of monasticism. If he failed, Saint Francis failed also, and both were sublime in their failure.

It is noteworthy that Saint Theodosius preceded Saint Francis by some one hundred and fifty years.

In the Western Catholic world, the revival of the Christ of the Gospel was a great discovery of the twelfth century. Saint Francis closed the movement, not as a precursor but as a fulfiller. The Russian saint, alone, without any support of tradition, himself began the tradition: not a fulfiller but a founder.

It is noteworthy that Saint Theodosius preceded Saint Francis by some one hundred and fifty years. In the Western Catholic World, the revival of the Christ of the Gospel was a great discovery of the twelfth century. Saint Francis closed the movement, not as a precursor but as a fulfiller. The Russian saint, alone, without any support of tradition, himself began the tradition: not a fulfiller but a founder.

In connecting Theodosius, the monk, with Princes Boris and Gleb under the heading of kenoticism, we do no violence to their individual ways. The suffering of the princes is, indeed, the expression of the same kenotic "following Christ" (the Eastern Church does not like to speak of "imitating" Christ). Boris and Gleb followed Christ in their sacrificial deaths—the climax of His kenosis—as Theodosius did in his poverty and humiliation. Humility and love, if not poverty, are present also in the suffering of the princes. We have seen their eloquent expression. Humility and self-offering are the very core of Boris's action. His death is not the summit of a struggle, of an heroic action. From the outside, it must give the impression of weakness as Theodosius's poverty must appear foolish to the outsider. Weak and foolish—such is Christ in His kenosis to the eyes of a Nietzsche just as he was to the eyes of the ancient pagan world. The semipagan Christian societies, such as in Byzantium or the Western Dark Ages, turned away with fear and discomfort from the face of the humiliated God. Typical for the whole millennium is what Gregory of Tours in the sixth century tells about one of his contemporary bishops who ordered that the image of the nude Christ on the cross be hidden under a veil. In the light of this, it is even more amazing and significant to view the great discovery of the first Christian generation in Russia: the kenotic Christ of the Russian saints.

Saint Francis and Sri Ramakrishna

GUIDO FERRANDO

While reading the *Gospel of Sri Ramakrishna*, a truly remarkable book that brings so vividly before our eyes the figure of the great Indian saint, I was continually reminded of the purest, the gentlest, the most beloved and lovable of all the Christian saints, Francis of Assisi. There is a striking similarity between these two divine men who belong to different ages, different races, and different faiths; a similarity that is most illuminating as it proves the fundamental unity of true religion.

There is a striking similarity between these two divine men who belong to different ages, different races, and different faiths; a similarity that is most illuminating as it proves the fundamental unity of true religion.

They both seem to have had the same mission in this world. They were not founders of a *new* religion, but rather revivers and restorers of the eternal faith in an all-pervading God who can and must be realized in our earthly life. They were "living embodiments of godliness," as Mahatma Gandhi says of Ramakrishna, or, to use a beautiful expression of one of Saint Francis's biographers, they were "perfect images of God in the mirror of humanity." Saint Francis, at the beginning of the thirteenth century, was the Savior of the Christian Church, then on the verge of collapse, threatened outwardly by the struggle with the emperor and inwardly by corruption, dissension, and heresy; and he saved the Christian religion simply by living the Gospel of Christ in a spirit of obedience, of purity and love. Ramakrishna, during the latter part of the nineteenth century, played the "noble role of the Savior of the Eternal Religion of India, and fulfilled the spiritual aspirations of three hundred millions of Hindus for the last two thousand years."

They both had followers: Saint Francis founded a religious order that spread rapidly all over the world, exercised an incalculable influence on Western civilization, and is still flourishing after more than seven centuries. Sri Ramakrishna had a number of devoted disciples who, after the death of the master, renounced the world and formed a monastic Order that is spreading over land and sea, bringing the message of India to Europe and America, and helping toward the spiritual unity of mankind.

When we consider these two great teachers in their human aspect, we find that they both had the purity and the simplicity of a child. It was the child in them that gave them their irresistible charm, their instinctive ability of winning the hearts of those around them. They never lost the sublime naïveté of childhood; they were happy natures always desirous to share their joys with others. They were also intellectually simple; they were not scholars and did not attach any importance to learning; on the contrary, they sometimes looked upon it as an obstacle to God. Ramakrishna was an almost illiterate man and was always telling his disciples not to waste time in reasoning and worldly knowledge. Francis, in an age of great theologians, was not a man of great culture; true knowledge for him consisted in being, not in possessing intellectual learning.

I do not mean to say that these two supreme religious masters were ignorant men; they had a marvelous spiritual intelligence and possessed the divine wisdom that comes from the love of God. And they never attacked learning. Francis was most respectful to the Doctors of the Church and, when compelled to relinquish the active leadership of the Order, chose as his successor a man thoroughly versed in theology and canon law. He did not scorn culture; he merely felt that it was impossible for one to be devoted both to the pursuit of learning and to the cultivation of the mystical side of one's nature. Moreover, among his followers were some of the famous scholars of his age, and he became the inspirer of the greatest of poets, Dante, and of one of the supreme artists of all times, Giotto, both of whom painted for us, one in exquisite lines and the other in marvelous frescoes, the life of their spiritual master. Ramakrishna, though he was not a cultivated man and took no interest in science and philosophy, had among his dearest friends some learned pundits and teachers; and his most beloved disciple, Narendra—universally known under his monastic name of Swami Vivekananda—whom he chose to carry on his teaching and to bring his message to the Western world, was one of the most brilliant and scholarly minds of our time.

Saint Francis believed that the greatest obstacles to God were lust and greed, which Ramakrishna so vividly personified in "woman and gold"; and he founded his Order on chastity, poverty, and obedience. It is in the interpretation of these spiritual rules that the medieval Italian and the modern Hindu masters reveal their likeness. Chastity for Saint Francis is not simply a negative virtue, the refraining from lust; and it is much more than a mode of living; chastity is the broadening of the scope of life so as to take in the whole world. It is carnal passion that fetters love. No one who looks back on his own life, can fail to realize what vast stores of enthusiasm, faith, and gaiety are dissipated through the betrayal of our senses. Francis, in the vow of chastity, saw the means of preserving for, or of restoring to oneself, the purity, the intensity, and the independence of the child who is always free to pursue any object of his affections. Also for Ramakrishna chastity was much more than abstinence from carnal love. "To me," he used to say over and over again, "every woman is a mother." And the image of a mother, the idea of motherhood, lifted his mind to the vision of the divine Mother, Kali, to whom he was completely devoted.

Poverty, for the Italian saint, was not merely renunciation of earthly riches and power. No one saw more clearly than Saint Francis how most of us are slaves to money, whether we possess it or not, and how the accumulation of riches corrupts the soul more than anything else; for him riches and fetters are synonymous. But it is most important to understand that for Francis poverty was a spiritual attitude, not a material state. Fidelity to poverty signified for him the negation of all desire for worldly honor or bodily comfort, since this alone was the soul's freedom to be secured. The external sacrifice was a mere symbol of the inward renunciation. It was not only a casting away of worldly encumbrance for a life of liberty, it was also a shedding of spiritual obstructions for the soul's union with God. Ramakrishna undoubtedly had the same understanding of the great spiritual meaning of poverty.

The vow of obedience, which has as its symbol a yoke, serves not to fetter, but to free the soul. It is only through spiritual obedience that one can attain complete freedom from the illusion of the ego. Just as moral freedom is the result of our obedience to reason, so spiritual freedom, the surrender of our individual self, comes to us only through renunciation of our personal will and obedience to the will of God. Francis saw very clearly how necessary it is for all who seek union with God to be humble, to trust divine Providence, to obey their spiritual guide. Ramakrishna, in his talks with his disciples, continually reminds them that they cannot attain divine wisdom without the help and the guidance of a guru, and that they must obey their master completely, with the same trust that a child has for its mother. It is, however, in another trait of their nature that these two great masters revealed their wonderful likeness; both were unconsciously supreme religious artists. An English biographer of the Italian saint rightly emphasizes this quality of Saint Francis. "Probably the particular human quality," he says,

in which Francis lives with the modern world, is as a supreme religious artist, with an exquisite sensibility as to spiritual value and a unique power of dramatic self-expression. All through his life he is either the hero of episodes that seize the imagination and impress themselves indelibly upon the memory, or he is uttering parables or inventing images, which no one, having read or heard them, can easily forget. It is manifest he had all the shining virtues: courage and humility, love and purity, joy and compassion, courtesy and holiness; so had other saints. It is in the expression of these qualities that he excels them all. No human soul so bright as his ever shone out so clearly through the fleshly veil; there seems to be an actual radiance about him. By reason of this heavenly quality he ranks with the great poets as the creator of the common imagination of mankind; and the simple stories of his life take their place in the world's literature with those of Dante and the Bible.

Ramakrishna shared with Francis this divine quality; he was a poet at heart, and he explained to his disciples the deepest truths of religion, not in an abstruse, philosophic language, but by using, with telling effect, simple and homely parables and images full of charm and beauty.

They both loved music and song, because, living in direct communion with God, only in song could they express, at least in part, the ecstatic love and the unutterable joy that filled their hearts. Ecstatic love and joy is probably the nearest description we can give of the plane of consciousness on which they lived. Ramakrishna saw God in everything, in the loftiest and noblest as well as in the humblest and meanest form; he believed in the Absolute, indivisible and formless, but he loved His manifested world the *lila*, with its infinite variety of created forms. He especially loved and worshipped Kali, the divine mother, a living reality for him, full of compassion and tenderness for all; and it was through this all-permeating and embracing love for every single manifestation of God that he attained union with the Absolute. He used to sing many times a day hymns of praise to God and chant His name and glory, and he used to ask his devotees and his visitors to join in the songs, and, almost invariably, while singing or listening to a beautiful song, he entered *samadhi*, communion with God.

Among the many songs recorded in the *Gospel of Sri Ramakrishna*, there is one, especially dear to the master, who loved to sing it while dancing in a circle with his disciples, which recalls to our minds the Italian saint, as it is full of the Franciscan spirit:

In Wisdom's firmament the moon of Love is rising full
And Love's flood-tide, in surging waves,
   is flowing everywhere.
O Lord, how full of bliss thou art! Victory unto thee!

On every side shine devotees, like stars around the moon;
Their Friend, the Lord All-merciful,
   joyously plays with them.
Behold! the gates of paradise today are open wide.

The soft spring wind of the New Day
   raises fresh waves of joy;
Gently it carries to the earth the fragrance of God's love,
Till all the yogis, drunk with bliss, are lost in ecstasy.

Upon the sea of the world unfolds the
   lotus of the New Day,
And there the Mother sits enshrined in blissful majesty.
See how the bees are mad with joy,
   sipping the nectar there!

Behold the Mother's radiant face,
   which so enchants the heart
And captivates the universe! About her lotus feet
Bands of ecstatic holy men are dancing in delight.

What matchless loveliness is hers! What infinite content
Pervades the heart when she appears!
   O brothers, says Premdas,
I humbly beg you, one and all,
   to sing the Mother's praise!

Francis would have loved this beautiful song; it has something in common with his great hymn: *"Laudes Creaturarum,"* the "Praises of Creatures." *
Francis was a born poet. As a young man, before his conversion, he loved the troubadours' songs, which he probably learned from the lips of his mother, who was French by birth; later on, after he

* "The Canticle of Brother Sun."

had renounced the world, he went on singing—no longer the praise of woman, but of God. Among his followers there was a brother who, before he entered the Order, had been a troubadour; and it was he who set to music the songs that Francis composed, so that the brethren might chant them morning and night in praise of God. Of all his songs, the most famous and the only one (sic) that has been preserved to us in its complete form, is the "Canticle of Brother Sun," a poem beyond the realms of art, in which one senses immediately the simplicity and spirituality of the author. It was composed shortly after Francis had attained the highest state of samadhi, the complete realization of God, of which he bore a visible sign in the stigmata. "I will make a new song," he said to his brethren, "a praise of all creatures that daily minister to us and without which we could not live, and among which man much offendeth his Creator by reason of his gross ingratitude, though in the midst of so much grace and benefit."

Thomas of Celano, his first biographer, says that he invited the creatures and the elements to praise God, their Creator, in certain verses that he composed after the manner of the *"Benedicite."* The title of the poem explains the aim: it is the praises *of* the creatures, and not merely the praise of man *for* them; and the creatures consist of the heavenly bodies and the four elements. To these praises, which form the main body of the hymn, Francis added later on two brief stanzas, one in praise of those who suffer in peace all human infirmities, and the other, composed just before his passing away, in praise of bodily death.

This beautiful hymn, which expresses in a naïve and moving way the true religious spirit, and which, I recall with deep emotion, was chosen at the World Congress of Religion held in London in the summer of 1931 as the one song that representatives of all creeds would gladly sing together in praise of God, has been often misunderstood by modern interpreters. The majority of the students of Saint Francis believe that for him the heavenly bodies and the elements were brothers and sisters of man: our Brother Sun, our Sister Moon, and so on; which is not correct. Only one verse of the poem contains the possessive pronoun "our," and that is in the praise of Mother Earth, "our mother," as he calls her, and not "our sister," because she could not be both. For Francis, "our brothers and sisters" were the animals, especially the birds, the larks above all, to which he used to preach and which he dearly loved because they soar up into the sky and express in their song the joy of life and their gratitude to the Creator. The heavenly bodies and the elements, in Francis's poetic imagination, formed a divine order which was, in a certain sense, a counterpart of the religious order he had founded on earth. It is the brethren and sisters of this higher and far more glorious Order that he invites to praise his Lord as men could not do worthily.

Muhammad and Saint Francis

GIULIO BASETTI-SANI, O.F.M.

When we look at the geographical map revealing the diffusion of Islam, we cannot remain indifferent to the disturbing problem raised by the mysterious presence of a phenomenon so important for the history of Christianity and of humanity. It is our most cherished longing to create in the Christian conscience an interest in these millions of people.

Too often one hears repeated by the very persons who live in the lands of Islam: "There is nothing that can be done!" How many times, in the course of seventeen years spent in Muslim territory, have I heard my own confreres enunciate this sad conclusion as the final lesson of their practical experience. The more I meditate, however, the more the verdict strikes me as unacceptable. It appears to me that the contrary must be said: "There is everything that can be done with Muslims." Without contesting the merit and the honor due to those who in the past, at the price of their lives, have preached the Gospel to our Muslim brothers, we must realize that, from the failure of so many attempts, it is not to be concluded that grace has been denied to so many people who likewise are called to salvation.

We are, therefore, convinced that to arrive at a more Christian understanding of our brothers in Islam, it is important for us to adopt the attitude adopted by Saint Francis of Assisi and meditate on a phase of his life that has perhaps escaped a number of biographers and admirers: namely, the mysterious bonds that united the Poverello to the founder of Islam, the Arab prophet Muhammad.

No one disputes that in the thirteenth century divine Providence sent Saint Francis to His Church to bring the world back to fidelity to the Gospel. The vision of Innocent III expressed that mission of the Poor Man, who as a prophet, spoke to the people the language of God.

We shall especially discover that Saint Francis approached Islam with an entirely new spirit, with spiritual attitudes completely unknown to medieval Christendom. In this we are once again led to think that Saint Francis received the prophetic mission to bring the Christian conscience back to a more just and more evangelical understanding of its relations with Muslims.

For the medieval conscience, Muslims were the "unbelieving profaners of the Holy Places." The papal documents themselves designate them in terms that could not fail to create a strong impression on the imagination of the faithful: "enemies of the Cross of Christ," "dogs," "the most wicked lot of warriors," "a wicked people," and so forth. Islam was presented not only as a politico-military power against which it was necessary to defend oneself, but above all as the most diabolically anti-Christian force. The popes and bishops many a time stirred the zeal of the faithful by the ideal of the Crusade.

It is in this environment of anti-Muslim reaction that Saint Francis appeared, as the inspired prophet, sent by God to His Church in order that Christians might regard the followers of Islam with a more evangelical outlook. Continual meditation on the Passion of Christ made Saint Francis understand that God brought about the salvation of man through annihilation and affliction, through the death of His divine Son, and not through violence and the deployment of material power. The Christian attitude toward Islam ought to conform itself to that evangelical outlook.

Consequently Francis discovered in Muslims not the terrible enemies against whom it had to be a question of taking up swords, because they themselves took up the sword, but alienated brothers who had to be led to their Father's house through kindness and goodness. Jesus treated men with love and saved them by giving himself on the Cross. The Church, which is his Mystical Body, cannot pursue another way; she must treat Muslims with charity and understanding and save them by prayer and suffering.

In the redaction of his first Rule, Saint Francis gave to his friars—"those who wish to go among the Saracens"—a program so far removed from the mentality of that time that it could not have been impressed upon his mind without an inspiration from above. It was impossible for him to look upon Muslims as "enemies of the Cross of Christ," profaners of the Holy Sepulcher. He saw in them only brothers of God, redeemed by the Blood of Jesus, called to share in the kingdom of God, more precious than the mounds of earth covered with the Blood of the Son and still more precious than the stone of the Sepulcher.

But let us hear Saint Francis as he proposed his program of apostolic conquest. He divided it into two periods. The first period (which, we add, could eventually last for centuries, since in the eyes of God a thousand years are as yesterday already passed), is that in which the evangelical message is announced in the land of Isalm by the practice of Christian virtues. The brothers (who go among the Saracens) must not take action against them, nor cause disputes, but must submit themselves to all (and therefore even to the Muslim authorities). It was considered to be humanly impossible to live in the Orient without taking such action; in the light of this the value of the attitude prescribed by the Franciscan precept is more clearly apparent. After an assiduous practice had shown that humility, poverty, and gentleness were the superior spiritual values, the ground would be well prepared. It would be easier for Islam to accept and understand the humiliation of the Son of God.

If the testimony that they tried for centuries to render to Christ in the lands of Islam has not produced the expected result, that derives precisely from being preoccupied in looking for immediate results.

The second period, that of external manifestation and preaching, is determined by the choice of God. In this respect we should heed the words of Jesus to his Apostles: "It is not for you to know the times or the seasons that the Father has fixed by his own authority" (Acts 1:7).

The hour for action is determined by divine mercy. The Apostle must be ready to execute that second part of his mission. To announce the word of God presupposes, besides the spiritual preparation required for the first period, a serious intellectual preparation: the Lord is in no way bound to give all messengers of his Word the gift of tongues. On the other hand, no one can pretend to announce the Gospel to a people, without first knowing the language and the mentality of that people in order to be able, according to the teaching of Saint Paul, to become all things to all men—a Jew among Jews, a Greek among Greeks, and so an Arab among the Arabs, in order to draw all to Christ. No

one before Saint Francis understood the apostolate among Muslims in this way. He remained unique among his contemporaries, the rest of whom viewed the problem of Islam in a pessimistic light.

It is necessary here to underline an important eventual consequence of the attitude encouraged for the first period of the apostolic mission: the testimony of blood realized in union with the sacrifice of the Savior for the redemption of our brothers the Muslims. That supreme expression of charity taught by Christ will manifest to the world that we consider Muslims as true brothers. Saint Francis affirmed in his rule that it is precisely because Muslims make us suffer and because they inflict suffering and death upon us, that they must be considered as our dearest friends. In these words is embodied the answer to be given to all those who invoke the malice of the Saracens and their obstinacy in refusing the teachings of the Gospel. Nothing can belittle for Saint Francis the value of the words of Christ that he repeated to his own sons: "Behold, I send you as sheep among wolves."

It was in that spirit that he was able to see in Muslims his own brothers. He would not have dared to consider himself a friend of Christ if he had not felt himself animated with zeal for the salvation of all those whose brother Christ had become before the Father. For Saint Francis and for whoever wishes to remain faithful to the seraphic spirit, Muslims must be the object of a constant love, even if in return they hate us. Did not Christ go even further, He who loved Judas?

Saint Francis, by a special illumination that conferred upon him a prophetic mission, understood that Islam could not be won over by contempt, still less by threats and violence. One of his most ardent preoccupations had been to make the Gospel known to Muslims. He devoted his life to that ideal; he offered it to God as living sacrifice for his Muslim brethren in union with the dying Christ, in order to redeem humanity. To this end, he set out three times to seek martyrdom among them.

The prophetic character of the mission of Saint Francis for Islam was confirmed by the connection —evident to us—between certain events in the history of Muhammad and two events in the life of the seraphic father. By relating them we are able to acquire a full understanding of these. In so doing, we discover the particular vocation of the Franciscan apostolate in Islam. It is only with the heart and spirit of a Francis of Assisi or of a Charles de Foucauld that one can understand the mind of Muslims and draw near to them.

It is impossible to understand the profound and supernatural meaning of the apostolate of Saint Francis at Damietta, the reaction of the Sultan Melek-el-Kamil and the Muslim doctors to the proposition of the saint, if one does not compare the happening at Damietta with what occurred at Medina, in the tenth year of Hegira.

At that time Muhammad had practically extended his authority over all of Arabia; numbers of tribes had spontaneously submitted. Although he was still far from knowing the true Christianity, Muhammad manifested more sympathy for the Christians than for the Jews. The official meeting with a delegation of the Christians of Najran and their conduct strongly modified his personal judgment on Christianity, and afterward the personal judgment of all Muslims who saw in the conduct of Muhammad the rule to be observed before every Christian desirous of engaging in a religious discussion.

The Christian delegation was led by the Bishop Abu-l-Harith ibn Aqamah. Muhammad summoned the delegation to the burial ground at Medina; and there, in the presence of the dead, after a discussion on the Passion of Jesus, asked the Christians to prove the truth of the Incarnation, inviting them to invoke together with him and his five companions the malediction of God on those who would be wrong, by means of the *mubahalah* or ordeal, consisting of passing through fire.

These Christians did not accept the challenge and did not wish to recognize the prophetic mission. However, they declared themselves ready to negotiate a compromise with Muhammad, who then conceded the first "capitulation of Islam." The

faithful of the two Abrahamic monotheisms, Jews and Christians, because of their holy books (the Bible), should have the right to refuse to embrace Islam, by paying a tribute (the *jizyah*), by which means their life, property, and entire communal autonomy would be guaranteed them.

This event is very important for many reasons. In the first place it is a manifestation of the complete faith of Muhammad in his mission; it likewise shows that the Prophet did not admit the manifestation of God in his creation except by thunder that strikes the guilty, as previously on Mount Carmel in the presence of Elijah (2 Kings 1:10–12; Luke 9:54).

In addition, this event truly reveals a particular attitude of Muhammad and of Islam toward the mystery of the Incarnation. Perhaps the refusal of the Christians to give him what he demanded in all sincerity of faith—namely, the proof of the Divinity of Jesus Christ—barred the Prophet's way to the Christian faith.

In this first and solemn meeting of Islam and the Christians, the latter incurred a heavy responsibility in lacking courage to bear witness to the truth and to the sincerity of their faith, in failing in charity, by their contempt of that nonbaptized person who pretended "foolishly" to make himself recognized as messenger of Allah, while they themselves judged him excluded from the privileged participation: the adoration of the Son of God. That pusillanimity and, at the same time, that pride of believing themselves the only privileged ones, scandalized Muhammad, who, having retired to pray, should have been strengthened by the word of God. The desired answer was remitted to the day of the Last Judgment. And Islam still waits!

The ordeal asked for in vain by Muhammad was proposed by Saint Francis at Damietta, since he had wished to repair and to make up for the unfortunate behavior of the Christians of Najran.

The action of Saint Francis, brought closer and placed in direct relation with the happenings at Medina, takes on a profound meaning that biographers have habitually failed to perceive. While it gives an indication of the greatness of the soul of Saint Francis, it announces at the same time the new attitude that the Lord demands of Christians toward Islam: reparation in a suffering that, in life and death, bears witness to the faith; Christian charity that condemns no one, leaves the judgment of intention to God, knows how to discover and recognize in all, even in the greatest sinners, the gifts of God, and incites the apostle to love the brother in whom he sees the image and likeness of Christ, even so far as immolating himself for his salvation and substituting himself for him before the Savior.

Muhammad, animated with a deep and sincere faith in the living God of Abraham, believed in the original equality of the three Abrahamic religions: Judaism, Christianity, and Islam, and he knew that, referring all to the same God the Creator—God-Truth—the pure souls (tahirat) of the Jews or of the Christians could also be for him the instrument through which God communicated truth to him.

The refusal of the Christians to Najran to bear witness to Christ, while scandalizing Muhammad, demanded for many centuries a reparation on the part of the Christians: St. Francis of Assisi gave it, providentially, in the name of true Christianity.

In July of 1219, Saint Francis landed in Egypt. It was the third time that he had resolved to go among the Saracens, driven by the ardent desire of sacrificing his life for them.

The sincerity with which Saint Francis presented himself to the Sultan Melek-el-Kamil to announce to him his mission as the envoy of God, could not but elicit and win sympathy and respect. The religious conscience of Melek-el-Kamil, a just and pious man, did not refuse a priori the testimony of any member of the "people of the Book," bringing to him the words of God. A frank, humble, and courageous affirmation of the Christian faith, without any offense to the Muslim conscience, is respectfully heard in Muslim circles. According to the biographers of the saint, it seems that the Sultan was personally aware of the fervor of spirit and the sanctity of Francis, who had no word of contempt

for Muhammad, nor for the Islamic faith, but only professed himself ready to remain among Muslims for the love of Christ, prepared to preclude their every hesitation by means of the ordeal of fire.

The ordeal, like the *mubahalah* that Muhammad had asked of the Christians of Najran, would have to show the intervention of God, who would thus declare which is the truest and holiest faith.

In conformity with the rule of action prescribed by the Koran, the Muslims refused the challenge. Saint Francis then declared himself ready to enter the fire alone. Humbly, he forewarned them that if the Lord did not assist him, those present should attribute that to his sins and not consider it as a divine condemnation of Christianity. If, on the contrary, the power of God should be miraculously manifested by leaving him unharmed in the midst of the flames, he asked the Sultan and his people to hear the message of God.

The conduct of the Sultan and the attitude of the doctors of the Koran who, upon declining the first proposition, had backed out, must be interpreted in the light of psychology and the Muslim law. After the incident that occurred between Muhammad and the Christians of Najran, especially after the answer that the Prophet received from the Lord (Sura 3:48–55), the Muslim was not able to accept anticipating the judgment that God had reserved to himself to give to the angels and to men in the presence of Jesus Christ, when, on the last day, he will judge both angels and men.

Taking into account these characteristics of the Muslim conscience, we must, of necessity, evaluate both the Sultan's response and the doctors' conduct properly. The refusal did not signify contempt—neither of Saint Francis, nor of the Christian religion. On the contrary, the Sultan, in conformity with his faith, professed publicly the divine origin of Christianity: "I believe that your faith is good and true."

Islam at Damietta did not accept the proof that Saint Francis, in order to make reparation for the refusal of the Christians of Najran, desired to give of belief in Christ's Divinity and in the Trinity. It would appear that at Damietta Islam refused the absolute gift of love that Saint Francis was ready to make by exposing his life in the hope of martyrdom. But this interior disposition of sublime charity toward his Muslim brothers did not diminish in the heart of the seraphic father; on the contrary, the attitude of the Sultan, one that was most generous and courteous, incited in his soul the great suffering of the apostolate; it verified the difficulties that men oppose to the triumph of grace. Then Saint Francis returned to Italy.

The hour of God had not yet arrived. A long maturing of suffering and of immolation impelled by the love of Christ was necessary, the presence of which he recognized even in his distant brothers.

We do not believe that Saint Francis, after that experience, was convinced that there was nothing that could be done with Muslims. On the contrary, that direct and personal experience made him understand more clearly, with the aid of grace, that Islam is a mystery. Even more than before, that thought became one of the profoundest themes of his interior life. Henceforth, those distant brothers could no longer be excluded from his prayers; they, who continued to be looked upon by other Christians as enemies, remained for him true friends. The first Rule, redacted after that first apostolic experience, is the best proof of all that has been said here. Now, more than ever, Saint Francis substituted himself for thousands of Muslim souls. That supreme immolation, which continued during the years, received the divine seal of acceptance on Mount Alvernia. Thus, the stigmata of Saint Francis were intimately related to the mystery of Islam and in particular to an important event in the religious experience of the Prophet Muhammad.

Prompted and guided by a deep sense of the divine transcendence, Muhammad gathered in his "conversion" the spiritual and personal character of his relation with the living God of Abraham, understood as the sovereign freedom and absolute will, to whom we must respond by the total abandonment of self (Sura 3:77).

The fact of the nocturnal ascension of Muhammad—an ecstasy to which the Koran twice alludes—was in his calling a central event that ruled the entire legislative activity of Medina. It was to this that, seeking to rediscover and revive the dispositions of Muhammad's heart in his search for God, fervent Muslims turned over the centuries and gave their concentrated thought.

When the angel to whom the Prophet was entrusted had transported him from Mecca, first onto the esplanade of the temple of the destroyed Jerusalem and thence to the inaccessible Holy City—the heavenly Jerusalem, where the glory of God resides—Muhammad reached beyond the "supreme horizon," up to the "lotus of delay," close to which was found the garden of eternal sojourn, while a host of angels covered the tree (Sura 3:14–16). Behind that mystical tree, at an interval of two bowshots, God was hidden. Muhammad desired and attempted to reach God through the mystery, but his angelic guide was unable to introduce him into the embracing union, for the completely naked angelic nature, which his guide had assumed, did not normally represent the type of intimate union with God that is possible only through the crucified humanity of Christ.

Ignorant of the true meaning and purpose of the mystery of the Incarnation, Muhammad remained excluded from the divine union reserved to the adoration of sons. In all sincerity he asked the Divinity to manifest Himself to him, at least under the appearance of an angel; but under the features of the angel who guided him he could discover and proclaim only the inaccessibility of the divine essence. Thus he remained on the threshold and did not try to advance into the eternity of Divine Fire, thus too renouncing the knowledge *ab intra* [from within] of the personal life of God through the only Mediator, Christ, who would have sanctified him.

There was in that outpouring of Muhammad's faith the expression of a desperate desire that he kept during his whole life: "to contemplate God, at least under the form of an angel." This desire was to remain unsatisfied over the centuries; yet we may hope that Saint Francis's complete sacrifice of himself at Damietta for the salvation of all Muslims will bring about, thanks to his merits, the most unexpected answer to Muhammad's prayer and desire.

The event that took place on Alvernia toward the middle of September 1224, is well known. Franciscan tradition, from the very beginning, has meditated on the mystery of the stigmata of Saint Francis, confining itself to the consideration of what it signified for the person of the saint; but it seems to us that it has neglected the problems raised by the mysterious significance of the apparition of the Crucified under the features of a seraph. Saint Francis himself had been left confused. All the biographers of Saint Francis see in the stigmata the answer to that desire for martyrdom that had driven Saint Francis on to offer himself in the land of Islam. Saint Bonaventure, in particular, established the relation between the two events: the preaching before the Sultan from whom he awaited martyrdom and the stigmatization.

The offering of self made by the saint at Damietta for the salvation of the Muslims had been accepted by the Lord, but the martyrdom he desired to undergo in the land of Islam had to receive a new and deeper meaning. While it was Francis's desire to make reparation by his courage and char-

ity for the Najran Christians' refusal to Muhammad, the Lord reserved for him a more extraordinary martyrdom on Mount Alvernia.

That generous offer of intercession and of substitution for the Muslims echoed in the heart of God. Saint Francis was therefore recognized by God as the greatest aspirant for the salvation of Islam. Thanks to him, the expression "brothers and friends" is found in the Church—an expression to which the Muslims have a right. But it was especially in the person of Francis that the Lord willed to satisfy Muhammad's sincere and ardent desire to see God manifested under the form of an angel. In the miracle of Mount Alvernia, the stigmata of Saint Francis, uniting in some way the angelic nature to the Crucifixion, appear precisely as a supernatural compensation for that which was wanting in Muhammad.

The Arab race, excluded in Ishmael its father from the offering of Abraham, remains to this day in an almost invincible ignorance of the Crucifixion in all its sad reality. For Muhammad and all Islam after him, Jesus Christ, the Holy One of God, could not suffer in such an ignominious manner; the "Judge" could not submit to a condemnation inflicted by men because all that appeared as a defeat inflicted upon God.

To that protestation of earthly wisdom, scandalized by the folly of the Cross, Saint Francis himself was the answer: he offered himself at Damietta to bear witness to both the sufferings and the Divinity of Christ, and he obtained on Mount Alvernia the visible sign of divine mercy for the descendants of Ishmael.

While all Christianity was wont to see in Muslims the worst enemies of the Cross of Christ, Saint Francis, through his love for them, was permitted by the Lord to be the first to suffer visibly with the Crucified. Thus was the prophetic mission accomplished by him in some way authenticated and consecrated when he showed what the evangelical attitude should be toward Islam and condemned by his own action the bellicose violence of the Crusades. Through the five wounds imprinted on the body of Francis in fulfillment of his desire for the offering of his life for Islam, Islam will be able one day to recognize the value of the five wounds of Christ, the only source of Redemption.

For a more Christian understanding of our Muslim brothers—more imperative and urgent than ever—it remains for us to meditate upon the example left by St. Francis and to enter into his spirit.

For a more Christian understanding of our Muslim brothers—more imperative and more urgent than ever—it remains for us to meditate upon the example left by Saint Francis and to enter into his spirit.

When Christians, especially those who live in direct contact with Muslims, nurture on their part such a love that they can even desire to immolate themselves for them in a spirit of substitution, then will Islam perceive the call to grace.

Jesus, Francis, Buddha: The Challenge of Tomorrow

ARNOLD TOYNBEE

Long before the Industrial Revolution, mankind's greatest spiritual leaders perceived and proclaimed that the prostitution of human power to serve human greed is immoral and is also suicidal. The peasantry of India is one of the less greedy sections of the human race; yet one of the first of those spiritual leaders who have warned us to mortify our appetites was an Indian, the Buddha Gau-

189

tama, a king's son who voluntarily became a mendicant monk. The bourgeoisie of Western Europe and of its modern extensions overseas in the Americas, southern Africa, and Australasia is one of the greedier sections of the human race. It is therefore significant that, in Italy at the turn of the twelfth and thirteenth centuries, Saint Francis of Assisi, the son of a successful wholesale dealer in textiles, embraced economic poverty for himself and founded an order of monks who, like the members of the Buddhist Sangha, are dedicated to the renunciation of the pursuit of wealth. Unfortunately for the West and for the world, the West, and eventually the world as well, has chosen, so far, to follow the example of Saint Francis's father, instead of following the contrary example set by Saint Francis himself and, before Saint Francis's day, by Jesus, by whom Saint Francis was inspired, and by the Buddha earliest of all. . . .

Unfortunately for the West and for the rest of the world, the West, and eventually the world as well, has chosen so far, to follow the example of Saint Francis's father, instead of following the contrary example set by Saint Francis himself.

Not every human being is an intellectual or artistic genius. Our degree of intellectual and artistic endowment varies between one person and another. But religion is a field that every human being is bound to enter as a consequence of his being endowed with human consciousness. We are conscious that we have come to life in a universe that is both mysterious and formidable. We are not fully, or even mainly, masters of the situation in which we find ourselves. The ultimate mastery lies with powers other than ourselves, with which we have to bring ourselves into harmony in order to make human life viable.

In the past, religion, not economics, has been mankind's paramount concern. The substitution of economics for religion as our master activity is a modern aberration. We have now to reorient our course. We have to turn away from this aberration and return to the right path. This is possible; for our right path is our ancestors' traditional path. But are we going to make this salutary but difficult change of direction? This question is "the challenge of tomorrow."

Saint Francis, Buddha, and Confucius

LIAM BROPHY

Fanciful or fantastic as it may seem, the Franciscan spirit offers a bridge of complete understanding between China and the West. The character of her people—those who are not corrupted by Communism—and the works of her sages reveal naturally Franciscan traits, which are not in keeping with the conduct of her present rulers. If and when the Communist stranglehold is relaxed or released from China, the way will be open to appeal to her by a seraphic approach. Though it may strike some as a paradox, Orientals in general and the Chinese in particular are nearer the Franciscan spirit than the great bulk of people in the Western nations who have put material prosperity and aggressiveness before mysticism and peace.

That non-Catholic author of *Little Plays of Saint Francis,* Laurence Housman, wrote in an essay on the Poverello:

Saint Francis of Assisi had the extraordinary notion (to which in actual practice we are being gradually converted) that man is more inclined to do good than to do evil; that, given a fair chance of choosing under equal conditions, he will prefer to do right than to do wrong. He believed that the equal condition necessary for man's salvation was merely a free offer of love and the service to his fellow-man. To that he believed that human nature would respond in so overwhelming a majority of cases as to solve the problem of social evil.

That is perfectly true. Saint Francis *did* believe in the fundamental goodness of the human heart, not in the manner of Rousseau, who believed that man was born good and remained good until civilization degraded him, nor yet after the manner of the Reds, who fondly believe that human nature will be perfected in the proletarian utopia. Saint Francis insisted on the natural goodness of man because he recognized that evil and sin are negations. He might quite conceivably have written:

Be careful not to interfere with the natural goodness of the heart of man. Man's heart may be forced down or stirred up. In each case the issue is fatal. By gentleness, the hardest heart may be softened. But try to cut and polish it, and it will glow like fire or freeze like ice.

This passage occurs, in fact, in the writings of Lao-tzu, the founder of Taoism, one of the three main religions of China. The two others, similar in many ways, are Confucianism and Buddhism. In all three religions we find insistence on the virtues of courtesy, gentleness, peacefulness, and cheerfulness —eminently Franciscan virtues.

One of the most searching and searing books on Western civilization as it now stands, or totters, has been written by a Chinese philosopher who is a scholarly citizen of both East and West. He is Lin Yutang, and the book is entitled *Between Tears and Laughter*. He quotes his own religious leaders and sages to demonstrate his thesis that Western thinking has become crudely materialistic and mathematical, with the inevitable result of wars and social unrest. He cites Mencius to prove again the Chinese belief in the goodness of the human heart: "The heart of mercy is in all men; the sense of shame is in all men; the sense of courtesy and respect is in all men; the sense of right and wrong is in all men."

Our Western mathematical thinking disregards the human heart and tends to reduce people to mere statistics. The ultimate logical working-out of that attitude is the levelling Socialist process culminating in the Communist collective. Belief in free will has become dim and ineffectual. Science has come to hasten and harden the process. "The dead hand of Science is upon the West." Science or the objective study of matter has colored man's thinking and brought us Naturalism, Determinism, and Materialism. These have destroyed the human values. Naturalism has destroyed the belief in the power for good and cooperation. Materialism has destroyed subtlety, insight, and faith in things unseen. Determinism has destroyed the capacity for hope.

As the Chinese philosopher sees it, the fundamental question for the West is the question of the freedom of the will versus Determinism, the question of whether goodwill has power to change the world. "Peace on earth, I repeat, is an act of faith, and without faith we shall not be saved. It boils down almost to this: Jesus, the Prince of Peace, was a liar, or he was not. We've got to make up our minds." Franciscan spirituality has always placed special emphasis on the will, which is regarded as the free and responsible ruler of all man's abilities. This primacy of the will is stressed by all the Franciscan doctors and needs to be repeated in a world that is allowing itself to be dragged down to a Deterministic philosophy of its own contrivance.

Lin Yutang assures us that the Chinese used to call their country "The Country of Courtesy (*li*) and Accommodation (*jang*)." They held that manners make not only a man but also a civilization. The fact is that thousands of years before the flowering of Western culture, the highly refined Chinese civilization had insisted on courtesy and consideration for others as the marks of a civilized people. It was this that distinguished them from "barbarians," who placed aggressiveness and go-getter tactics to the forefront. The inference for the West is clear. The three Chinese religions agreed in their emphasis on the importance of courtesy, not merely in everyday life but in government and administration. One happy consequence of this was the significant fact that "China has lived for four thousand years without police and lawyers, and the soldier is despised." And again: "Ultimately, the problem of peace is the problem of general education in good manners and music." That is the core of Confucianism.

To practical and efficient minds, Confucianism must seem as quixotic as Franciscanism in its emphasis on manners and music. Yet, courtesy, after all, is but charity in action. And by music the saint and the sage referred to that culture and refinement of the spirit that abhors all sin and evil as base and discordant. There is also the implication that they held cheerfulness to be next to Godliness, and that it is the insensitive who are given to cruelty, which they both abhorred. Of Saint Francis and Confucius it is recorded that they sang in the rain.

There is an even greater similarity between Saint Francis and Buddha. The similarity has been noticed by scholars of the last century. Henry Thode, whose *Franz von Assisi* (Berlin, 1855) initiated the whole modern cult of St. Francis, was the first to make a detailed comparison:

Buddha and Francis! Both arose to oppose a religion reduced to mere formulas and to a spirit of caste; both, impressed by the awful forebodings of death, renounced a life of pleasure and sensuality; to both, absolute poverty appeared as a means of freedom from all things earthly. Both attained a depth of spiritual insight that led them to absolute control over the body. . . . Both had a community of homeless, wandering monks who spread their doctrines through the country and soon seemed to fill the world.

Both were filled with great compassion for others, especially the unfortunate. Buddha taught: "Being delivered, deliver others; having arrived at the other shore, bring others there; being consoled, console others; having attained perfect Nirvana, bring others there." Saint Francis spoke often to his followers on the theme of "freely have you received; freely give."

Buddha's "Bhikkus," or mendicant monks, resembled the early followers of Saint Francis. Poverty, simplicity, and humility distinguished both. Buddha introduced an element that till then was novel. The Brahmanism he reformed would allow only members of the superior castes to join, but he declared: "My law is a law of grace for all; it is a law under which beggars as miserable as Duragata and others may become religious." Class distinction was very strong in Saint Francis's day. It existed between the nobles, with an abundance of wealth, and the serfs. There was no middle class till the merchants, of whom Saint Francis's father was one, rose in power and prominence, making a new caste system of the bourgeois kind. Francis, as we know, admitted all classes to his ranks. From the wealthy Bernard of Quintavalle and the knight Angelo Tancredi to the simple peasant Brother Juniper, who distinguished himself for his simplicity—all were welcome to that happy democracy by the Rivo Torto.

Buddha's obvious sincerity attracted so many men to follow him in a mode of life dedicated to poverty and celibacy that he was asked to create "orders" that should include women and married people. After some deliberation, he instituted communities for women as well as lay Buddhistic communities similar to the Franciscan Third Order.

There were other points of similarity between the Franciscan and Buddhist organizations. Both guarded against undue asceticism, which can often be a cloak for curious perversions.

There are two extremes, [said Buddha] which he who has given up the world should avoid: a life given to pleasure, which is degrading, sensual, vulgar, ignoble, and profitless; and a life of mortification, which is painful, ignoble, and profitless.

On one occasion Saint Francis made all his followers deliver up their instruments of mortification to make a bonfire of them. True asceticism, as both men taught, is of the spirit.

Compassion was another characteristic of the followers of the saint and the sage. Saint Francis's disciples went about tending the sick, dressing lepers' wounds, just as the Buddhist monk carried his medicine chest about with him to care for whatever afflicted persons he met on his way. Their compassion extended even to animals. We know from the *Fioretti* and the early accounts of the Poverello how great his tenderness was for all animal creation, how he set free birds from their cages, and hares from their traps, and how, on a famous occasion, he invited the birds to join him in praise of their Creator. Buddhist monks trod warily lest they crush a worm or insect under their sandaled feet. Courtesy was the natural concomitant of compassion in both Franciscans and Buddhists.

There were, of course, certain basic differences between the Buddhist and Franciscan movements. For instance, the Buddhist believed, and still believes, in the transmigration of souls, and he also holds to the pessimistic philosophy that existence, as such, is evil, that it is a punishment for some past evil in another state of being. Again, Buddha condemned marriage and procreation, since existence was something to be escaped from rather than promoted. Besides this, he despised labor. It is obvious that in these things he was absolutely opposed to the attitude of Saint Francis, who regarded existence as a wonderful gift of God and enjoined labor on his friars, giving very good example himself.

What we wish to stress is the readiness with which the Chinese adopted and adapted Buddhism because so many of its doctrines appealed to the Chinese character—courtesy, gentleness, simplicity of life, and the accumulation of spiritual riches rather than wealth and material advantage. The Orient and China need to be reassured that Christianity has not come to destroy but rather to fulfill the finer tenets of Taoism, Confucianism, and Buddhism; and, as Franciscanism is the marrow of the Gospel, we hold it would be a splendid thing if the Chinese could come to know and appreciate the Franciscan spirit. They would feel immediately "at home" with it.

Great advantages have been lost to missionary effort in the East, not through lack of devotion and heroic endeavor, but through lack of tact. That has been stressed in two books published within a short period of each other: *Through Eastern Eyes*, by Father van Straelen, and *Beyond East and West*, by John Wu.

Ramon Lull, that strange, highly gifted, and versatile Franciscan Tertiary who lived in the troubled thirteenth century, anticipated the methods of the propaganda by centuries in his plans for Christianizing the Arab nations. He believed and showed by his own practical example that missionaries should learn the language of the Arabs as well as their way of life and of thinking. After that, the missionary should show the Arabs how much latent Christianity lay in the Koran. We feel if some Lull should arise in our time and approach the Chinese, he could do nothing better than use that same simple and effective missionary technique.

At the present time, one solution to the Chinese problem would be a prayerful appeal to Saint Francis, because for four thousand years the Chinese have been "naturally Franciscan."

There appears to be a marvelous resurgence of the Franciscan spirit throughout the world. We dare hope that when the Chinese people have cast off Communism, which does such violence to their character and traditions, there will be some means of getting our bridge across to them, the bridge of the Franciscan spirit. Just as M. Jordain spoke prose for the greater part of his life without knowing it, so the Chinese have been naturally Franciscan for thousands of years without realizing it. The solution to the Chinese problem, as to all the world's great problems, lies not with the statesmen or soldiers, but with the simple and saintly of heart who have discovered the good that is common in all hearts.

An Experience of Saint Francis in India

ARTHUR LITTLE

Like many Protestant laymen, especially Quakers, I have long been fond of Francis of Assisi. My knowledge of him was not very deep, and my response for the most part at least romantic, if not downright sentimental. A kind of pilgrimage to Assisi some twenty years ago strengthened my feeling. But it was the shock of Calcutta that brought a strong sense of recognition.

During our Great Depression in the thirties, I was living in New York City. I had very little money. But as the streets had many beggars and the lines of unemployed were very long, I knew that however uneasy I might feel, there were others much more unfortunate. And I had to make some gesture to ease my conscience. So I established a kind of ritual. To the first person who begged of me each morning, I gave a nickel. (A little bit! but it bought more in 1935, and it was a high percent of my income.) And to all the others who came after on that day, I gave a real look of recognition and said, "I'm sorry." I did not plan it as a technique for getting rid of them; but it worked that way. They said something like "That's O.K., bud," and went away.

Such a pitiful crew. I was indeed overwhelmed. I looked at them and hurt. Suddenly, I knew clearly the choice of Saint Francis. I had either to reject them or join them. If there were another choice, I did not know it. I ran.

When I was going to India in the sixties, my friends in Japan warned me about many difficulties I would encounter—among them the beggars. "Do not give anything to anybody," they warned, "or you will be overwhelmed." But nothing they said really prepared me for the shock of Calcutta. When I saw the appalling number of beggars, and their miserable condition, I knew that I could do nothing to alleviate the situation by casual giving on the street, and I heeded my friends' advice to give nothing. But I fell into my old New York habit: I looked. And that was a tactical error. When I looked at someone and he saw a gleam of sympathy, he attached himself to me. Within my first hour on the streets of Calcutta, I had an entourage of a score of people, all holding out their hands, all whining piteously, some clutching at my coat.

Such a pitiful crew. I was indeed overwhelmed. I looked at them and hurt. Suddenly, I knew clearly the choice of Saint Francis. I had either to reject them or join them. If there were another choice, I did not know it. I ran. I ran back to the hotel, retreated to my room, and prayed.

My prayer may have been sacrilegious. It was certainly tinged with conscious irony. But it was also certainly fervent and sincere.

"Dear Lord," I prayed, "please do not give me a religious experience. I have a wife and children; I have other worldly responsibilities. Surely it will do no one any good for me to become one of the poor of Calcutta."

And the Lord withheld from me the total experience. But it was a close thing, and I felt a passionate communion with my old friend Francis of Assisi.

I made the other choice: I rejected them. After several hours of prayer—and a meal—I walked boldly onto the streets of Calcutta, and in no uncertain tones I said, "Go away." And they went.

The experience haunted me. I could not join Saint Francis, but I had a deeper understanding with him ("of him" I had intended to write, but perhaps the slip is an reflection of the truth; perhaps I have a deeper understanding *with* him).

Saint Francis: A Noh Play

ARTHUR LITTLE

Preface

Though the Noh theater, which developed in Japan at the end of the fourteenth and the beginning of the fifteenth centuries, generally reflected Buddhist philosophy, the plays were by no means moralities or homilies designed to teach; the aim was to provide an esthetic experience, or rather to create a thing of beauty from which one might derive an esthetic experience. Sight and sound contribute as much to a Noh play as does the text. Details of movement, of gesture, of costumes, masks and stage properties, of choral chanting and orchestration are handed down in the Noh families with the same respect as are the scripts, and any least departure from tradition is unthinkable.

It is only American gall, then, that permits me to offer a new script based on a Christian theme, and that gall is not strong enough to prevent my blushes as I humbly bow in apology to the modern masters of Noh who have helped in my attempt to appreciate their ancient art. To them and to whoever reads the lines presented herewith, I would like to say that this play was begun as a purely academic exercise in a dewy-eyed attempt to understand the various parts of a Noh play and how they fit together.

But then, as the words were formed, partly because the inciting incident is based on a personal experience, I began to visualize the play as a whole, to see the movement, the color of the costumes, the shape of the masks—and to realize that, as in so many of the authentic Noh plays I have studied, the climax is not in the poetry but in the dance. Or rather, perhaps it would be more accurate to say that my great hope is that in any production of *Saint Francis* the poetry, the music, the acting will all move toward that point in the play when the chorus says, "A saint has come among us." By then, the spirit of Saint Francis should have been evoked, and all elements of the production should be a celebration of that spirit, creating a passing moment of beauty.

This may sound like, and indeed may be, an excuse for weak poetry. But I believe it to be true to the spirit of Noh, which dictates that no one element shall take precedence over another, but that all should blend into one esthetic whole.

The structure of the written script follows an orthodox pattern, the names of the various parts being indicated in the left margin, and brief explanations of those names being given in notes. I hope that one reading the play for the first time will ignore the notes, reading straight through. This should not take long, though a conventional presentation by an authentic Noh troupe would require about an hour and fifteen minutes. The "Americanized" production at Earlham College took fifty-five minutes.

For the Earlham production, Leonard Holvik, composer, and Eleanor King, choreographer, did their work so well that however else the enterprise might be judged, the true synthesis that is an ideal of Noh was achieved, and the play that was once mine has become ours.

ARTHUR LITTLE

SAINT FRANCIS: A NOH PLAY

Persons [1]

A Weighty Friend	WAKI
An Old Man	SHITE
Member of Meeting	KYOGEN
Saint Francis	NOCHI-SHITE
Members of Meeting Gathered for Worship	JI

Part I

On the back wall of the stage is represented Penn's Oak,[2] beneath which William Penn signed a treaty with the Indians. On stage left, a two- or three-tiered Quaker "facing bench." On stage right, sufficient space to function as the Noh stage's *hashigakari*, or entranceway.

When it is time to begin, the orchestra comes on in single file, ceremonially spaced, from stage right and proceeds to its place upstage, slightly to the right to give some balance to the facing bench. At the same time, the chorus comes on from upstage left, also in single file, but more-closely spaced. Members of the chorus seat themselves on the facing benches, entering from the upstage side and leaving empty one seat on the first bench.

While the entrance music Shin-No-Shidai is being played, the WAKI enters from stage right, walks slowly to the acting area, faces the front, hesitates, walks toward the front of the stage, turns slowly, proceeds on a straight line to the empty seat on the first bench, turns slowly, and sits.

Meanwhile, the KYOGEN, coming on behind the WAKI, proceeds directly to a stool upstage right and sits.

When the WAKI sits, the entrance music stops. Silence is maintained as long as bearable. Suddenly, but slowly and with dignity, the WAKI stands.

SHIDAI [3]

WAKI:
Re-cent-ly in In-di-a   an ex-pe-ri-ence.

JIDORI [4]

JI:
Recently in India   an experience.

NANORI [5]

WAKI:
Recently in India   an experience.
It happened in Calcutta   where I met a man.
        [WAKI X R]

I was at the time on a special mission to study the effect of Christianity on the Hindus, an arduous task, and I talked with many men; still I found time to enjoy the beauties of the place, to keep at arm's length, as it were, the pressing problems of the poor. There were attractions and distractions, but as it was not my task to solve unsolvable problems, I kept my mind on things the tourists enjoy.
[*The* WAKI *begins his journey around the stage.*]

MICHIYUKI [6]

India is a strange land   full of strange beauty
A strange land full of
strange beauty.

In the caves of Ajunta   voluptuous stones
Swarm before the
  swarming crowd   sinuous heaving.
Moonlit Taj Mahal
  becomes   a marble sonnet.
O Agra is a lotus   its green pad withered
And like a desert flower   blooms the Red Fort.
Along broken paths of a
  once-tended garden   hardy buds persist.
While tendrils of
  poverty strangle
  all—obliterating
As a jungle smothers
  ancient cities
  obliering all.

Let us then move on: [WAKI X to seat.]
Home of Tagore: Here at last is Calcutta:
  Home of Holy
  Ganges and of the
  Black Hole.
It happened in Calcutta   where I met a man
                              [WAKI sits.]

While the entrance music Shin-No-Issei is being played, the SHITE enters stage right and stops at what would be the first pine position on the traditional Noh stage. He is wearing beautifully draped soft rags in browns and yellows, with an outer covering of muted saffron draped over one shoulder. He wears an old man mask and wig.

ISSEI [7]

SHITE:
The song of the bord
Lifts my eyes up to
  heaven   I do not see thee
But "Hail to thee, blithe
  spirit"   whether bird or not
Singing o'er the parched
  land,   thou art a maiden
JI:
Bringing water from the
  well,   grapes from the vineyard.
                              [SHITE X onto stage
                                           proper.]

SASHI [8]

SHITE:
Deep in the jungle
Hidden deep in the
  jungle,   the plumage of birds
Is obscured by the
  shadows,   till piercing the shade
The sun like
  scythe-cutting   clears a path of light.
Then can the feathers be
  seen   in all their glory.
Before the sun shone on
  them   were the colors there?
What happens to bright
  colors   in a darkened room?
And you, O little brown
  birds,   hopping in the street,
What are your honest
  colors?   Are you really brown?
Perhaps my poor eyes
  can see   Only brown in you.

SAGEUTA [9]

Dear little brothers,
                              JI: [10]
You make such a
  raucous noise,   Dear little brothers
Chattering so together   in no govern'd tune.
Hopping about on the
  ground,   foolishly you chirp.

AGEUTA

SHITE:
How wonderful is the
  sound   of one unseen bird
JI:
Filling the empty sky.   O let us join him:
Raise now our voices on
  high   with clear notes only;
Praise now the
  everlasting—   that which cannot die.
Stretch your feathers,
  little friends,   receive the sunlight.
And singing now with
  one voice   let our spirits soar;
And though we leave
  our bodies   drooping in the dust,
Long will the world
  remember   our transcendental
                                           song—
Long find comfort in   our heaven-seeking song.

MONDO [11]

WAKI:
I beg your pardon,
  friend: Excuse me if I interrupt
                              [WAKI rises, steps be-
                              low the facing bench.]

196

Oh, I have scattered the
  birds—

SHITE:
It is no interruption and the birds will return.

[SHITE *turns toward* WAKI.]

WAKI:
I beg your pardon, but you seem to be preaching to the birds. Is that your practice?

SHITE:
Preaching? Perhaps. They are my companions. I, too, am a little brown bird, grubbing in the dust.

[SHITE *walks to C, facing* WAKI.]

WAKI:
Perhaps, as a stranger, I am too personal.

SHITE:
No encounter can be too personal, and we are all strangers: strangers and brothers. What is it you wish to know?

WAKI:
Though you look poor, friend, as poorly clad and thin as all the rest we see about us everywhere, you do not seem to ask for alms; your hands do not supplicate, nor do your eyes plead. Are you not one of the poor?

SHITE:
I am one of the poor. Though I do not beg, I receive. Daily I receive my daily needs, and more. Daily I give thanks. Daily the birds sing to me. Daily we raise our voices in praise and thanksgiving.

WAKI:
Tell me your history, friend. Surely you were not born among the poor?

SHITE:
To be born in this world is to be born among the poor. But I did not always know it. Like you, I came from a more abundant land, and my eyes were not opened for many years. My earthly father's business prospered and with his money I set out to see the world. Happily, for my soul's sake, I saw. It happened in Calcutta.

[WAKI *sits.*]

When I came to this city
The multitude of people
and saw in the street
how some slept, some ate,

All pushing for space to
  breathe,
Living out their daily
  lives.
some defecating,

It was too much to
  receive:
As I walked along the
  street
some ill, some dying,
My breath seemed to stop.

seeing what I saw,

But not wishing to
  believe
one beggar approached

[SHITE *begins to dance.*]

AGEUTA

JI:
One beggar approached;
  then two;
four, eight, sixteen came.

Bony hands outstretched,
  pleading
bony babies held

Hungry against empty
  breasts:
bony faces hung

Like masks on wooden
  poles
bony bodies hung

With rags not fit for
  scarecrows;
no sense of flesh but

Skin stretched tight as
  catgut
My spirit rebelled:

"Take away this evil
  sight,
for this cannot be!"

SHITE:
It was and I knew it was:
My eyes were opened.

MONDO

JI:
It was and I knew it was:
These were the blessed
  poor;
These were the poor.

And I a chastened man.

[WAKI *stands.*]

WAKI:
Tell me, friend,
  o tell me:
What did you do?

[WAKI *sits.*]

KURI 12

JI:
"Sell all that thou hast,
Yet when he sells all he
  has
He becomes one of the
  poor;
And give to the poor"

a man becomes poor.

he joins the poor.

SASHI

SHITE:
Hearken ye unto the
  word:
"Blessed are the poor—

JI:
Blessed are the poor in
  spirit:
Blessed are they that
  mourn:
theirs is the kingdom.

they shall be comforted.

Blessed are the meek　for they shall inherit the earth.

Blessed are they who hunger　and thirst after righteousness for they shall be fulfilled.

Blessed are the merciful　for they shall obtain mercy.

Blessed are the pure in heart　for they shall see God.
Blessed are the peacemakers　for they shall be called the children of God.
Blessed are ye when men revile　and persecute you
And say all manner of evil:　Rejoice and be glad."

KUSE [13]

SHITE:

JI:

Suffering must be endured
Only in the agony
Can man　No cross—no crown.
Only in darkness open　of humility
Only in the dust　shed his cloak of pride;
Only in tumult open　his eyes to the light.
Only in confusion's din　breathe the purest air
Receive God's quiet word.　his ears to the word.
　will reluctant ear

O in hot tears away;　his sins will be washed
His soul will be purged—way.　In the crucible
Lying in the ashes　the dross burned a-
The pit thinking all is lost　At the bottom of
Reduced to nothingness　in great despair
　beyond the power of thought

With hope neither for himself　nor for the world
Faintly at first　then with clarity
He will hear a soothing voice
From the bottom of the pit　calling to him
Sweet as a lark in the sky　he will hear the voice
He will hear　heralding joy.
　will heed.
Then from the ground he will rise
To receive the Holy Ghost,　swift as a swallow
Amen　bringing perfect joy.

SHITE:
O whirling moment　O moment of truth

JI:
When skies are opened　when earth heaves up
When self is lost　and self is found
In one moment I knew　O mystical truth
God is my father　All men are my brothers
All that is mine is theirs all
Mine is their hunger and thirst　that is theirs mine
I have no joy but in them　mine is their nakedness
All creatures brothers　we are of one blood
Animate, inanimate　All that is on earth created by God.
[WAKI rises.]

RONGI [14]

All men are brothers, 'tis true
But what you say is madness　and God, the father
Must one be mad to be good?　it cannot be so.
All would be lost if all fol-　it cannot be so.
It cannot be so　low the way you lead.
His creation lost　that God desires
Surely to prevent
on his chosen stewards who　it he put a trust
Who must tend the vineyard　render account.
Prune the orchard, feed the flock;　water the garden;
Store up grain against famine.　count the harvest and
SHITE:
Take thought for the morrow?　Is it not they who
JI:　Store up riches?
It is enough to obey
Give a tenth of thy riches　the law as written
SHITE:
JI:　It costs nothing.
Share of thy labor.
SHITE:
JI:　SHITE:　Art truly weary?
Fast　Dost thou know true hunger?　JI:
　Pray.
[WAKI sits.]
SHITE:
dost thou submit?
When I was a rich man's son　JI:
I walked abroad, doing good　Money in my purse,
　doing charity

<table>
<tr><td>

SHITE:
O what a good man,

Truly they have their
  reward
The charitable have eyes
Ears to hear the outward
  cries
Hands to offer lovingly

Tears to shed in pity;
  and
But they do not know
Of compassion
Whose indiscriminate
  flame
So saying, he
  disappeared:

Leaving me a-
If I had encountered
Francis of Assisi

</td><td>

[SHITE *moves about.*]

JI:
they said. It was sweet to
  hear.

who give to the poor
to see the surface;

of suffering souls;
balm for skin-deep
  wounds
they have their reward.
the sweet pain
the fiery furnace

makes of all men one.

melted in the crowd;
  [SHITE *moves down*
    entranceway.]
mazed for it was as

the saint himself
  [SHITE *disappears.*]

</td></tr>
</table>

Now Francis saw a bright light, and he turned it on the world about him. He did not try to keep it for himself, but he held it aloft for all to see.

The KYOGEN rises, stands still for a second, moves into the acting area, and faces front.[15]

KYOGEN:

Friends: Let's not forget that Francis was a gay bird. He was no long-faced goon; though some of the people of his own time thought him rather a loony bird, and his followers, after his death, tried to pluck his feathers, so to speak, and dress him in borrowed plumage. Many men whom we call good—even saints— have been wild in their youth, have repented and given over their former ways. They have, we say, "seen the light." And after their lives have been exemplary, and for the most part, dull. The light they saw was evidently dim, or else they managed to hide it under a bushel.

Now Francis saw a bright light, and he turned it on the world about him. He did not try to keep it for himself, but held it aloft for all to see. He did not shun the dark corners, but rather explored them.

And his light went with him. He did not turn his eyes away from misery, but looked straight at it. Indeed, he concentrated on it so hard, and his compassion was so great, that he received the stigmata, duplicates of the very wounds received by Christ himself. He took on every pain, every sorrow, every doubt, and somehow in him these things were transmuted, so that receiving pain, he gave back comfort; receiving sorrow, gave back joy; receiving doubt, radiated certainty. He was a loving man with joy at the core of his being. A gay bird, even after he had moulted, so to speak; had shed his brilliant trappings and clothed himself in the brown Franciscan habit.

It is recorded that even after he became a holy man and was allowed to set up an order, he continued to shock his neighbors. This may not have amused Saint Francis, but it still delights poor sinners like me. "Good men are so pious. They need a jolt once in a while for the sake of their souls." Oh,

Francis was a gay bird; a gay dog, to change the metaphor. He was a gay dog who knew he was a dog, and took on a dog's life without a whimper. That was not his vision of the way the world ends. I feel sure that however you wish to explain it, however you understand it, however you rationalize—I feel sure that it was Saint Francis, miles from Assisi, whom our friend met in Calcutta.

[KYOGEN *returns to seat.*]

Part II

While the entrance music Issei is being played, the spirit of Saint Francis appears from right and dances onto the stage. He wears a Kantan Otoko mask (or an especially made Saint Francis mask), and a brightly colored costume taken from one of Giotto's paintings. His head is covered with a Dantesque toque.

ISSEI

SHITE:

In youth I was a gay bird   flitting round the town
Flashing my splendid
    feathers   brilliant in the sun
     [SHITE *dances.*] [16]

JI:

Spreading my powerful
    wings   soaring now on high,
Now swooping low to
    conquer   a butterfly.

AGEUTA

Lifting the hearts of all
    who   saw me on the wing
Lifting high the spirits of   all who heard me sing.
Preening my gorgeous
    feathers   lazy in the sun
I ruffle restless feathers,   sprinkle them with dust
Then suddenly
    responding   to some inner urge
I fly again toward heaven   to the very sun
Till from the earth my
    colors   seem one crimson speck.
Affectionate and carefree   a covey of cads
I chose as my
    companions   scarlet tanagers
Peacocks and popinjays,
Painted with all the
    pigments   of great God's palette.
But scattering before us,   Hov'ring on the fringe
Were little common
    sparrows,   and I saw them not.

SHITE:

Mine was a god of
    pleasure,   god of fleshly love.
JI:
The earth a spacious
    ballroom   life itself like a ball
     [SHITE *performs a*
     chu-no-mai.] [17]

SASHI

JI:

Mine was a god of
    pleasure   god of profane love.
My light foot followed
    heedless   of the path it trod.
Mindless,
    uncomprehending,   unaware of pain,
I stomped on crawling
    creatures,   insects underfoot,
Inflicting pain,
    unknowing   in a dance of death.
     [*Drum beat, foot*
     beat together.]

SHITE:
O Holy Lord, forgive me   for my innocence.
JI:
He had eyes, yet he saw
    not;   neither did he hear
The cry of the suffering   loud in Assisi.
But God, being merciful,   granted salvation
For, lo, his eyes were
    opened;   his ears unstopped.

The SHITE stands awhile C, then turns and walks with dignity upstage R, where assistants help him change his bright garments for a Franciscan robe. His headdress being removed reveals the tonsure.

The orchestra meanwhile continues playing. When he is ready, the SHITE takes the stage in a *jo-no-mai.* [18]

RONGI

JI:
O blessed vision: a saint has come among
     us

See how quickly he
    moves,   alarming no one,
Neither the birds nor the
    beasts   nor frightened sinners.
SHITE: JI:
Hear ye, O hear God's
    message.   God has not called you
Solely for your salvation.   He has summoned you

To gather a harvest of souls / That many may be saved.

SHITE:
Let us go forth in the name / of God the Father.

JI:
In the name of God he heals / the sore afflicted,
Gathers the poor about him, / comforts the grieving,
He kneels before the humble / and washes their feet,
He orders the swallows to / cease their twittering
And to keep silent until / he ends his sermon
And they obey him.

WAKA [19]

SHITE:
O come let us sing:
"Praise the Lord, all ye nations, / O praise him all ye people.

JI:
For his merciful kindness / is great toward us
And the truth of the Lord en- / dureth forever."

KIRI [20]

SHITE:
Hear the song of Brother Sun

JI:
Song of Brother Sun

Most High Almighty, / Thine be the praise, the glory.

SHITE:
Thine be the praise, glory, hon- / or and all blessings.

JI:
Thine be the praise, glory, hon- / or and all blessings.
To thee alone, O Most High / they are due. No man
Is worthy to speak thy name. / Praise to thee, my Lord,
For all thy creatures. Above / all for Brother Sun.
'Tis he who brings us the day, / And lends us his light;
O lovely he is, radi- / ant with great splendor.
And he speaks to us of thee, / O Most High.
Praise to Thee, my Lord, for Sis- / ter Moon and the Stars
Thou hast set in the heavens, / clear, precious, and fair.
Praise to thee, my Lord, for Sis- / ter Water, she who
Is so useful and humble, / so precious and pure.
Praise to thee, my Lord, for Bro- / ther Fire, by whom
Thou lightest nightly, lovely, plea- / sant, mighty and strong.
Praise to thee, my Lord, for those / who pardon for love
Of thee and endure sickness / and tribulation.
Blessed are they who shall en- / dure these things in peace.

For they shall be crowned by thee, / O Most High.
Praise to thee, my Lord, for Sis- / ter Bodily Death.
None escapes. Woe to those who / die in mortal sin.
Blessed are they who are found / in thy holy will,
For even the second death / can do them no harm.
Praise and bless my Lord; / Thank him and serve him,
With humility.
Rejoice in the love of God / through eternity.
Though flesh and temporal things / may be snatched away
The spirit stands firm. / The spirit stands firm.

The SHITE stamps his feet twice, and the play is over.[21]

Notes

It is to be hoped that anyone attempting to produce this play will acquaint himself at least rudimentarily with Noh. The handiest sources for this acquaintance are Arthur Waley's *The Noh Plays of Japan* (New York, Grove Press—E-62, paperback); Donald Keene's *Noh: The Classical Theater of Japan* (Tokyo & Palo Alto, 1966); the Nippon Gakujutsu Shinkokai's *The Noh Drama* (Rutland, VT: Charles E. Tuttle Co., 1955); two subsequent volumes of the latter, published in Japan, available through Tuttle; and William Malm's *Japanese Music*, chapter 4 (Tuttle, 1959). The definitions below will refer to these volumes as Waley, Keene, and Malm.

1 Persons: Every Noh play has at least a WAKI, a SHITE, and a chorus (JI).

The WAKI is the secondary actor who usually introduces a play. He does not wear a mask, but his face is impassive. He in no way competes with the SHITE for attention.

The SHITE (pronounced "shtay") is the leading character. He usually wears a mask, and dominates the play from his entrance until the end.

The NOCHI-SHITE is played by the same actor as the SHITE, appearing in the second half of a two-part play with a different mask and costume. Most of the time, he represents the spirit of the character played by the SHITE in part one.

The KYOGEN is a comic actor used most frequently to bridge parts one and two. He does not wear a mask, and speaks in a tone distinct from the SHITE and WAKI.

The JI is the chorus. In Noh it does not represent a distinct group as in Greek drama, but is abstract. It takes over for the SHITE in certain passages, though occasionally it will hold a kind of dialogue with the SHITE in something resembling a Greek *agon*.

2 Penn's Oak: This is for the Earlham production. As Earlham is a Quaker school, it seemed appropriate to substitute the oak for the traditional Noh pine that is always on the back wall of a Noh stage. For Earlham, too, the chorus has been set up as if it constituted a meeting for worship in the traditional Quaker style. There is no reason intrinsic to *Saint Francis* why the play should be set in a meeting.

3 *Shidai:* The entrance music, and the WAKI's entrance song in English in Japanese form is illustrated here by the necessity of counting "-ence" as one syllable. In Japanese, if such a strange word should find its way into that language, "experience" which has here been counted as four syllables would be seven (Keene, pp. 55, 76).

4 *Jidori:* A line or passage repeated by the chorus *sotto voce*. It is here a part of the *shidai*.

5 *Nanori:* Name-telling passage. Usually in prose. Sometimes "*accompanied*" by flute or drums, but never in the same rhythm or pitch as the speaker's voice (Keene, p. 76).

6 *Michiyuki:* Travel-song, during which the WAKI usually moves from one part of the stage to another. His motions are stylized, rhythmic, but not "dance" that might compete with the SHITE's subsequent performance.

7 *Issei:* Literally, "first voice." There are several kinds of *issei*. Here it is the SHITE's entrance song (Keene, p. 55; Malm, pp. 110, 112, 129).

8 *Sashi:* A type of heightened speech, somewhat like a recitative, spoken on one pitch. Uusually about ten lines of seven to five syllables (Keene, pp. 55–56).

9 *Sageuta and Ageuta:* The former is low in pitch and usually short; the latter is higher in pitch and longer, usually sung by the chorus, but sometimes by the SHITE (Malm, pp. 111, 145).

10 *Ji:* Here is a case of the chorus taking over for the SHITE, who usually pantomimes (in a very abstract way) the action.

11 *Mondo:* A passage of dialogue, usually, as here, between the SHITE and the WAKI. It usually begins in "recitative" style, rises to a melody that is taken up and completed by the chorus (Malm, pp. 111–12).

12 *Kuri:* A short, lively passage of no fixed meter. This one, however, follows the regular 7-5 form (Malm, pp. 111–12, 120, 128; Keene, pp. 56, 76).

13 *Kuse:* The dance section of the first part of a play. Frequently the core of the story on which the play is based is presented here. I have used it to express the central paradox of the Saint Francis experience. During this particular kuse the SHITE might sit or stand still, meditating (Malm, pp. 111, 120).

14 *Rongi:* Usually a dialogue: sometimes in the form of question and answer; sometimes ends with the chorus sing-ing, as here, the final passage of an act (Malm, pp. 111–12; Keene, p. 56).

15 KYOGEN: See note 1. This passage should be in a lighter, more colloquial manner than any other part of the play.

16 SHITE *dances:* This should be very much "illustrative" of the words and not so much a formal dance set apart as the two that follow.

17 *Chu-no-mai:* A lyric and elegant dance, usually performed by female deities; but it seems to me appropriate for the effete, pleasure-loving Francis. Most of it should be performed without the accompaniment of words, the chorus coming in only at the end of the dance, which is finished with the words: "dance of death." The SHITE should stand still during the next five lines (Keene, p. 80; Malm, p. 266).

18 *Jo-no-mai:* This is an elegant dance in the slowest tempo (Keene, pp. 81, 120).

19 *Waka:* This is not strictly a *waka*, which is composed of thirty-one syllables. Most frequently a famous poem is quoted here, and I have shown a passage from Psalm 117.

20 *Kiri:* The finale. Sung by the chorus, usually with increasing tempo to the end.

21 The SHITE usually ends a play by stamping his foot twice, standing near the upstage right pillar (known as the SHITE-pillar). He then folds his fan and walks slowly out the long entranceway. After he leaves, the orchestra members bow and exit ceremoniously as they entered. While they are making their exits, the chorus leaves in orderly fashion by the upstage left.

About the Music of *Saint Francis*

Although the music of *Saint Francis* is not the same as the music of a real Japanese Noh drama, I have attempted to adhere to some of the same basic principles and to use some of the essential sounds of the Noh theater. Other aspects of the music were not used, however, usually because they did not seem appropriate to the English language, the abilities of American performers, or the background of an American audience.

The chief principle, without which anything like Noh would be impossible, is the subordination of everything to one entity: the whole play. None of the elements of dance, music, mime, poetry, or costume is allowed to develop forms that exist for their own sake. This is most crucial in the case of the music, where temptations to arialike development or even to overt interpretation of the words through purely musical expansion must be resisted. On the other hand, every moment must be set to "music," since no passage in a Noh play is without rhythmical design.

One should expect neither an opera, nor a play with incidental music, nor a dance, nor a poetry reading, but a Noh play, which is different from any of them.

Arthur Little's poetry was written in the metrical forms of the Noh and was conceived with the aural environment of the Noh theater in mind. The music is meant to be faithful to that concept. The rhythmical nature of the Noh and the tone colors and musical techniques of that theater provide a kind of suggestive background. There are several actual transcriptions of passages from Noh plays, chiefly instrumental introductions, interludes, and dances. Almost all of these, however, have been modified by newly composed music extending or changing the original models. Also, the performance employs different instruments and, most important, Western performers. In general, the attempt has been to deviate in about the same sense and to about the same degree as the play deviates by being in English and about subjects from Western tradition. Some departures have not been as great as I expected. For example, a young American flutist (using a flute with open holes) produced remarkably well effects reminiscent of the tonally indistinct Noh flute, and our drummers used their voices as well as their hands without the difficulties I had expected.

Some specific characteristics which come from the nature of Noh music are these:

• Pitch varies from clearly defined intervals on the one hand to extremely indistinct and shifting relationships on the other. (This includes portamento microtonal effects in the flute part and sometimes in the singing and free, unspecified relationships of pitch and rhythm between the singing and the flute.)
• Rhythms vary from passages of metrical regularity to very flexible "follow-the-leader" sections, sometimes avoiding exact agreement even among the drums.
• The Noh scale system is used in part and at times, but it is not applied strictly, and it is intermixed with references to plainsong and medieval polyphony of the West.
• Percussion sounds are dry and have fairly short reverberation times; the vocal calls of the drummers are rhythmical and expressive in function. They are essential to the aural environment for which *Saint Francis* was conceived.

Saint Francis is not offered as an example of a Japanese Noh play. For that you will have to depend on the real thing, performed by the professional masters of the Japanese theater. It is not even based on thorough knowledge of the details of the tradition. For that you need the lifelong study of those masters. It is based on respect for that great art and on the belief that some of its principles and practices may be translated and combined with ours in a way that will be of value for its own sake.

LEONARD HOLVIK

The Dance In Noh

Western dancing is traditionally noted for emphasis on the personality of the dancer, athleticism of the body, exploitation of techniques of motion, and superficial effects. In Noh dance, the masked player, whose body is concealed, whose dancing expresses the meaning of the play, is singing and dancing to us of the world of the spirit—he is himself a god, sometimes a ghost who returns to the world to relive his passion. To understand *Saint Francis* we need to put on a different pair of glasses, a new set of lenses, for that eyeopening that a Noh performance gives of the life of the soul. We also need a clock without hands to enter this world of timelessness, of motion stretched to sometimes excruciating lengths, of the stillness of the Noh dancer, whose concentration of being invites our imagination as in no other theatre.

The essence of the cohesive rhythm of Noh is a gradual acceleration, a sophisticated and subtle rise and fall that is in every step of the dances, every movement phrase, every section, and the play as a whole. Maintaining and building this rhythmic form challenges equally the chorus, the musicians, the dancer, for together only, they weave the magic spell.

As Arthur Little's poetry and Leonard Holvik's music are both structured rhythmically and metrically in the true form of Noh, the dance necessarily conforms to associated movement conventions—some, but not all of them, particularly Japanese. The Japanese conventions are these:

• The posture of the disciplined courtier-warrior, and the deportment that requires the extremities to be used as little as possible (not "Look Ma, I'm dancing"; but "Reflect upon the beauty of these passing forms").
• The walk, called the priest's walk, based on one of the mental and physical exercises of priests who are undergoing meditative discipline for achievement of *sartori*, or enlightenment.
• Stamping, the most characteristic gesture found in all Japanese dance, functionally related to the rice field, mythically to the first created dance in

the world, performed by Uzume dancing on a tub, which succeeded in luring the Sun Goddess from her hiding place.

- The use of the fan. When Noh was crystallized in the fourteenth century, it embedded in its heart the sum of a thousand years of previous dance forms, one of the earliest of which was ceremonial Shrine Kagura, the music and dance performed in the presence of a god. Virgin priestesses or attendants of shrines still perform ritual blessing or prayer dances. These require that some sacred object be held in the hands. In Noh, the secular theater, the sacred object becomes the fan, used to denote the elements or ideas expressed in the text. *Saint Francis* uses the fan with a variety of meanings: now the abstract symbol of Brother Sun, or Sister Moon, the Stars, of Sister Water, of states of feeling of exultation and joy, or symbols of compassion and blessing.

With Arthur Little's *Saint Francis* having a Western subject, and Western speech, no attempt is made to keep to Japanese conventions of mime in the critical passages where the SHITE dances his trauma in Calcutta, the climactic *Kuse* section, "Suffering must be endured," or the preceding "Blessed are the poor in spirit." Here we have thought in terms of universal gesture, hoping to achieve, as with all Noh plays, a maximum of experience with a minimum of means, to create beauty within a few forms, which touch on the imperishable spirit.

ELEANOR KING

The Stone

ANNE MORROW LINDBERGH

There is a core of suffering that the mind
Can never penetrate or even find;
A stone that clogs the stream of my delight,
Hidden beneath the surface out of sight,
Below the flow of words it lies concealed.
It blocks my passage and it will not yield
To hammer blows of will, and still resists
The surgeon's scalpel of analysis.
Too hard for tears and too opaque for light,
Bright shafts of prayer splinter against its might.
Beauty cannot disguise nor music melt
A pain, undiagnosable but felt.

No sleep dissolves that stony stalagmite,
Mounting within the unconscious caves of night.

No solvent left but love. Whose love? My own?
And is one asked to love the harsh unknown?
I am no Francis who could kiss the lip
Of alien leper. Caught within the grip
Of world unfaith, I cannot even pray,
And must I love? Is there no other way?
Suffering without name or tongue or face,
Blindly I crush you in my dark embrace!

Kazantzakis and Saint Francis

Review of *Saint Francis,* a Novel by Nikos Kazantzakis
Time magazine

When the Victorians "discovered" Saint Francis in the last century, they were charmed by his gentleness, fashioned an image of an almost sickly sweet saint who slipped effortlessly through life. In his last novel, Greece's late, great Nikos Kazantzakis has restored agony of soul to the story of Saint Francis. Like Jesus in Kazantzakis's *The Last Temptation of Christ* and Ulysses in his epic poem, *The Odyssey,* Francis struggles to shed earthly desires for a harder, truer life of the spirit.

SWEAT AND LUST "We, as human beings, are all miserable persons, heartless, small, insignificant," wrote Kazantzakis in his personal credo, *The Saviors of God.* "But within us a superior essence drives us ruthlessly upward. From within this human mire divine songs have welled up, great ideas, violent loves, an unsleeping assault full of mystery."

In Kazantzakis's imaginative reconstruction, Saint Francis searches for God in these commonly human terms. His Francis sweats with lust for the lovely Clare, dreams of wrestling with a naked woman and other demons, and wakes "beating his hands against the floor, bellowing, his hair sodden and dripping." About to kiss a leper, he blanches at the putrescent nose, the fingerless hands, spits, and is nauseated. Clothed always in rags, he smells. "What pigsty did you come from?" the Pope sardonically asks on meeting Francis. "I suppose you think you're duplicating the aroma of paradise?"

God gives Francis no rest or comfort. "You know how a lion seizes a hare and bangs him playfully against the ground?" he tells one of his Brothers. "Well, God has seized me in the same way. I am writhing in God's claws and cannot escape." Making the "terrible" discovery that God is never satisfied, he takes on one task after another—building a church, founding an order, risking his life in the Crusades, fasting for almost a year on a bitter cold mountaintop. On Mount Albernia, he receives the stigmata in a vision that is pure Kazantzakis. Seeing the crucified Christ wrapped in flames, Francis cries in anguish: "I want more, more! The Resurrection!" But Christ, echoing Kazantzakis's own belief, stonily replies: "Crucifixion, Resurrection, and paradise are identical."

But Francis's charm is as richly portrayed as his torments. He preaches by ringing a bell, dancing in the streets, clapping, and singing. His sermon to the swallows, his conversion of his friends are as beautifully rendered as they are in *The Little Flowers of Saint Francis*. "God forgive me," Francis tells his Sisters, "I feel sorry even for Satan. There is no creature more unfortunate, more wretched than he, because he was once with God, but now he has left him, denied him, and he roams the air inconsolable."

To his eye, the Francis of legend was too mild to be a saint. In his retelling, he endows the saint with a human vulnerability that gives Francis a new universality.

Kazantzakis's prose moves with the stateliness of a funeral dirge as Francis, bleeding from the stigmata and nearly blind, moves to his death with childlike dignity. When a mouse gnaws at his toes one night, Francis whispers softly, "as though he had been speaking to a child, 'Brother Mouse, I am suffering! For the love of God, go away! I am suffering!'"

Kazantzakis knew something of suffering himself. By stifling his own physical desires, he contracted a savage skin disease of the same type that used to rack medieval ascetics. Neither its origin nor its cure is known, and it is commonly called the Saint's Disease. "My dear sir," psychoanalyst Wilhelm Stekel once scolded him, "you are trying to live out of your century. Your body is suffering from remorse of spirit." It was Kazantzakis's belief that only through soul-searing struggle could man approach God. To his eye, the Francis of legend was too mild to be a saint. In his retelling, he endows the saint with a human vulnerability that gives Francis a new universality.

Alien

MARY BRENT WHITESIDE

He crouches in the chapel, on his knees,
    With matted hair that hangs in dusky strands;
    Apart and strange, among the little bands
Of worshipers, for he is not as these.
Alone! and yet a deeper vision sees
    That near this alien with his grimy hands,
    The Little Poor Man of Assisi stands,
As Giotto painted him upon a frieze.

I knew one luminous Italian spring!
    "Your province? Is it Umbria?" I ask.
    The weariness falls from him like a mask,
And all his visage is a shining thing,
    As though some deathless master of his race
    Inscribed a sudden message on his face.

Saint Francis

ALFRED LORD TENNYSON

. . . Are we devils? Are we men?
Sweet Saint Francis of Assisi,
Would that he were here again,
He who in his catholic wholeness
Called the very birds and flowers
Brothers, sisters.

Epilogue

Would I Might Wake Saint Francis in You All

VACHEL LINDSAY

Would I might wake Saint Francis in you all,
Brother of birds and trees,
God's Troubadour,
Blinded with weeping for the sad and the poor:
Our wealth undone, all strict Franciscan men,
Come, let us chant the canticle again
Of mother earth and the enduring sun.
God make each soul
The lowly leper's slave:
God make us saints, and brave.

A Final Word

"I have done what was mine to do; may Christ teach you what you are to do."

SAINT FRANCIS OF ASSISI

EICHENBERG

Text Sources
and Permissions

Sources and permissions are expressed in their entirety only the first time they appear. Sources are listed in the order in which they appear in the text.

p. 1. Nikos Kazantzakis, *St. Francis*. Copyright © 1962 by Simon & Schuster, Inc., a Division of Gulf & Western Corporation, pp. 22–29. Reprinted with permission.

p. 4. Raphael Brown, *True Joy from Assisi*. Chicago: Franciscan Herald Press, 1978.

p. 5. *Fodor's Italy, 1978*. New York: David McKay Co.

p. 7. *St. Francis and the Poet*, Elizabeth Patterson, editor, copyright © 1956 by The Devin-Adair Co., Old Greenwich, CT 06870. Reprinted with permission.

p. 7. W. Stephen Bush, "Simple Homage Is Paid to Saint Francis." © 1926 by *The New York Times* Company. Reprinted by permission.

p. 8. Pope John Paul II, *L'Osservatore Romano*, November 13, 1978.

p. 10. Francis and Helen Line, *Man with a Song*. Chicago: Franciscan Herald Press, 1972.

p. 10. Ernest Raymond, *In the Steps of St. Francis*. Chicago: Franciscan Herald Press, 1975.

p. 12. Omer Englebert, *Saint Francis of Assisi*. Chicago: Franciscan Herald Press, 1965.

p. 15. Colman McCarthy, "St. Francis: The Eccentric Realist." The *Washington Post*, December 25, 1972.

p. 18. G. K. Chesterton, *St. Francis of Assisi*. Garden City, NY: Doubleday Image Books, 1957.

p. 21. Joseph Roddy, "The Hippie Saint." *Look* magazine, April 20, 1971.

p. 25. Thomas of Celano, "An Eyewitness Description of Saint Francis's Appearance and Personality." In *Saint Francis of Assisi: Omnibus of Sources*. Chicago: Franciscan Herald Press, 1972.

p. 26. Reprinted with permission of Macmillan Publishing Co., Inc., from *The Saints Through Their Handwriting* by Girolamo Moretti. Copyright © 1964 by Macmillan Publishing Co., Inc.

p. 28. Ernest Raymond, *In the Steps of St. Francis*.

p. 29. From *Francis of Assisi* by Anthony Mockler. Copyright © 1976 by Phaidon Press Ltd. Reprinted by permission of the publisher in the United States, E. P. Dutton.

p. 31. John Ruskin, *Mornings in Venice*. New York: John Wiley & Sons, 1891.

p. 33. Marion A. Habig, O.F.M., "Dante on Saint Francis." In *The Cord*, April 1960.

p. 34. Omer Englebert, *Saint Francis of Assisi*.

p. 37. Roy M. Gasnick, O.F.M., "Franciscan Witness in the World." *Good News*, May 1972.

p. 40. Frances Frost, "Prayer to St. Francis." In *St. Francis and the Poet*.

p. 40. G. K. Chesterton, *St. Francis of Assisi*.

p. 42. Mario von Galli, S.J., *Francis of Assisi and the Church Tomorrow*. Chicago: Franciscan Herald Press, 1972.

p. 46. Thomas Merton, "Franciscan Eremitism." In *The Cord*, December 1966.

p. 49. Romano Guardini, "St. Francis and Self-achievement." In *The Focus of Freedom*. Copyright © translation 1966 by Helicon Press, Inc.

p. 52. Dan Mauk, "Poor Man of God." In *The Catholic Worker*, October–November 1975.

p. 53. Philip Scharper, "Francis of Assisi: A Search for the Man and His Meaning." Produced by the Public Affairs Department of N.B.C. News in association with the Office for Film and Broadcasting of the U.S. Catholic Conference, Martin Hoad, producer, 1977.

p. 54. Liam Brophy, "Lenin Was Right." In *St. Anthony's Messenger*, October 1949.

p. 56. Peter Maurin, "We Seem to Think." *Easy Essays*, Chicago: Franciscan Herald Press, 1977.

p. 56. Evelyn Underhill, "The Lady Poverty." In Thomas Walsh's *Catholic Anthology*, New York: Macmillan Publishing Co., Inc., 1927.

p. 57. Oscar Wilde, *De Profundis*. Union City, NJ: William H. Wise & Co., 1923.

p. 57. William Wordsworth, "The Cuckoo at Lavernia." In *St. Francis and the Poet*.

p. 58. G. K. Chesterton, "The Ungloomy Ascetic." In *St. Francis of Assisi*.

p. 58. Constantine Koser, O.F.M., "Saint Francis and Man." *Our Life with God*. Pulaski, WI: Franciscan Publishers, 1971.

p. 60. G. K. Chesterton, "Monks Versus Slippery Fishes." *St. Francis of Assisi*.

p. 63. John O'Connor, S.M., "The Religious Life and the Religious Layman." In *The Catholic World*, February 1969.

p. 64. Rudolf Harvey, O.F.M., "A Third Order." In the *Friar*, February 1968.

p. 69. Murray Bodo, O.F.M., *Clare, A Light in the Garden*. Cincinnati: St. Anthony Messenger Press, 1979.

p. 72. Phyllis McGinley, "The Good Companions." In *Saint Watching*, Garden City, NY: Doubleday Image Books, 1975.

p. 74. Joan Mowat Erikson, "The Lady Clare, His Daughter." *St. Francis Et His Four Ladies*, New York: W. W. Norton & Company, Inc. Copyright © 1970 by Joan Mowat Erikson. Selection is used with the permission of the publisher.

p. 75. *The Fioretti*, "How Saint Clare Ate a Meal with Saint Francis and His Friars." Translated by Raphael Brown in *St. Francis of Assisi: Omnibus of Sources*.

p. 76. Sister Mary Seraphim, P.C.P.A., "Feminine and Franciscan. In *The Franciscan Herald*, January 1972.

p. 79. Donovan, "There's a Shape in the Sky." From the Franco Zefirelli film, *Brother Sun, Sister Moon* (Paramount Pictures), 1973. Copyright © 1973 and 1974 by Famous Music Corporation.

p. 81. Phyllis McGinley, "Kind Men and Beasts." In *Saint Watching*.

p. 82. Paul Gallico, "Saint Francis of Assisi." In *Saints for Now*, edited by Clare Boothe Luce, New York: Sheed and Ward, 1952.

p. 84. P. Pourrat, *Christian Spirituality*. London: Burns, Oates and Washbourne, Ltd., 1924.

p. 86. Roy McFadden, "Saint Francis and the Birds." In *Flowers for a Lady*, London: Routledge Ltd., 1964.

p. 88. Lynn White, "A Patron Saint of Ecologists." As condensed by Francis and Helen Line in *Man with a Song*.

p. 89. Henry Wadsworth Longfellow, "The Sermon of Saint Francis." *The Complete Works of Henry Wadsworth Longfellow*, Boston: Houghton & Mifflin Co., 1881.

p. 90. Clement Wood, "The Minstrel of God." In *Commonweal*, October 1926.

p. 91. Marion Doyle, "Prayer Against Hunters." © 1933 by *The New York Times* Company. Reprinted by permission.

p. 91. Philip Murray, "A Little Litany to Saint Francis." In Rolfe Humphries' *New Poems by American Poets*, Ballantine Books, 1953.

p. 92. P. Pourrat, *Christian Spirituality*.

p. 94. John R. Moorman, "Crisis in the Order." *Saint Francis of Assisi*, London: The Society for Promoting Christian Knowledge, 1972.

p. 97. Omer Englebert, "The Stigmata." *Saint Francis of Assisi*.

p. 101. Francis Thompson, "Franciscus Christificatus." In *St. Francis and the Poet*.

p. 101. Reprinted with permission of Macmillan Publishing Co., Inc., from *Collected Poems*, by Vachel Lindsay. Copyright © 1920 by Macmillan Publishing Co., Inc., renewed in 1948 by Elizabeth C. Lindsay.

p. 102. Frederick Ozanam, *The Franciscan Poets*. London: David Nutt, Ltd., 1914.

p. 104. Eloi Leclerc, O.F.M., *The Canticle of Creatures*. Chicago: Franciscan Herald Press, 1977.

p. 107. "Il Cantico del Sole." In Eloi Leclerc, *The Canticle of Creatures*.

p. 107. "The Canticle of Brother Sun." From *Saint Francis of Assisi: Omnibus of Sources.*

p. 108. "The Canticle of Brother Sun" (verse translation by William H. Draper), © J. Curwen & Sons, Ltd. Used by permission.

p. 108. "The Canticle of Brother Sun." As paraphrased by *The Catholic Worker.*

p. 109. "The Canticle of Brother Sun." As adapted by Ken Ford and Richard Duprey for the musical *Francis*, originally produced and directed by Frank A. Martin.

p. 110. John Bannister Tabb, "Brother Ass and Saint Francis." In *St. Francis and the Poet.*

p. 110. Johannes Jorgensen, "La Verna and the Stigmata." *Saint Francis of Assisi*, New York: Longman, Inc., quoted from the Doubleday Image Book edition, 1955.

p. 112. Emile Ripert, "Francis, Dying, Blesses Assisi." In Raphael Brown, *True Joy from Assisi.*

p. 113. Ernest Raymond, "Festa di San Francesco." *In the Steps of Saint Francis.*

p. 116. Vitale Bommarco, O.F.M., Conv., "Opening the Tomb of Saint Francis." *The Franciscan Herald*, April 1978.

p. 121. Ernest Raymond, "A Fourth Order?" *In the Steps of St. Francis.*

p. 121. John R. Moorman, "Francesco Bernardone." *A History of the Franciscan Order*, Oxford: at the Clarendon Press, 1968. By permission of the Oxford University Press.

p. 122. P. Pourrat, *Christian Spirituality.*

p. 122. James J. Walsh, "Origin of the Drama." *The Thirteenth, Greatest of Centuries*, New York: AMS Press, Inc., 1913.

p. 125. Reinhold Schneider, *Saint Francis*. Freiburg: Herder Art Series, 1954.

p. 127. William Fleming, *Arts and Ideas*. New York: Holt, Rinehart & Winston, Inc., 3rd edition, 1968.

p. 128. Frederick Ozanam, *The Franciscan Poets.*

p. 132. James J. Walsh, *The Thirteenth, Greatest of Centuries.*

p. 133. Matthew Arnold, *Lectures and Essays in Criticism*. University of Michigan Press, 1962. Used with permission.

p. 135. Ernst Renan, *Studies in Religious History*. As quoted in Omer Englebert, *Saint Francis of Assisi.*

p. 135. Albert Camus, *Notebooks, 1935–1942*. New York: Alfred A. Knopf, 1963.

p. 136. Anne O'Hare McCormick, "Fascism Takes Francis as Patron Saint." © 1926 by *The New York Times* Company. Reprinted by permission.

p. 139. Luis Anibal Sanchez, "Brother Dog." In *St. Francis and the Poet.*

p. 139. From *Civilization*, by Kenneth Clark, pp. 74–79. Copyright © 1969 by Kenneth Clark. Reprinted by permission of Harper & Row, Publishers, Inc.

p. 142. Leonard John Frankish, "The First of the First Californians." *Sunset* magazine, August 1927.

p. 142. Francis and Helen Line, "His Name Is on America." *Man with a Song.*

p. 143. Catherine De Hueck Doherty, "Saint Francis in Modern Times." In *The Lamp*, 1965.

p. 144. Francis and Helen Line, "Miracle of 32nd Street." *Man with a Song.*

p. 145. Declan Madden, O.F.M., "My Southwest Canticle." In the *Friar* magazine, April 1976.

p. 147. Luke R. Power, "Il Poverello and Technology." In *The Cord*, May 1966.

p. 149. Reprinted with permission of Macmillan Publishing Co., Inc., from *Collected Poems*, by Vachel Lindsay. Copyright © 1920 by Macmillan Publishing Co., Inc., renewed in 1948 by Elizabeth C. Lindsay.

p. 150. Peter Maurin, "What a Fine Place This World Would Be." *Easy Essays.*

p. 150. Dorothy Day, "Troubadors of Christ." *Meditations*, Paramus, NJ: Newman Press. Copyright © Paulist Press, 1970. Used with permission.

p. 150. Mario von Galli, S.J., "Francis, the Revolutionary." *Francis of Assisi and the Church Tomorrow.*

p. 154. Enid Dinnis, "A Franciscan Prayer." In *Saint Francis and the Poet.*

p. 154. Enzo Natta, "Young Friars of Assisi Ask Franco Zeffirelli About His New Film on Saint Francis." *L'Osservatore Romano*, June 16, 1971.

p. 157. John Felice, O.F.M. and Roy M. Gasnick, O.F.M., "Brother Sun, Sister Moon: A Review." *Good News*, May 1973.

p. 161. Anthony Scannell, O.F.M., Cap., "The Franciscan Style of Communications." In *The Franciscan Herald*, February 1977.

p. 163. Arlo Guthrie, "Peace: How Much Do You Let God Love You?" In *The Franciscan Herald*, October 1978.

p. 163. Gene Pelc, "Saint Francis of Assisi . . . Superhero." In *The Tokyo Weekender*, November 9, 1979.

p. 166. Colin Eisler, "In Detail: Bellini's Saint Francis." *Portfolio*, April-May 1979.

p. 169. John Garvey, "Francis of Assisi." *Saints for Confused Times*, © Thomas More Press, Chicago, 1976.

p. 176. Excerpt from *The Sufis* by Idries Shah. Copyright © 1964 by Idries Shah. Reprinted by permission of Doubleday & Company, Inc.

p. 179. Excerpt from G. P. Fedotov, "Russian Kenoticism." *The Russian Religious Mind*, New York: Harper Torchbooks, Harper & Row, Inc., 1960.

p. 181. Guido Ferrando in Christopher Isherwood, *Vedanta for the Western World*. Hollywood: Vedanta Press, 1973, pp. 253–259.

p. 184. Giulio Basetti-Sani, O.F.M., "Muhammad and Saint Francis." In *The Cord*, March 1958.

p. 189. Arnold Toynbee, "The Challenge of Tomorrow." As quoted in the *Japan Times*, October 4, 1972. Used with permission of the Oxford University Press.

p. 190. Liam Brophy, "Saint Francis, Buddha, and Confucius." In *St. Anthony Messenger*, October 1959.

p. 193. Arthur Little, "An Experience of Saint Francis in India." In *Forum* (an internal publication of the Franciscan Communications Office of New York), March 1974.

p. 194. Arthur Little, *St. Francis: A Noh Play*. International Programs, Earlham College, Richmond, IN, 1970. Permission must be sought for any performance of this play.

p. 204. Anne Morrow Lindbergh, "The Stone." Copyright © 1951 by Anne Morrow Lindbergh. Reprinted from *The Unicorn and Other Poems* by Anne Morrow Lindbergh, by permission of Pantheon Books, a Division of Random House, Inc.

p. 204. An unsigned review in *Time* magazine, June 1, 1962. Reprinted by permission from *Time*, The Weekly Magazine, copyright © Time, Inc., 1962.

p. 205. Mary Brent Whiteside, "Alien." In *St. Francis and the Poet.*

p. 205. Alfred Lord Tennyson, "Saint Francis." In *St. Francis and the Poet.*

p. 206. Reprinted with permission of Macmillan Publishing Co., Inc., from *Collected Poems*, by Vachel Lindsay. Copyright © 1920 by Macmillan Publishing Co., Inc., renewed in 1948 by Elizabeth C. Lindsay.

p. 206. Thomas of Celano, "A Final Word." *Second Life of Saint Francis*, 214, in *Saint Francis of Assisi: Omnibus of Sources.*

Illustration Sources and Permissions

p. iii. Drawing by Gregory Zoltowski, O.F.M. Used with permission.

p. vi. Detail from El Greco's *Francis and Brother Rufo*. Religious News Service Photo. Used with permission.

p. xi. Painting by Rembrandt. Religious News Service Photo. Used with permission.

' p. 2. The crucifix of San Damiano that spoke to Francis; it is now in the Basilica of St. Clare, Assisi. Photograph by Salvator Fink, O.F.M. Used with permission.

p. 4. Basilica of St. Francis, Assisi. Alitalia Airlines. Used with permission.

p. 6. Panorama of Assisi. Alitalia Airlines. Used with permission.

p. 7. A characteristic arch, Assisi. Alitalia Airlines. Used with permission.

p. 8. Panoramic view of Assisi. Alitalia Airlines. Used with permission.

p. 9. Another panoramic view of Assisi. Alitalia Airlines. Used with permission.

p. 12. Drawing by Mary Whelan. *The Catholic Worker.* Used with permission.

p. 14. From *Brother Sun, Sister Moon.* Copyright © 1972 by Euro International Spa. All rights reserved. Still furnished by Paramount Pictures Corporation.

p. 16. Watercolor by Subercaseaux Errazuriz, O.S.B. Used with permission.

pp. 18–19. Panels from the Francis window in the Zouche chapel of York Minster, England. With permission of the Dean and Chapter of York.

p. 22. Drawing by Gregory Zoltowski, O.F.M. Used with permission.

p. 26. Painting done by Cimabue no more than two years after Francis's death; it is now in the lower Basilica of St. Francis, Assisi. Photograph by Salvator Fink, O.F.M. Used with permission.

p. 27. Reprinted with permission of Macmillan Publishing Co., Inc., from *The Saints Through Their Handwriting* by Girolamo Moretti. Copyright © 1964 by Macmillan Publishing Co., Inc.

p. 30. From *The Franciscan Herald.* Used with permission.

p. 32. From *The Cord.* Used with permission.

pp. 34–36. From *The Franciscan Herald.* Used with permission.

p. 37. Artist unknown.

p. 39. Mexican sculpture now residing in the Tumacari National Historical Monument, Arizona. Photograph by Capistran Hanlon, O.F.M. Used with permission.

pp. 40–41. Drawings by Sister Kay Francis Berger, OSF. Used with permission.

p. 44. Drawing by Gregory Zoltowski, O.F.M. Used with permission.

pp. 47–48. From *The Franciscan Herald.* Used with permission.

p. 51. Drawing by John Quigley, O.F.M. Used with permission.

p. 52. Drawing by Sister Kay Francis Berger, OSF. Used with permission.

p. 55. From the *Friar.* Used with permission.

p. 61. Woodcut by Fritz Eichenberg. Used with permission.

p. 62. Cartoon by Rodrigues. From the *Friar.* Used with permission.

p. 63. Irish postage stamp, 1926. Used with permission.

pp. 64–66. Copyright © 1980 Marvel Comics Group, a division of Cadence Industries Corp.; all rights reserved.

p. 68. From *Brother Sun, Sister Moon.* Copyright © 1972 by Euro International Spa. All rights reserved. Still furnished by Paramount Pictures Corporation.

p. 70. Clare meeting her brother; painting by unknown thirteenth-century artist; it resides in the Basilica of St. Clare. Photograph by Salvator Fink, O.F.M. Used with permission.

p. 71. Francis receiving Clare into the Order; painting by an unknown artist; it resides in the Basilica of St. Clare, Assisi. Photograph by Salvator Fink, O.F.M. Used with permission.

p. 73. From *Brother Sun, Sister Moon.* Copyright © 1972 by Euro International Spa. All rights reserved. Still furnished by Paramount Pictures Corporation.

p. 74. Painting by Tiberus of Assisi now hanging in the Basilica of St. Mary of the Angels, Assisi. Photograph by Salvator Fink, O.F.M. Used with permission.

p. 76. St. Clare repelling the Saracens at San Damiano with the Blessed Sacrament. Painting by Diotallevi now hanging in the Church of St. Anthony, Rome. Photograph by Salvator Fink, O.F.M. Used with permission.

p. 78. From *Brother Sun, Sister Moon.* Copyright © 1972 by Euro International Spa. All rights reserved. Still furnished by Paramount Pictures Corporation.

p. 80. Woodcut by Fritz Eichenberg. Used with permission.

p. 84. Fourteenth-century stained glass, Konigsfeld, Switzerland. Photograph by Salvator Fink, O.F.M. Used with permission.

p. 85. Drawing by Gregory Zoltowski, O.F.M. Used with permission.

p. 86. The only public statue of St. Francis in London. The sculpture, by A. Fleischmann, is at the friary opposite Westminster Cathedral. Religious News Service Photo. Used with permission.

pp. 87–88. Woodcuts by Fritz Eichenberg. Used with permission.

p. 89. Wood carving by New Mexican Ben Ortega. Religious News Service Photo. Used with permission.

p. 90. (*Left*) From *The Franciscan Herald.* Used with permission.

p. 90. (*Right*) *St. Francis near the Jewel Box* in Forest Park, Illinois, sculpted by Carl Mose. Photograph by Robert C. Holte, Jr.; courtesy of the *St. Lous Post-Dispatch.*

p. 91. From the *Friar.* Used with permission.

p. 93. Mural by John LaFarge in St. Matthew's Cathedral, Washington, D.C. Photograph by Salvator Fink, O.F.M. Used with permission.

p. 95. *The Ecstasy of St. Francis* by Giovanni Baglione. Religious News Service Photo. Used with permission.

p. 96. From *The Franciscan Herald.* Used with permission.

p. 99. Woodcut by Fritz Eichenberg. Used with permission.

pp. 102, 103, 105. Drawings by Gregory Zoltowski, O.F.M. Used with permission.

p. 106. From *Brother Sun, Sister Moon.* Copyright © 1972 by Euro International Spa. All rights reserved. Still furnished by Paramount Pictures Corporation.

p. 110. Drawing by Kelly Freas. From *The Franciscan Herald.* Used with permission.

p. 111. From the *Friar.* Used with permission.

p. 112. From *The Franciscan Herald.* Used with permission.

p. 115. *Death of Francis* by Bernard Hofmann, O.F.M. Used with permission.

p. 117. *Francis Lying Dead.* Painting by Giotto in the church of Santa Croce, Florence. Photograph by Salvator Fink, O.F.M. Used with permission.

p. 118. Silvio Cardinal Oddio and other prelates view the bones of St. Francis when they were exhumed in 1978. Religious News Service Photo. Used with permission.

NOTE: Woodcuts on pages 61, 80, 87, 90, and 99 copyright Fritz Eichenberg. All rights reserved. Woodcut on page 88 copyright Harper & Row. All rights reserved.

p. 120. Drawing by R. Powell, O.F.M. From *The Franciscan Herald*. Used with permission.

p. 124. *Christmas at Greccio*. Painting by Giotto in the Basilica of St. Francis, Assisi. Photograph by Salvator Fink, O.F.M. Used with permission.

p. 126. Painting, one of the earliest of Francis, by an unknown artist on a wall in the church of Sacro Speco in Subiaco. Photograph by Salvator Fink, O.F.M. Used with permission.

p. 129. Painting by Ludovico Cardi da Cigoli. Religious News Service Photo. Used with permission.

p. 130. Drawing by Daniel Mauk. From *The Catholic Worker*. Used with permission.

p. 137. Woodcut by Fritz Eichenberg. Used with permission.

p. 138. Fifteenth-century canvas in the heritage of Greccio, artist unknown. Photograph by Salvator Fink, O.F.M. Used with permission.

p. 140. Detail of *St. Francis of Assisi Receiving the Stigmata*, a painting by Jan van Eyck. Religious News Service Photo. Used with permission.

p. 144. Statue in St. Francis Courtyard, West 32nd Street, New York City. Used with permission.

p. 149. Copyright © 1978 *The Los Angeles Times;* reprinted with permission.

p. 151. *St. Francis of the Guns*. Sculpture by Beniamino Bufano; metal for the sculpture came in part from guns turned in by San Franciscans after the assassination of Robert Kennedy. Religious News Service Photo. Used with permission.

p. 154. *Francis and the Robbers*. Watercolor by Eugene Burnand. Used with permission.

pp. 156, 158, 159, 160. From *Brother Sun, Sister Moon*. Copyright © 1972 by Euro International Spa. All rights reserved. Stills furnished by Paramount Pictures Corporation.

p. 162. From the *Friar*. Used with permission.

p. 163. From *The Franciscan Herald*. Used with permission.

p. 164–165. Copyright © 1980 Marvel Comics Group, a division of Cadence Industries Corp;. all rights reserved.

p. 167. *St. Francis in Ecstasy*. Painting by Giovanni Bellini. Copyright © 1936 by The Frick Collection. Used with permission.

p. 170. Drawing by Meinrad Craighead. From *The Catholic Worker*. Used with permission.

pp. 171, 172, 175, 176, 185, 186. From the *Friar*. Used with permission.

p. 189. From *The Franciscan Herald*. Used with permission.

p. 199. Statue in Kiryu, Japan. Photograph by Flavian Walsh, O.F.M. Used with permission.

p. 207. Woodcut by Fritz Eichenberg. Used with permission.

NOTE: Woodcuts on pages 137 and 207 copyright Fritz Eichenberg. All rights reserved.